VOLUME ONE

The Birth
of
Britain

A HISTORY OF THE
ENGLISH-SPEAKING PEOPLES

The Birth of Britain

Winston S. Churchill

DODD, MEAD & COMPANY · NEW YORK

1956

ACKNOWLEDGMENTS

I desire to record my thanks to Mr. F. W. Deakin and Mr. G. M. Young for their assistance before the Second World War in the preparation of this work, to Mr. Alan Hodge, to Mr. A. R. Myers of Liverpool University, who has scrutinised the text in the light of subsequent advances in historical knowledge, and to Mr. Denis Kelly and Mr. C. C. Wood. I have also to thank many others who have read these pages and commented on them.

Preface

IT is nearly twenty years ago that I made the arrangements which resulted in this book. At the outbreak of the war about half a million words were duly delivered. Of course, there was still much to be done in proof-reading when I went to the Admiralty on September 3, 1939. All this was set aside. During six years of war, and an even longer period in which I was occupied with my war memoirs, the book slumbered peacefully. It is only now when things have quietened down that I present to the public. A HISTORY OF THE ENGLISH-SPEAKING PEOPLES.

If there was need for it before, that has certainly not passed away. For the second time in the present century the British Empire and the United States have stood together facing the perils of war on the largest scale known among men, and since the cannons ceased to fire and the bombs to burst we have become more conscious of our common duty to the human race. Language, law, and the processes by which we have come into being already afforded a unique foundation for drawing together and portraying a concerted task. I thought when I began that such a unity might well notably influence the destiny of the world. Certainly I do not feel that the need for this has diminished in any way in the twenty years that have passed.

On the contrary, the theme of the work has grown in strength and reality and human thought is broadened. Vast numbers of people on both sides of the Atlantic and throughout the British Commonwealth of Nations have felt a sense of brotherhood. A new generation is at hand. Many practical steps have been taken which carry us far. Thinking primarily of the English-speaking peoples in no way implies any sense of restriction. It does not mean canalising the development of world affairs, nor does it prevent the erection of structures like United Europe or other similar groupings which may all find their place in the world organisation we have set on foot. It rather helps to invest them with life and truth. There is a growing feeling that the English-speaking peoples might point a finger showing the way if things went right, and could of course defend themselves, so far as any of us have the power, if things went wrong.

This book does not seek to rival the works of professional historians. It aims rather to present a personal view on the processes whereby English-speaking peoples throughout the world have achieved their distinctive position and character. I write about the things in our past that appear significant to me and I do so as one not without some experience of historical and violent events in our own time. I use the term "English-speaking peoples" because there is no other that applies both to the inhabitants of the British Isles and to those independent nations who derive their beginnings, their speech, and many of their institutions from England, and who now preserve, nourish, and develop them in their own ways.

This first volume traces the story of the English-speaking peoples from the earliest times to the eve of the European discovery of the New World. It concludes upon the field of Bosworth, the last battle of the tumultuous English Middle Ages. The year is 1485, and a new dynasty has just mounted the English throne. Seven years later Columbus landed in the Americas, and from this date, 1492, a new era in the history of mankind takes its beginnings.

*   *   *   *   *

Our story centres in an island, not widely sundered from the Continent, and so tilted that its mountains lie all to the west and north, while south and east is a gently undulating landscape of wooded valleys, open downs, and slow rivers. It is very accessible to the invader, whether he comes in peace or war, as pirate or merchant, conqueror or missionary. Those who dwelt there are not insensitive to any shift of power, any change of faith, or even fashion, on the mainland, but they give to every practice, every doctrine that comes to it from abroad, its own peculiar turn and imprint. A province of the Roman Empire, cut off and left to sink or swim in the great convulsion of the Dark Ages; reunited to Christendom, and almost torn away from it once more by the heathen Dane; victorious, united, but exhausted, yielding, almost without resistance, to the Norman Conqueror; submerged, it might seem, within the august framework of Catholic feudalism, was yet capable of reappearing with an individuality of its own. Neither its civilisation nor speech is quite Latin nor quite Germanic. It possesses a body of custom which, whatever its ultimate sources may be—folkright brought from beyond the seas by Danes, and by Saxons before them, maxims of civil jurisprudence culled from Roman codes—is being welded into one Common Law. This is England in the thirteenth century, the century of Magna Carta, and of the first Parliament.

As we gaze back into the mists of time we can very faintly discern the men of the Old Stone Age, and the New Stone Age; the builders of the great megalithic monuments; the newcomers from the Rhineland, with their beakers and tools of bronze. Standing on a grassy down where Dover now is, and pointing to the valley at his feet, one of them might have said to his grandson, "The sea comes farther up that creek than it did when I was a boy," and the grandson might have lived to watch a flood-tide, a roaring swirl of white water, sweeping the valley from end to end, carving its grassy sides into steep chalk edges, and linking the North Sea with the Channel. No wanderings, henceforth, of little clans, in search of game or food-yielding plants, from the plains of France or Belgium, to the wooded valleys and downs of Southern England; no small ventures in dugout canoes across narrow inlets at slack water. Those who come now must come in ships, and bold and wary they must be to face and master the Channel fogs and the Channel tides, and all that may lie beyond them.

Suddenly the mist clears. For a moment the Island stands in the full light of historic day. In itself the invasion of Britain by Julius Cæsar was an episode that had no sequel; but it showed that the power of Rome and the civilisation of the Mediterranean world were not necessarily bounded by the Atlantic coast. Cæsar's landing at Deal bridged the chasm which nature had cloven. For a century, while the Roman world was tearing itself to pieces in civil war, or slowly recovering under a new Imperial form, Britain remained uneasily poised between isolation and union with the Continent, but absorbing, by way of trade and peaceful intercourse, something of the common culture of the West. In the end Rome gave the word and the legions sailed. For nearly four hundred years Britain became a Roman province. This considerable period was characterised for a great part of the time by that profound tranquillity which leaves little for history to record. It stands forth sedate, luminous, and calm. And what remained? Noble roads, sometimes overgrown with woodland; the stupendous work of the Roman Wall, breached and crumbling; fortresses, market towns, country houses, whose very ruins the next comers contemplated with awe. But of Roman speech, Roman law, Roman institutions, hardly a vestige. Yet we should be mistaken if we therefore supposed that the Roman occupation could be dismissed as an incident without consequence. It had given time for the Christian faith to plant itself. Far in the West, though severed from the world by the broad flood of barbarism, there remained, sorely beset, but defended by its mountains, a tiny Christian realm. British Christianity converted Ireland. From Ireland the faith recrossed the seas to Scotland. Thus the newcomers were enveloped in the old civilisation; while at Rome men remembered that Britain had been Christian once, and might be Christian again.

This island world was not wholly cut off from the mainland. The south-east at all events kept up a certain intercourse with its Frankish cousins across the straits, and hence came the Roman missionaries. They brought with them a new set of beliefs, which, with some brief, if obstinate, resistance here and there, were accepted with surprising readiness. They brought a new political order, a Church which was to have its own rulers, its own officers, its own assemblies, and make its own laws, all of which had somehow or other to be fitted into the ancient customs of the English people. They planted the seed of a great problem, the problem of Church and State, which will grow until a thousand years later it almost rives the foundations of both asunder. But all this lies in the future. What mattered at the moment was that with her conversion England became once more part of the Western World. Very soon English missionaries would be at work on the Continent; English pilgrims would be making their way across the Alps to see the wonders of Rome, among them English princes, who, their work in this world being done, desired that their bones should rest near the tomb of the Apostles.

Nor was this all, because the English people now have an institution which overrode all local distinctions of speech, or custom, or even sovereignty. Whatever dynastic quarrels might go on between the kingdoms, the Church was one and indivisible: its rites are everywhere the same, its ministers are sacred. The Kingdom of Kent may lose its ancient primacy, Northumbria make way for Mercia; but Canterbury and York remain.

The contrast is startling between the secular annals of these generations, with their meagre and tedious records of forays and slaughter, and the brilliant achievements of the English Church. The greatest scholar in Christendom was a Northumbrian monk. The most popular stylist was a West Saxon abbot. The Apostle of Germany was Boniface from Devon. The revival of learning in the Empire of Charlemagne was directed by Alcuin of York.

But this youthful, flourishing, immature civilisation lacked any solid military defence. The North was stirring again: from Denmark up the Baltic, up the Norwegian fiords, the pirate galleys were once more pushing forth in search of plunder, and of new homes for a crowded people. An island without a fleet, without a sovereign to command its scattered strength, rich in gold pieces, in cunning metal-work, and rare embroideries, stored in defenceless churches and monasteries, was a prize which the heathen men might think reserved for them whenever they chose to lay hands on it. Those broad, slow rivers of the English plain invited their galleys into the very heart of the country, and once on land how were rustics hurriedly summoned from the plough to resist the swift and disciplined march of armed bands, mounted or on foot? When the storm broke the North, the Midlands, the East, went down under its fury. If Wessex had succumbed all would have been lost. Gradually however it became manifest that the invaders had come not only to ravage but to settle.

At last the hurricane abated and men could take count of their losses. A broad strip of land along the middle of the eastern coast and stretching inland as far as Derby was in Danish hands; seafarers turned farmers were still holding together as an army. But London, already one of the great ports of Northern Europe, had been saved, and all the South, and here was the seat and strength of the royal house. The tie with the mainland had not been severed. Year by year, sometimes by treaty, sometimes by hard fighting, King Alfred's dynasty laboured to establish its ascendancy and reunite the land; so successfully that the temporary substitution of a Danish for an English king made little mark on history. He too was a Christian; he too made the pilgrimage to Rome. After this brief interlude the old line returned to the throne, and might have remained there from one generation to another. Yet in three short winter months, between October and Christmas Day in 1066, the astounding event had happened. The ruler of one French province—and that not the largest or most powerful—had crossed the Channel and made himself King of England.

*   *   *   *   *

The structure into which the Norman enters with the strong hand was a kingdom, acknowledged by all who spoke the King's English, and claiming some vague sovereignty over the Welsh and the Scots as well. It was governed, we may say, by the King in Council, and the Council consisted of his wise men, laymen and clerics; in other words, bishops and abbots, great landowners, officers of the Household. In all this it departed in no way from the common pattern of all kingdoms which had been built out of fragments of the Roman Empire. It had also been showing, since the last of the strong kings died, a dangerous tendency to split up into provinces, or earldoms, at the expense of the Crown and the unity of the nation; a tendency only, because the notion still persisted that the kingdom was one and indivisible, and that the King's Peace was over all men alike. Within this peace man was bound to man by a most intricate network of rights and duties, which might vary almost indefinitely from shire to shire, and even from village to village. But on the whole the English doctrine was that a free man might choose his lord, following him in war, working for him in peace, and in return the lord must protect him against encroaching neighbours and back him in the courts of law. What is more, the man might go from one lord to another, and hold his land from his new lord. And these lords, taken together, were the ruling class. The greatest of them, as we have seen, sat in the King's Council. The lesser of them are the local magnates, who took the lead in shire or hundred, and when the free men met in the shire or hundred court to decide the rights and wrongs of a matter it was their voice which carried weight. We cannot yet speak of a nobility and gentry, because the Saxons distinguished sharply between nobles and peasants and there was no room for any middle rank. But there were the makings of a gentry, to be realised hereafter.

Such was the state of England when the new Norman order was imposed on it. The Conqueror succeeded to all the rights of the old kings, but his Council now is mainly French-born, and French-speaking. The tendency to provincialisation is arrested; the King's Peace is everywhere. But the shifting pattern of relationships is drastically simplified to suit the more advanced, or more logical, Norman doctrine, that the tie of man to lord is not only moral and legal, but material, so that the status of every man can be fixed by the land he owns, and the services he does for it, if he is a tenant, or can demand, if he is a lord. In Norman days far more definitely than in Saxon the governing class is a landowning class.

In spite of its violent reannexation to the Continent, and its merger in the common feudalism of the West, England retained a positive individuality, expressed in institutions gradually shaped in the five or six hundred years that had passed since its severance, and predestined to a most remarkable development. The old English nobility of office made way for the Norman nobility of faith and landed wealth. The lesser folk throve in a peaceful but busy obscurity, in which English and

Norman soon blended, and from them will issue in due course the Grand Jurors, the Justices of the Peace, the knights of the shire; ultimately overshadowing, in power if not in dignity, the nobility, and even the Crown itself. These days are far off. In the meantime we may picture the Government of England in the reign of Henry II, let us say, somehow thus. A strong monarchy, reaching by means of its judges and sheriffs into every corner of the land; a powerful Church that has come to a settlement with the Crown, in which the rights of both sides are acknowledged; a rich and self-willed nobility, which the Crown is bound by custom to consult in all matters of State; a larger body of gentry by whom the local administration is carried on; and the king's Household, his personal staff, of men experienced in the law and in finance. To these we must add the boroughs, which are growing in wealth and consequence now that the peace is well kept, the roads and seaways safe, and trade is flourishing.

*   *   *   *   *

Standing at this point, and peering forward into the future, we see how much depends on the personality of the sovereign. In the period after the Conquest we have had three powerful rulers: in William a ruthless and determined soldier-prince who stamped the Norman pattern on the land; in his son Henry I a far-sighted, patient administrator; in Henry's grandson, the second Henry, a great statesman who had seen that national unity and the power of the Crown hung together, and that both could only be served by offering, for a price, even justice to all men, and enforcing it by the royal authority. Certain strains are developing in that compact fabric of Plantagenet England. The Crown is pressing rather hard on the nobility; the king's Household is beginning to oust the ancient counsellors of the kingdom. We need a strong king who will maintain the law, but a just king who will maintain it for the good of all, and not only for his private emolument or aggrandisement. With King John we enter on a century of political experiment.

Anyone who has heard from childhood of Magna Carta, who has read with what interest and reverence one copy of it was lately received in New York, and takes it up for the first time, will be strangely disappointed, and may find himself agreeing with the historian who proposed to translate its title not as the Great Charter of Liberties, but the Long List of Privileges—privileges of the nobility at the expense of the State. The reason is that our notion of law is wholly different from that of our ancestors. We think of it as something constantly changing to meet new circumstances; we reproach a Government if it is slow to pass new legislation. In the Middle Ages circumstances changed very gradually; the pattern of society was settled by custom or Divine decree, and men thought of the law rather as a fixed standard by which rights and duties could in case of wrongdoing or dispute be enforced or determined.

The Great Charter therefore is not in our sense of the word a legislative or constitutional instrument. It is an agreed statement of what the law is, as between the king and his barons; and many of the provisions which seem to us to be trifling and technical indicate the points at which the king had encroached on their ancient rights. Perhaps, in their turn, the victorious barons encroached unduly on the rights of the Crown. No one at the time regarded the Charter as a final settlement of all outstanding issues, and its importance lay not in details but in the broad affirmation of the principle that there is a law to which the Crown itself is subject. *Rex non debet esse sub homine, sed sub Deo et lege*—the king should not be below man, but below God and the law. This at least is clear. He has his sphere of action, within which he is free from human control. If he steps outside it he must be brought back. And he will step outside it if, ignoring the ancient Council of the kingdom, and refusing to take the advice of his wise men, he tries to govern through his Household, his favourites, or his clerks.

In other words, personal government, with all its latent possibilities of oppression and caprice, is not to be endured. But it is not easy to prevent. The King is strong, far stronger than any great lord, and stronger than most combinations of great lords. If the Crown is to be kept within its due limits some broader basis of resistance must be found than the ancient privileges of the nobility. About this time, in the middle of the thirteenth century, we begin to have a new word, Parliament. It bears a very vague meaning, and some of those who first used it would have been startled if they could have foreseen what it would some day come to signify. But gradually the idea spreads that if it is not enough for the King to "talk things over" with his own Council; so, on the other hand, it is not enough for the barons to insist solely on their right to be considered the Council of the kingdom. Though they often claim to speak for the community of the realm, in fact they only represent themselves, and the King after all represents the whole people. Then why not call in the lesser gentry and the burgesses? They are always used in local matters. Why not use them in national concerns? Bring them up to Westminster, two gentlemen from every shire, two tradesmen from every borough. What exactly they are to do when they get there no one quite knows. Perhaps to listen while their betters speak; to let them know what the grievances of the country are; to talk things over with one another behind the scenes; to learn what the king's intentions are in Scotland and France, and to pay the more cheerfully for knowing. It is a very delicate plant, this Parliament. There is nothing inevitable about its growth, and it might have been dropped as an experiment not worth going on with. But it took root. In two or three generations a prudent statesman would no more think of governing England without a Parliament than without a king. What its actual powers are it would be very hard to say. Broadly, its consent is necessary to give legal sanction to any substantial act of authority: an important change of ancient custom can only be effected by Act of Parliament; a new tax can only be levied with the approval of the Commons. What more it can do the unfolding of time will show. But its authority is stabilised by a series of accidents. Edward III needed money for his French wars. Henry IV needed support for his seizure of the crown. And in the Wars of the Roses both the contending parties wanted some sort of public sanction for their actions, which only Parliament could provide.

Thus when in the fifteenth century the baronial structure perished in faction and civil war there remained not only the Crown, but the Crown in Parliament, now clearly shaped into its two divisions, the Lords sitting in their own right, and the Commoners as representatives of the shires and boroughs. So far nothing has changed. But the destruction of the old nobility in battle or on the morrow of battle was to tip the balance of the two Houses, and the Commons, knights and burgesses, stood for those elements in society which suffered most from anarchy and profited most by strong government. There was a natural alliance between the Crown and the Commons. The Commons had little objection to the Crown extending its prerogative at the expense of the nobility, planting Councils of the North and Councils of Wales, or in the Star Chamber exercising a remedial jurisdiction by which the small man could be defended against the great. On the other hand, the Crown was willing enough to leave local administration to the Justices of the Peace, whose interest it was to be loyal, to put down sturdy beggars, and to grow quietly and peacefully rich. As late as 1937 the Coronation service proclaimed the ideal of

Tudor government in praying that the sovereign may be blessed with "a loyal nobility, a dutiful gentry, and an honest, peaceable, and obedient commonalty." Some day perhaps that commonalty might ask whether they had no more to do with Government than to obey it.

*   *   *   *   *

Thus by the end of the fifteenth century the main characteristics and institutions of the race had taken shape. The rough German dialects of the Anglo-Saxon invaders had been modified before the Norman conquest by the passage of time and the influence of Church Latin. Vocabularies had been extended by many words of British and Danish root. This broadening and smoothing process was greatly hastened by the introduction into the islands of Norman French, and the assimilation of the two languages went on apace. Writings survive from the early thirteenth century which the ordinary man of to-day would recognise as a form of English, even if he could not wholly understand them. By the end of the fourteenth century, the century of Geoffrey Chaucer, it is thought that even the great magnates had ceased to use French as their principal language and commonly spoke English. Language moreover was not the only institution which had achieved a distinctively English character. Unlike the remainder of Western Europe, which still retains the imprint and tradition of Roman law and the Roman system of government, the English-speaking peoples had at the close of the period covered by this volume achieved a body of legal and what might almost be called democratic principles which survived the upheavals and onslaughts of the French and Spanish Empires. Parliament, trial by jury, local government run by local citizens, and even the beginnings of a free Press, may be discerned, at any rate in primitive form, by the time Christopher Columbus set sail for the American continent.

Every nation or group of nations has its own tale to tell.

Knowledge of the trials and struggles is necessary to all who would comprehend the problems, perils, challenges, and opportunities which confront us to-day. It is not intended to stir a new spirit of mastery, or create a mood in the study of history which would favour national ambition at the expense of world peace. It may be indeed that an inner selective power may lead to the continuous broadening of our thought. It is in the hope that contemplation of the trials and tribulations of our forefathers may not only fortify the English-speaking peoples of to-day, but also play some small part in uniting the whole world, that I present this account.

W.S.C.

Chartwell
Westerham
Kent
January 15, 1956

Contents

BOOK I

THE ISLAND RACE

BOOK II

THE MAKING OF THE NATION

CONTENTS

BOOK III

THE END OF THE FEUDAL AGE

BOOK ONE

THE
ISLAND RACE

Britannia

IN the summer of the Roman year 699, now described as the year 55 before the birth of Christ, the Proconsul of Gaul, Gaius Julius Cæsar, turned his gaze upon Britain. In the midst of his wars in Germany and in Gaul he became conscious of this heavy Island which stirred his ambitions and already obstructed his designs. He knew that it was inhabited by the same type of tribesmen who confronted the Roman arms in Germany, Gaul, and Spain. The Islanders had helped the local tribes in the late campaigns along the northern coast of Gaul. They were the same Celtic stock, somewhat intensified by insular life. British volunteers had shared the defeat of the Veneti on the coasts of Brittany in the previous year. Refugees from momentarily conquered Gaul were welcomed and sheltered in Britannia. To Cæsar the Island now presented itself as an integral part of his task of subjugating the Northern barbarians to the rule and system of Rome. The land not covered by forest or marsh was verdant and fertile. The climate, though far from genial, was equable and healthy. The natives, though uncouth, had a certain value as slaves for rougher work on the land, in mines, and even about the house. There was talk of a pearl fishery, and also of gold. "Even if there was not time for a campaign that season, Cæsar thought it would be of great advantage to him merely to visit the island, to see what its inhabitants were like, and to make himself acquainted with the lie of the land, the harbours, and the landing-places. Of all this the Gauls knew next to nothing." [1] Other reasons added

[1] Cæsar, *The Conquest of Gaul,* translated by S. A. Handford, Penguin Classics, 1951.

their weight. Cæsar's colleague in the Triumvirate, Crassus, had excited the imagination of the Roman Senate and people by his spirited march towards Mesopotamia. Here, at the other end of the known world, was an enterprise equally audacious. The Romans hated and feared the sea. By a supreme effort of survival they had two hundred years before surpassed Carthage upon its own element in the Mediterranean, but the idea of Roman legions landing in the remote, unknown, fabulous Island of the vast ocean of the North would create a novel thrill and topic in all ranks of Roman society.

Moreover, Britannia was the prime centre of the Druidical religion, which, in various forms and degrees, influenced profoundly the life of Gaul and Germany. "Those who want to make a study of the subject," wrote Cæsar, "generally go to Britain for the purpose." The unnatural principle of human sacrifice was carried by the British Druids to a ruthless pitch. The mysterious priesthoods of the forests bound themselves and their votaries together by the most deadly sacrament that men can take. Here, perhaps, upon these wooden altars of a sullen island, there lay one of the secrets, awful, inflaming, unifying, of the tribes of Gaul. And whence did this sombre custom come? Was it perhaps part of the message which Carthage had given to the Western world before the Roman legions had strangled it at its source? Here then was the largest issue. Cæsar's vision pierced the centuries, and where he conquered civilisation dwelt.

Thus, in this summer fifty-five years before the birth of Christ, he withdrew his army from Germany, broke down his massive and ingenious timber bridge across the Rhine above Coblenz, and throughout July marched westward by long strides towards the Gallic shore somewhere about the modern Calais and Boulogne.

Cæsar saw the Britons as a tougher and coarser branch of

the Celtic tribes whom he was subduing in Gaul. With an army of ten legions, less than fifty thousand soldiers, he was striving against a brave, warlike race which certainly comprised half a million fighting men. On his other flank were the Germans, driven westward by pressure from the East. His policy towards them was to hurl their invading yet fleeing hordes into the Rhine whenever they intruded beyond it. Although all war was then on both sides waged only with tempered iron and mastery depended upon discipline and generalship alone, Cæsar felt himself and his soldiers not unequal to these prodigies. A raid upon Britannia seemed but a minor addition to his toils and risks. But at the seashore new problems arose. There were tides unknown in the Mediterranean; storms beat more often and more fiercely on the coasts. The Roman galleys and their captains were in contact with the violence of the Northern sea. Nevertheless, only a year before they had, at remarkable odds, destroyed the fleet of the hardy, maritime Veneti. With sickles at the end of long poles they had cut the ropes and halyards of their fine sailing ships and slaughtered their crews with boarding-parties. They had gained command of the Narrow Seas which separated Britannia from the mainland. The salt water was now a path and not a barrier. Apart from the accidents of weather and the tides and currents, about which he admits he could not obtain trustworthy information, Julius Cæsar saw no difficulty in invading the Island. There was not then that far-off line of storm-beaten ships which about two thousand years later stood between the great Corsican conqueror and the dominion of the world. All that mattered was to choose a good day in the fine August weather, throw a few legions on to the nearest shore, and see what there was in this strange Island after all.

While Cæsar marched from the Rhine across Northern Gaul, perhaps through Rheims and Amiens, to the coast, he sent an officer in a warship to spy out the Island shore, and when he arrived near what is now Boulogne, or perhaps the mouth of the Somme, this captain was at hand, with other knowledgeable persons, traders, Celtic princes, and British traitors, to greet him. He had concentrated the forces which had beaten the Veneti in two ports or inlets nearest to Britannia, and now he awaited a suitable day for the descent.

* * * * *

What was, in fact, this Island which now for the first time in coherent history was to be linked with the great world? We have dug up in the present age from the gravel of Swanscombe a human skull which is certainly a quarter of a million years old. Biologists perceive important differences from the heads that hold our brains to-day, but there is no reason to suppose that this remote Palæolithic ancestor was not capable of all the crimes, follies, and infirmities definitely associated with mankind. Evidently, for prolonged, almost motionless, periods men and women, naked or wrapped in the skins of animals, prowled about the primeval forests and plashed through wide marshes, hunting each other and other wild beasts, cheered, as the historian Trevelyan finely says,[1] by the songs of innumerable birds. It is said that the whole of Southern Britain could in this period support upon its game no more than seven hundred families. Here indeed were the lords of creation. Seven hundred families, all this fine estate, and no work but sport and fighting. Already man had found out that a flint was better than a fist. His descendants would burrow deep in the chalk and gravel for battle-axe flints of the best size and quality, and gained survival thereby. But so far he had only learned to chip his flints into rough tools.

At the close of the Ice Age changes in climate brought about the collapse of the hunting civilisations of Old Stone

[1] *History of England.*

Age Man, and after a very long period of time the tides of invasion brought Neolithic culture into the Western forests. The newcomers had a primitive agriculture. They scratched the soil and sowed the seeds of edible grasses. They made pits or burrows, which they gradually filled with the refuse of generations, and they clustered together for greater safety. Presently they constructed earthwork enclosures on the hilltops, into which they drove their cattle at night-time. Windmill Hill, near Avebury, illustrates the efforts of these primitive engineers to provide for the protection of herds and men. Moreover, Neolithic man had developed a means of polishing his flints into perfect shape for killing. This betokened a great advance; but others were in prospect.

It seems that at this time "the whole of Western Europe was inhabited by a race of long-headed men, varying somewhat in appearance and especially in colouring, since they were probably always fairer in the north and darker in the south, but in most respects substantially alike. Into this area of long-headed populations there was driven a wedge of round-headed immigrants from the east, known to anthropologists as 'the Alpine race.' Most of the people that have invaded Britain have belonged to the Western European long-headed stock, and have therefore borne a general resemblance to the people already living there; and consequently, in spite of the diversities among these various newcomers, the tendency in Britain has been towards the establishment and maintenance of a tolerably uniform long-headed type." [1]

A great majority of the skulls found in Britain, of whatever age, are of the long- or medium-headed varieties. Nevertheless it is known that the Beaker people and other round-headed types penetrated here and there, and established themselves as a definite element. Cremation, almost universal in the Later

[1] Collingwood and Myres, *Roman Britain.*

· 7 ·

Bronze Age, has destroyed all record of the blending of the long-headed and round-headed types of man, but undoubtedly both persisted, and from later traces, when in Roman times burials were resumed instead of cremation, anthropologists of the older school professed themselves able to discern a characteristic Roman-British type, although in point of fact this may have established itself long before the Roman conquest. Increasing knowledge has rendered these early categories less certain.

In early days Britain was part of the Continent. A wide plain joined England and Holland, in which the Thames and the Rhine met together and poured their waters northward. In some slight movement of the earth's surface this plain sank a few hundred feet, and admitted the ocean to the North Sea and the Baltic. Another tremor, important for our story, sundered the cliffs of Dover from those of Cape Gris Nez, and the scour of the ocean and its tides made the Straits of Dover and the English Channel. When did this tremendous severance occur? Until lately geologists would have assigned it to periods far beyond Neolithic man. But the study of striped clays, the deposits of Norwegian glaciers, shows layer by layer and year by year what the weather was like, and modern science has found other methods of counting the centuries. From these and other indications time and climate scales have been framed which cover with tolerable accuracy many thousand years of prehistoric time. These scales enable times to be fixed when through milder conditions the oak succeeded the pine in British forests, and the fossilised vegetation elaborates the tale. Trawlers bring up in their nets fragments of trees from the bottom of the North Sea, and these when fitted into the climatic scale show that oaks were growing on what is now sixty fathoms deep of stormy water less than nine thousand years ago. Britain was still little more than a promontory of Europe, or divided from it by a narrow tide race which has gradually enlarged into the Straits of Dover, when the Pyramids were a-building, and when learned Egyptians were laboriously exploring the ancient ruins of Sakkara.

While what is now our Island was still joined to the Continent another great improvement was made in human methods of destruction. Copper and tin were discovered and worried out of the earth; the one too soft and the other too brittle for the main purpose, but, blended by human genius, they opened the Age of Bronze. Other things being equal, the men with bronze could beat the men with flints. The discovery was hailed, and the Bronze Age began.

The invasion, or rather infiltration, of bronze weapons and tools from the Continent was spread over many centuries, and it is only when twenty or thirty generations have passed that any notable change can be discerned. Professor Collingwood has drawn us a picture of what is called the Late Bronze Age. "Britain," he says, "as a whole was a backward country by comparison with the Continent; primitive in its civilisation, stagnant and passive in its life, and receiving most of what progress it enjoyed through invasion and importation from overseas. Its people lived either in isolated farms or in hut-villages, situated for the most part on the gravel of river-banks, or the light upland soils such as the chalk downs or oolite plateaux, which by that time had been to a great extent cleared of their native scrub; each settlement was surrounded by small fields, tilled either with a foot-plough of the type still used not long ago by Hebridean crofters, or else at best with a light ox-drawn plough which scratched the soil without turning the sod; the dead were burnt and their ashes, preserved in urns, buried in regular cemeteries. Thus the land was inhabited by a stable and industrious peasant population, living by agriculture and the keeping of livestock, augmented no doubt by hunting and fishing. They made rude pottery without a wheel, and still used flint for such things as arrow-heads; but they were visited by itinerant bronze-founders able to make swords, spears, socketed axes, and many other types of implement and utensil, such as sickles, carpenter's tools, metal parts of wheeled vehicles, buckets, and cauldrons. Judging by the absence of towns and the scarcity of anything like true fortification, these people were little organised for warfare, and their political life was simple and undeveloped, though there was certainly a distinction between rich and poor, since many kinds of metal objects belonging to the period imply a considerable degree of wealth and luxury."

The Late Bronze Age in the southern parts of Britain, according to most authorities, began about 1000 B.C. and lasted until about 400 B.C.

At this point the march of invention brought a new factor upon the scene. Iron was dug and forged. Men armed with iron entered Britain from the Continent and killed the men of bronze. At this point we can plainly recognise across the vanished millenniums a fellow-being. A biped capable of slaying another with iron is evidently to modern eyes a man and a brother. It cannot be doubted that for smashing skulls, whether long-headed or round, iron is best.

The Iron Age overlapped the Bronze. It brought with it a keener and higher form of society, but it impinged only very gradually upon the existing population, and their customs, formed by immemorial routine, were changed only slowly and piecemeal. Certainly bronze implements remained in use, particularly in Northern Britain, until the last century before Christ.

The impact of iron upon bronze was at work in our Island before Julius Cæsar cast his eyes upon it. After about 500 B.C. successive invasions from the mainland gradually modified the whole of the southern parts of the Island. "In general," says Professor Collingwood, "settlements yielding the pottery characteristic of this culture occur all over the south-east, from Kent to the Cotswolds and the Wash. Many of these settlements indicate a mode of life not perceptibly differing from that of their late Bronze Age background; they are farms or villages, often undefended, lying among their little fields on river-gravels or light upland soils, mostly cremating their dead, storing their grain in underground pits and grinding it with primitive querns, not yet made with the upper stone revolving upon the lower; keeping oxen, sheep, goats, and pigs; still using bronze and even flint implements and possessing very little iron, but indicating their date by a change in the style of their pottery, which, however, is still made without the wheel." [1]

The Iron Age immigrations brought with them a revival of the hill-top camps, which had ceased to be constructed since the Neolithic Age. During the third and fourth centuries before Christ a large number of these were built in the inhabited parts of our Island. They consisted of a single rampart, sometimes of stone, but usually an earthwork revetted with timber and protected by a single ditch.

The size of the ramparts was generally not very great. The entrances were simply designed, though archaeological excavation has in some instances revealed the remains of wooden guardrooms. These camps were not mere places of refuge. Often they were settlements containing private dwellings, and permanently inhabited. They do not seem to have served the purpose of strongholds for invaders in enemy land. On the contrary, they appear to have come into existence gradually as the iron age newcomers multiplied and developed a tribal system from which tribal wars eventually arose.

[1] *Op. cit.*

The last of the successive waves of Celtic inroad and super-session which marked the Iron Age came in the early part of the first century B.C. "The Belgic tribes arrived in Kent and spread over Essex, Hertfordshire, and part of Oxfordshire, while other groups of the same stock . . . later . . . spread over Hampshire, Wiltshire, and Dorset and part of Sussex." [1] There is no doubt that the Belgæ were by far the most enlightened invaders who had hitherto penetrated the recesses of the Island. They were a people of chariots and horsemen. They were less addicted to the hill-forts in which the existing inhabitants put their trust. They built new towns in the valleys, sometimes even below the hilltop on which the old fort had stood. They introduced for the first time a coinage of silver and copper. They established themselves as a tribal aristocracy in Britain, subjugating the older stock. In the east they built Wheathampstead, Verulam (St Albans), and Camulodunum (Colchester); in the south Calleva (Silchester) and Venta Belgarum (Winchester). They were closely akin to the inhabitants of Gaul from whom they had sprung. This active, alert, conquering, and ruling race established themselves wherever they went with ease and celerity, and might have looked forward to a long dominion. But the tramp of the legions had followed hard behind them, and they must soon defend the prize they had won against still better men and higher systems of government and war.

Meanwhile in Rome, at the centre and summit, only vague ideas prevailed about the western islands. "The earliest geographers believed that the Ocean Stream encircled the whole earth, and knew of no islands in it." [2] Herodotus about 445 B.C. had heard of the tin of mysterious islands in the far West, which he called the Cassiterides, but he cautiously treated

[1] Darby, *Historical Geography of England*, p. 42.
[2] *Antiquity*, vol. i, p. 189.

them as being in the realms of fable. However, in the middle of
the fourth century B.C. Pytheas of Marseilles—surely one of
the greatest explorers in history—made two voyages in which
he actually circumnavigated the British Isles. He proclaimed
the existence of the "Pretanic Islands Albion and Ierne," as
Aristotle had called them. Pytheas was treated as a story-teller,
and his discoveries were admired only after the world he lived
in had long passed away. But even in the third century B.C.
the Romans had a definite conception of three large islands,
Albion, Ierne, and Thule (Iceland). Here all was strange and
monstrous. These were the ultimate fringes of the world. Still,
there was the tin trade, in which important interests were concerned, and Polybius, writing in 140 B.C., shows that this
aspect at least had been fully discussed by commercial writers.

* * * * *

We are much better informed upon these matters than was
Cæsar when he set out from Boulogne. Here are some of the
impressions he had collected:

"The interior of Britain is inhabited by people who claim,
on the strength of an oral tradition, to be aboriginal; the coast,
by Belgic immigrants who came to plunder and make war—
nearly all of them retaining the names of the tribes from which
they originated—and later settled down to till the soil. The
population is exceedingly large, the ground thickly studded
with homesteads, closely resembling those of the Gauls, and
the cattle very numerous. For money they use either bronze, or
gold coins, or iron ingots of fixed weights. Tin is found inland,
and small quantities of iron near the coast; the copper that
they use is imported. There is timber of every kind, as in Gaul,
except beech and fir. Hares, fowl, and geese they think it un-
lawful to eat, but rear them for pleasure and amusement. The
climate is more temperate than in Gaul, the cold being less
severe.

"By far the most civilised inhabitants are those living in Kent (a purely maritime district), whose way of life differs little from that of the Gauls. Most of the tribes in the interior do not grow corn but live on milk and meat, and wear skins. All the Britons dye their bodies with woad, which produces a blue colour, and this gives them a more terrifying appearance in battle. They wear their hair long, and shave the whole of their bodies except the head and the upper lip. Wives are shared between groups of ten or twelve men, especially between brothers and between fathers and sons; but the offspring of these unions are counted as the children of the man with whom a particular woman cohabited first."

*　　*　　*　　*　　*

Late in August 55 B.C. Cæsar sailed with eighty transports and two legions at midnight, and with the morning light saw the white cliffs of Dover crowned with armed men. He judged the placed "quite unsuitable for landing," since it was possible to throw missiles from the cliffs on to the shore. He therefore anchored till the turn of the tide, sailed seven miles farther, and descended upon Albion on the low, shelving beach between Deal and Walmer. But the Britons, observing these movements, kept pace along the coast and were found ready to meet him. There followed a scene upon which the eye of history has rested. The Islanders, with their chariots and horsemen, advanced into the surf to meet the invader. Cæsar's transports and warships grounded in deeper water. The legionaries, uncertain of the depth, hesitated in face of the shower of javelins and stones, but the eagle-bearer of the Tenth Legion plunged into the waves with the sacred emblem, and Cæsar brought his warships with their catapults and arrow-fire upon the British flank. The Romans, thus encouraged and sustained, leaped from their ships, and, forming as best they could, waded towards the enemy. There was a short, ferocious fight amid the waves, but the Romans reached the shore, and, once arrayed, forced the Britons to flight.

Cæsar's landing however was only the first of his troubles. His cavalry, in eighteen transports, which had started three days later, arrived in sight of the camp, but, caught by a sudden gale, drifted far down the Channel, and were thankful to regain the Continent. The high tide of the full moon which Cæsar had not understood wrought grievous damage to his fleet at anchor. "A number of ships," he says, "were shattered, and the rest, having lost their cables, anchors, and the remainder of their tackle, were unusable, which naturally threw the whole army into great consternation. For they had no other vessels in which they could return, nor any materials for repairing the fleet; and, since it had been generally understood that they were to return to Gaul for the winter, they had not provided themselves with a stock of grain for wintering in Britain."

The Britons had sued for peace after the battle on the beach, but now that they saw the plight of their assailants their hopes revived and they broke off the negotiations. In great numbers they attacked the Roman foragers. But the legion concerned had not neglected precautions, and discipline and armour once again told their tale. It shows how much food there was in the Island that two legions could live for a fortnight off the cornfields close to their camp. The British submitted. Their conqueror imposed only nominal terms. Breaking up many of his ships to repair the rest, he was glad to return with some hostages and captives to the mainland. He never even pretended that his expedition had been a success. To supersede the record of it he came again the next year, this time with five legions and some cavalry conveyed in eight hundred ships. The Islanders were overawed by the size of the armada. The landing was unimpeded, but again the sea as-

sailed him. Cæsar had marched twelve miles into the interior
when he was recalled by the news that a great storm had shattered or damaged a large portion of his fleet. He was forced to
spend ten days in hauling all his ships on to the shore, and in
fortifying the camp of which they then formed part. This done
he renewed his invasion, and, after easily destroying the forest
stockades in which the British sheltered, crossed the Thames
near Brentford. But the British had found a leader in the chief
Cassivellaunus, who was a master of war under the prevailing
conditions. Dismissing to their homes the mass of untrained
foot-soldiers and peasantry, he kept pace with the invaders
march by march with his chariots and horsemen. Cæsar gives
a detailed description of the chariot-fighting:

> In chariot fighting the Britons begin by driving all over the
> field hurling javelins, and generally the terror inspired by the
> horses and the noise of the wheels are sufficient to throw their
> opponents' ranks into disorder. Then, after making their way
> between the squadrons of their own cavalry, they jump down
> from the chariots and engage on foot. In the meantime their
> charioteers retire a short distance from the battle and place
> the chariots in such a position that their masters, if hard
> pressed by numbers, have an easy means of retreat to their
> own lines. Thus they combine the mobility of cavalry with the
> staying-power of infantry; and by daily training and practice
> they attain such proficiency that even on a steep incline they
> are able to control the horses at full gallop, and to check and
> turn them in a moment. They can run along the chariot pole,
> stand on the yoke, and get back into the chariot as quick as
> lightning.

Cassivellaunus, using these mobile forces and avoiding a
pitched battle with the Roman legions, escorted them on their
inroad and cut off their foraging parties. None the less Cæsar
captured his first stronghold; the tribes began to make terms

for themselves; a well-conceived plan for destroying Cæsar's base on the Kentish shore was defeated. At this juncture Cassivellaunus, by a prudence of policy equal to that of his tactics, negotiated a further surrender of hostages and a promise of tribute and submission, in return for which Cæsar was again content to quit the Island. In a dead calm, "he set sail late in the evening and brought all the fleet safely to land at dawn." This time he proclaimed a conquest. Cæsar had his triumph, and British captives trod their dreary path at his tail through the streets of Rome; but for nearly a hundred years no invading army landed upon the Island coasts.

Little is known of Cassivellaunus, and we can only hope that later defenders of the Island will be equally successful and that their measures will be as well suited to the needs of the time. The impression remains of a prudent and skilful chief, whose qualities and achievements, but for the fact that they were displayed in an outlandish theatre, might well have ranked with those of Fabius Maximus Cunctator.

Subjugation

URING the hundred years which followed Julius Cæsar's
invasion the British Islanders remained unmolested.
The Belgic cities developed a life of their own, and the warrior
tribes enjoyed amid their internecine feuds the comforting il-
lusion that no one was likely to attack them again. However,
their contacts with the mainland and with the civilisation of
the Roman Empire grew, and trade flourished in a wide range
of commodities. Roman traders established themselves in
many parts, and carried back to Rome tales of the wealth and
possibilities of Britannia, if only a stable Government were
set up.

In the year A.D. 41 the murder of the Emperor Caligula, and
a chapter of accidents, brought his uncle, the clownish scholar
Claudius, to the throne of the world. No one can suppose that
any coherent will to conquest resided in the new ruler, but the
policy of Rome was shaped by the officials of highly competent
departments. It proceeded upon broad lines, and in its various
aspects attracted a growing and strong measure of support
from many sections of public opinion. Eminent senators aired
their views, important commercial and financial interests were
conciliated, and elegant society had a new topic for gossip.
Thus, in this triumphant period there were always available
for a new emperor a number of desirable projects, well thought
out beforehand and in harmony with the generally understood
Roman system, any one of which might catch the fancy of the
latest wielder of supreme power. Hence we find emperors ele-

vated by chance whose unbridled and capricious passions were their only distinction, whose courts were debauched with lust and cruelty, who were themselves vicious or feeble-minded, who were pawns in the hands of their counsellors or favourites, decreeing great campaigns and setting their seal upon long-lasting acts of salutary legislation.

The advantages of conquering the recalcitrant island Britannia were paraded before the new monarch, and his interest was excited. He was attracted by the idea of gaining a military reputation. He gave orders that this dramatic and possibly lucrative enterprise should proceed. In the year 43, almost one hundred years after Julius Cæsar's evacuation, a powerful, well-organised Roman army of some twenty thousand men was prepared for the subjugation of Britain. "The soldiers were indignant at the thought of carrying on a campaign outside the limits of the known world." But when the Emperor's favourite freedman, Narcissus, attempted to address them they felt the insult. The spectacle of a former slave called in to stand sponsor for their commander rallied them to their duty. They taunted Narcissus with his slave origin, with the mocking shout of *"Io Saturnalia!"* (for at the festival of Saturn the slaves donned their masters' dress and held festival), but none the less they resolved to obey their chief's order.

"Their delay, however, had made their departure late in the season. They were sent over in three divisions, in order that they should not be hindered in landing—as might happen to a single force—and in their voyage across they first became discouraged because they were driven back in their course, and then plucked up courage because a flash of light rising in the east shot across to the west, the direction in which they were sailing. So they put in to the Island, and found none to oppose them. For the Britons, as the result of their inquiries, had not

expected that they would come, and had therefore not assembled beforehand." [1]

The internal situation favoured the invaders. Cunobelinus
(Shakespeare's Cymbeline) had established an overlordship
over the south-east of the Island, with his capital at Colchester.
But in his old age dissensions had begun to impair his
authority, and on his death the kingdom was ruled jointly by
his sons Caractacus and Togodumnus. They were not everywhere recognised, and they had no time to form a union of the
tribal kingdom before Plautius and the legions arrived. The
people of Kent fell back on the tactics of Cassivellaunus, and
Plautius accordingly had much trouble in searching them out;
but when at last he did find them he first defeated Caractacus,
and then his brother somewhere in East Kent. Then, advancing along Cæsar's old line of march, he came on a river he had
not heard of, the Medway. "The barbarians thought that the
Romans would not be able to cross without a bridge, and
consequently bivouacked in rather careless fashion on the opposite bank"; but the Roman general sent across "a detachment of Germans, who were accustomed to swim easily in full
armour across the most turbulent streams. These fell unexpectedly upon the enemy, but instead of shooting at the men
they disabled the horses that drew the chariots, and in the ensuing confusion not even the enemy's mounted men could save
themselves." [2] Nevertheless the Britons faced them on the second day, and were only broken by a flank attack, Vespasian—
some day to be Emperor himself—having discovered a ford
higher up. This victory marred the stage-management of the
campaign. Plautius had won his battle too soon, and in
the wrong place. Something had to be done to show that the
Emperor's presence was necessary to victory. So Claudius,

[1] Dio Cassius, chapter lx, pp. 19–20.
[2] *Ibid.*

who had been waiting on events in France, crossed the seas, bringing substantial reinforcements, including a number of elephants. A battle was procured, and the Romans won. Claudius returned to Rome to receive from the Senate the title of "Britannicus" and permission to celebrate a triumph.

But the British war continued. The Britons would not come to close quarters with the Romans, but took refuge in the swamps and the forests, hoping to wear out the invaders, so that, as in the days of Julius Cæsar, they should sail back with nothing accomplished. Caractacus escaped to the Welsh border, and, rousing its tribes, maintained an indomitable resistance for more than six years. It was not till A.D. 50 that he was finally defeated by a new general, Ostorius, an officer of energy and ability, who reduced to submission the whole of the more settled regions from the Wash to the Severn. Caractacus, escaping from the ruin of his forces in the West, sought to raise the Brigantes in the North. Their queen however handed him over to the Romans. "The fame of the British prince," writes Suetonius, "had by this time spread over the provinces of Gaul and Italy; and upon his arrival in the Roman capital the people flocked from all quarters to behold him. The ceremonial of his entrance was conducted with great solemnity. On a plain adjoining the Roman camp the Pretorian troops were drawn up in martial array. The Emperor and his court took their station in front of the lines, and behind them was ranged the whole body of the people. The procession commenced with the different trophies which had been taken from the Britons during the progress of the war. Next followed the brothers of the vanquished prince, with his wife and daughter, in chains, expressing by their supplicating looks and gestures the fears with which they were actuated. But not so Caractacus himself. With a manly gait and an undaunted countenance he marched up to the tribunal, where the Emperor was seated, and addressed him in the following terms:

"If to my high birth and distinguished rank I had added the virtues of moderation Rome had beheld me rather as a friend than a captive, and you would not have rejected an alliance with a prince descended from illustrious ancestors and governing many nations. The reverse of my fortune is glorious to you, and to me humiliating. I had arms, and men, and horses; I possessed extraordinary riches; and can it be any wonder that I was unwilling to lose them? Because Rome aspires to universal dominion must men therefore implicitly resign themselves to subjection? I opposed for a long time the progress of your arms, and had I acted otherwise would either you have had the glory of conquest or I of a brave resistance? I am now in your power. If you are determined to take revenge my fate will soon be forgotten, and you will derive no honour from the transaction. Preserve my life, and I shall remain to the latest ages a monument of your clemency.

"Immediately upon this speech Claudius granted him his liberty, as he did likewise to the other royal captives. They all returned their thanks in a manner the most grateful to the Emperor; and as soon as their chains were taken off, walking towards Agrippina, who sat upon a bench at a little distance, they repeated to her the same fervent declarations of gratitude and esteem." [1]

* * * * *

The conquest was not achieved without one frightful convulsion of revolt. "In this year A.D. 61," according to Tacitus, "a severe disaster was sustained in Britain." Suetonius, the new governor, had engaged himself deeply in the West. He trans-

---

[1] C. Suetonius Tranquillus, *The Lives of the Twelve Cæsars*, trans. by Alexander Thomson, revised by T. Forester.

ferred the operational base of the Roman army from Wroxeter to Chester. He prepared to attack "the populous island of Mona [Anglesey], which had become a refuge for fugitives, and he built a fleet of flat-bottomed vessels suitable for those shallow and shifting seas. The infantry crossed in the boats, the cavalry went over by fords: where the water was too deep the men swam alongside of their horses. The enemy lined the shore, a dense host of armed men, interspersed with women clad in black like the Furies, with their hair hanging down and holding torches in their hands. Round this were Druids uttering dire curses and stretching their hands towards heaven. These strange sights terrified the soldiers. They stayed motionless, as if paralysed, offering their bodies to the blows. At last, encouraged by the general, and exhorting each other not to quail before the rabble of female fanatics, they advanced their standards, bore down all resistance, and enveloped the enemy in their own flames.

"Suetonius imposed a garrison upon the conquered and cut down the groves devoted to their cruel superstitions; for it was part of their religion to spill the blood of captives on their altars, and to inquire of the gods by means of human entrails."

This dramatic scene on the frontiers of modern Wales was the prelude to a tragedy. The king of the East Anglian Iceni had died. Hoping to save his kingdom and family from molestation he had appointed Nero, who had succeeded Claudius as Emperor, as heir jointly with his two daughters. "But," says Tacitus, "things turned out differently. His kingdom was plundered by centurions, and his private property by slaves, as if they had been captured in war; his widow Boadicea [relished by the learned as Boudicca] was flogged, and his daughters outraged; the chiefs of the Iceni were robbed of their ancestral properties as if the Romans had received the whole country as

a gift, and the king's own relatives were reduced to slavery."
Thus the Roman historian.[1]

Boadicea's tribe, at once the most powerful and hitherto the
most submissive, was moved to frenzy against the Roman invaders. They flew to arms. Boadicea found herself at the head
of a numerous army, and nearly all the Britons within reach
rallied to her standard. There followed an up-rush of hatred
from the abyss, which is a measure of the cruelty of the conquest. It was a scream of rage against invincible oppression
and the superior culture which seemed to lend it power.
"Boadicea," said Ranke, "is rugged, earnest and terrible." [2]
Her monument on the Thames Embankment opposite Big Ben
reminds us of the harsh cry of liberty or death which has echoed down the ages.

In all Britain there were only four legions, at most twenty
thousand men. The Fourteenth and Twentieth were with Suetonius on his Welsh campaign. The Ninth was at Lincoln, and
the Second at Gloucester.

The first target of the revolt was Camulodunum (Colchester), an unwalled colony of Roman and Romanised
Britons, where the recently settled veterans, supported by the
soldiery, who hoped for similar licence for themselves, had
been ejecting the inhabitants from their houses and driving
them away from their lands. The Britons were encouraged by
omens. The statue of Victory fell face foremost, as if flying
from the enemy. The sea turned red. Strange cries were heard
in the council chamber and the theatre. The Roman officials,
business men, bankers, usurers, and the Britons who had par-
ticipated in their authority and profits, found themselves with
a handful of old soldiers in the midst of "a multitude of bar-

[1] Extracts from Tacitus' *Annals* are from G. G. Ramsay's translation;
passages from the *Agricola* come from the translation of Church and
Brodribb.

[2] *History of England,* vol. i, p. 8.

barians." Suetonius was a month distant. The Ninth Legion was a hundred and twenty miles away. There was neither mercy nor hope. The town was burned to ashes. The temple, whose strong walls resisted the conflagration, held out for two days. Everyone, Roman or Romanised, was massacred and everything destroyed. Meanwhile the Ninth Legion was marching to the rescue. The victorious Britons advanced from the sack of Colchester to meet it. By sheer force of numbers they overcame the Roman infantry and slaughtered them to a man, and the commander, Petilius Cerialis, was content to escape with his cavalry. Such were the tidings which reached Suetonius in Anglesey. He realised at once that his army could not make the distance in time to prevent even greater disaster, but, says Tacitus, he, "undaunted, made his way through a hostile country to Londinium, a town which, though not dignified by the title of colony, was a busy emporium for traders." This is the first mention of London in literature. Though fragments of Gallic or Italian pottery which may or may not antedate the Roman conquest have been found there, it is certain that the place attained no prominence until the Claudian invaders brought a mass of army contractors and officials to the most convenient bridgehead on the Thames.

Suetonius reached London with only a small mounted escort. He had sent orders to the Second Legion to meet him there from Gloucester, but the commander, appalled by the defeat of the Ninth, had not complied. London was a large, undefended town, full of Roman traders and their British associates, dependants, and slaves. It contained a fortified military depot, with valuable stores and a handful of legionaries. The citizens of London implored Suetonius to protect them, but when he heard that Boadicea, having chased Cerialis towards Lincoln, had turned and was marching south he took the hard but right decision to leave them to their fate. The commander of the Second Legion had disobeyed him, and he had no force to withstand the enormous masses hastening towards him. His only course was to rejoin the Fourteenth and Twentieth Legions, who were marching with might and main from Wales to London along the line of the Roman road now known as Watling Street, and, unmoved by the entreaties of the inhabitants, he gave the signal to march, receiving within his lines all who wished to go with him.

The slaughter which fell upon London was universal. No one was spared, neither man, woman, nor child. The wrath of the revolt concentrated itself upon all of those of British blood who had lent themselves to the wiles and seductions of the invader. In recent times, with London buildings growing taller and needing deeper foundations, the power-driven excavating machines have encountered at many points the layer of ashes which marks the effacement of London at the hands of the natives of Britain.

Boadicea then turned upon Verulamium (St Albans). Here was another trading centre, to which high civic rank had been accorded. A like total slaughter and obliteration was inflicted. "No less," according to Tacitus, "than seventy thousand citizens and allies were slain" in these three cities. "For the barbarians would have no capturing, no selling, nor any kind of traffic usual in war; they would have nothing but killing, by sword, cross, gibbet, or fire." These grim words show us an inexpiable war like that waged between Carthage and her revolted mercenaries two centuries before. Some high modern authorities think these numbers are exaggerated; but there is no reason why London should not have contained thirty or forty thousand inhabitants, and Colchester and St Albans between them about an equal number. If the butcheries in the countryside are added the estimate of Tacitus may well stand. This is probably the most horrible episode which our Island has known. We see the crude and corrupt beginnings of a higher civilisation blotted out by the ferocious uprising of the native tribes. Still, it is the primary right of men to die and kill for the land they live in, and to punish with exceptional severity all members of their own race who have warmed their hands at the invaders' hearth.

"And now Suetonius, having with him the Fourteenth Legion, with the veterans of the Twentieth, and the auxiliaries nearest at hand, making up a force of about ten thousand fully armed men, resolved . . . for battle. Selecting a position in a defile closed in behind a wood, and having made sure that there was no enemy but in front, where there was an open flat unsuited for ambuscades, he drew up his legions in close order, with the light-armed troops on the flanks, while the cavalry was massed at the extremities of the wings." The day was bloody and decisive. The barbarian army, eighty thousand strong, attended, like the Germans and the Gauls, by their women and children in an unwieldy wagon-train, drew out their array, resolved to conquer or perish. Here was no thought of subsequent accommodation. On both sides it was all for all. At heavy adverse odds Roman discipline and tactical skill triumphed. No quarter was given, even to the women.

"It was a glorious victory, fit to rank with those of olden days. Some say that little less than eighty thousand Britons fell, our own killed being about four hundred, with a somewhat larger number wounded." These are the tales of the victors. Boadicea poisoned herself. Pœnius Postumus, camp commander of the Second Legion, who had both disobeyed his general and deprived his men of their share in the victory, on hearing of the success of the Fourteenth and Twentieth ran himself through with his sword.

Suetonius now thought only of vengeance, and indeed there was much to repay. Reinforcements of four or five thousand men were sent by Nero from Germany, and all hostile or suspect tribes were harried with fire and sword. Worst of all was the want of food; for in their confident expectation of capturing the supplies of the Romans the Britons had brought every available man into the field and left their land unsown. Yet even so their spirit was unbroken, and the extermination of the entire ancient British race might have followed but for the remonstrances of a new Procurator, supported by the Treasury officials at Rome, who saw themselves about to be possessed of a desert instead of a province. As a man of action Suetonius ranks high, and his military decisions were sound. But there was a critical faculty alive in the Roman state which cannot be discounted as arising merely through the jealousies of important people. It was held that Suetonius had been rashly ambitious of military glory and had been caught unaware by the widespread uprising of the province, that "his reverses were due to his own folly, his successes to good fortune," and that a Governor must be sent, "free from feelings of hostility or triumph, who would deal gently with our conquered enemies." The Procurator, Julius Classicianus, whose tombstone is now in the British Museum, kept writing in this sense to Rome, and pleaded vehemently for the pacification of the warrior bands, who still fought on without seeking truce or mercy, starving and perishing in the forests and the fens. In the end it was resolved to make the best of the Britons. German unrest and dangers from across the Rhine made even military circles in Rome disinclined to squander forces in remoter regions. The loss in a storm of some of Suetonius's warships was made the pretext and occasion of his supersession. The Emperor Nero sent a new Governor, who made a peace with the desperate tribesmen which enabled their blood to be perpetuated in the Island race.

*   *   *   *   *

Tacitus gives an interesting account of the new province.

The red hair and large limbs of the inhabitants of Caledonia
[he says] pointed quite clearly to a German origin, while the
dark complexion of the Silures, their usually curly hair, and
the fact that Spain lies opposite to them are evidence that Ibe-
rians of a former date crossed over and occupied these parts.
Those who are nearest to the Gauls are also like them, either
from the permanent influence of original descent, or because
climate had produced similar qualities. . . . The religious
beliefs of Gaul may be traced in the strongly marked British
superstition [Druidism]. The language differs but little.
There is the same boldness in challenging danger, and when
it is near the same timidity in shrinking from it. The Britons
however exhibit more spirit, being a people whom a long
peace has not yet enervated. . . . Their sky is obscured by
continual rain and cloud. Severity of cold is unknown. The
days exceed in length those of our world; the nights are bright,
and in the extreme north so short that between sunset and
dawn there is but little distinction. . . . With the exception
of the olive and vine, and plants which usually grow in
warmer climates, the soil will yield all ordinary produce in
plenty. It ripens slowly, but grows rapidly, the cause in each
case being excessive moisture of soil and atmosphere.

In A.D. 78 Agricola, a Governor of talent and energy, was
sent to Britannia. Instead of spending his first year of office in
the customary tour of ceremony, he took field against all who
still disputed the Roman authority. One large tribe which had
massacred a squadron of auxiliary cavalry was exterminated.
The island of Mona, from which Suetonius had been recalled
by the rising of Boadicea, was subjugated. With military ability
Agricola united a statesmanlike humanity. According to
Tacitus (who had married his daughter), he proclaimed that
"little is gained by conquest if followed by oppression." He

mitigated the severity of the corn tribute. He encouraged and aided the building of temples, courts of justice, and dwelling-houses. He provided a liberal education for the sons of the chiefs, and showed "such a preference for the natural powers of the Britons over the more laboured style of the Gauls" that the well-to-do classes were conciliated and became willing to adopt the toga and other Roman fashions. "Step by step they were led to practices which disposed to vice—the lounge, the bath, the elegant banquet. All this in their ignorance they called civilisation, when it was but part of their servitude."

Although in the Senate and governing circles in Rome it was constantly explained that the Imperial policy adhered to the principle of the great Augustus, that the frontiers should be maintained but not extended, Agricola was permitted to conduct six campaigns of expansion in Britannia. In the third he reached the Tyne, the advances of his legions being supported at every stage by a fleet of sea-borne supplies. In the fifth campaign he reached the line of the Forth and Clyde, and here on this wasp-waist of Britain he might well have dug himself in. But there was no safety or permanent peace for the British province unless he could subdue the powerful tribes and large bands of desperate warriors who had been driven northwards by his advance. Indeed, it is evident that he would never of his own will have stopped in any direction short of the ocean shore. Therefore in his sixth campaign he marched northwards again with all his forces. The position had now become formidable. Past misfortunes had taught the Britons the penalties of disunion.

Agricola's son-in-law tells us:

> Our army, elated by the glory they had won, exclaimed that they must penetrate the recesses of Caledonia and at length in an unbroken succession of battles discover the farthest limits of Britain. But the Britons, thinking themselves baffled not

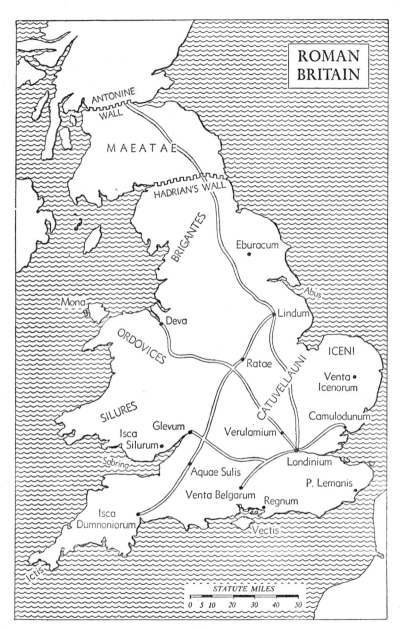

ROMAN
BRITAIN

ANTONINE
WALL

MAEATAE

HADRIAN'S WALL

BRIGANTES

Eburacum

Mona

Abus

Deva

Lindum

ORDOVICES

Ratae

ICENI

CATUVELLAUNI

Venta
Icenorum

SILURES

Glevum

Camulodunum

Isca
Silurum

Verulamium

Sabrina

Aquae Sulis

Londinium

P. Lemanis

Venta Belgarum

Regnum

Isca
Dumnoniorum

Vectis

Ictis

STATUTE MILES

0   5 10   20   30   40   50

· 31 ·

so much by our valour as by our general's skilful use of an opportunity, abated nothing of their arrogance, arming their youth, removing their wives and children to a place of safety, and assembling together to ratify, with sacred rites, a confederacy of all their states.

The decisive battle was fought at Mons Graupius, a place which remains unidentified, though some suggest the Pass of Killiecrankie. Tacitus describes in unconvincing detail the course of this famous struggle. The whole of Caledonia, all that was left of Britannia, a vast host of broken, hunted men, resolved on death or freedom, confronted in their superiority of four or five to one the skilfully handled Roman legions and auxiliaries, among whom no doubt many British renegades were serving. It is certain that Tacitus greatly exaggerated the dimensions of the native army in these wilds, where they could have no prepared magazines. The number, though still considerable, must have been severely limited. Apparently, as in so many ancient battles, the beaten side were the victims of misunderstanding and the fate of the day was decided against them before the bulk of the forces realised that a serious engagement had begun. Reserves descended from the hills too late to achieve victory, but in good time to be massacred in the rout. The last organised resistance of Britain to the Roman power ended at Mons Graupius. Here, according to the Roman account, "ten thousand of the enemy were slain, and on our side there were about three hundred and sixty men." Clive's victory at Plassey, which secured for the British Empire a long spell of authority in India, was gained against greater odds, with smaller forces and with smaller losses.

The way to the entire subjugation of the Island was now open, and had Agricola been encouraged or at least supported by the Imperial Government the course of history might have been altered. But Caledonia was to Rome only a sensation:

the real strain was between the Rhine and the Danube. Counsels of prudence prevailed, and the remnants of the British fighting men were left to moulder in the Northern mists.

Dio Cassius, writing over a century later, describes how they were a perpetual source of expense and worry to the settled regions of the South.

> There are two very extensive tribes in Britain, the Caledonians and the Mæatæ. The Mæatæ dwell close up to the cross-wall which cuts the island in two, the Caledonians beyond them. Both live on wild, waterless hills or forlorn and swampy plains, without walls or towns or husbandry, subsisting on pastoral products and the nuts which they gather. They have fish in plenty, but do not eat it. They live in huts, go naked and unshod; make no separate marriages, and rear all their offspring. They mostly have a democratic government, and are much addicted to robbery. . . . They can bear hunger and cold and all manner of hardship; they will retire into their marshes and hold out for days with only their heads above water, and in the forest they will subsist on bark and roots.

* * * * *

In the wild North and West freedom found refuge among the mountains, but elsewhere the conquest and pacification were at length complete and Britannia became one of the forty-five provinces of the Roman Empire. The great Augustus had proclaimed as the Imperial ideal the creation of a commonwealth of self-governing cantons. Each province was organised as a separate unit, and within it municipalities received their charters and rights. The provinces were divided between those exposed to barbarian invasion or uprising, for which an Imperial garrison must be provided, and those which required no such protection. The military provinces were under the direct supervision of the Emperor. The more sheltered were controlled, at least in form, through the medium of the Senate, but in all provinces the principle was followed of adapting the form of government to local conditions. No prejudice of race, language, or religion obstructed the universal character of the Roman system. The only divisions were those of class, and these ran unchallenged throughout the ordered world. There were Roman citizens, there was an enormous mass of non-Roman citizens, and there were slaves, but movement to full citizenship was possible to fortunate members of the servile class. On this basis therefore the life of Britain now developed.

The Roman Province

FOR nearly three hundred years Britain, reconciled to the Roman system, enjoyed in many respects the happiest, most comfortable, and most enlightened times its inhabitants have ever had. Confronted with the dangers of the frontiers, the military force was moderate. The Wall was held by the auxiliaries, with a legion in support at York. Wales was pinned down by a legion at Chester and another at Caerleon-on-Usk. In all the army of occupation numbered less than forty thousand men, and after a few generations was locally recruited and almost of purely British birth. In this period, almost equal to that which separates us from the reign of Queen Elizabeth I, well-to-do persons in Britain lived better than they ever did until late Victorian times. From the year 400 till the year 1900 no one had central heating and very few had hot baths. A wealthy British-Roman citizen building a country house regarded the hypocaust which warmed it as indispensable. For fifteen hundred years his descendants lived in the cold of unheated dwellings, mitigated by occasional roastings at gigantic wasteful fires. Even now a smaller proportion of the whole population dwells in centrally heated houses than in those ancient days. As for baths, they were completely lost till the middle of the nineteenth century. In all this long, bleak intervening gap cold and dirt clung to the most fortunate and highest in the land.

In culture and learning Britain was a pale reflection of the Roman scene, not so lively as the Gallic. But there was law; there was order; there was peace; there was warmth; there

was food, and a long-established custom of life. The population was free from barbarism without being sunk in sloth or
luxury. Some culture spread even to the villages. Roman habits
percolated; the use of Roman utensils and even of Roman
speech steadily grew. The British thought themselves as good
Romans as any. Indeed, it may be said that of all the provinces
few assimilated the Roman system with more aptitude than
the Islanders. The British legionaries and auxiliaries were
rated equal or second only to the Illyrians as the finest troops
in the Empire. There was a sense of pride in sharing in so noble
and widespread a system. To be a citizen of Rome was to be a
citizen of the world, raised upon a pedestal of unquestioned
superiority above barbarians or slaves. Movement across the
great Empire was as rapid as when Queen Victoria came to
the throne, and no obstruction of frontiers, laws, currency, or
nationalism hindered it. There is a monument at Norwich
erected to his wife by a Syrian resident in Britain. Constantius
Chlorus died at York. British sentinels watched along the
Rhine, the Danube, and the Euphrates. Troops from Asia
Minor, peering through the mists at the Scottish raiders, preserved the worship of Mithras along the Roman Wall. The
cult of this Persian Sun-god spread widely throughout the Roman world, appealing especially to soldiers, merchants, and
administrators. During the third century Mithraism was a powerful rival to Christianity, and, as was revealed by the impressive temple discovered at Walbrook in 1954, it could count
many believers in Roman London.

The violent changes at the summit of the Empire did not
affect so much as might be supposed the ordinary life of its
population. Here and there were wars and risings. Rival emperors suppressed each other. Legions mutinied. Usurpers
established themselves in the provinces affected on these occasions. The British took a keen interest in the politics of the

Roman world and formed strong views upon the changes in the Imperial power or upon the morale of the capital. Many thrusting spirits shot forward in Britain to play a part in the deadly game of Imperial politics, with its unparalleled prizes and fatal forfeits. But all were entirely reconciled to the Roman idea. They had their law; they had their life, which flowed on broad, and, if momentarily disturbed, in the main unaltered. A poll in the fourth century would have declared for an indefinite continuance of the Roman régime.

In our own fevered, changing, and precarious age, where all is in flux and nothing is accepted, we must survey with respect a period when, with only three hundred thousand soldiers, widespread the peace in the entire known world was maintained from generation to generation, and when the first pristine impulse of Christianity lifted men's souls to the contemplation of new and larger harmonies beyond the ordered world around them.

The gift which Roman civilisation had to bestow was civic and political. Towns were planned in chessboard squares for communities dwelling under orderly government. The buildings rose in accordance with the pattern standardised throughout the Roman world. Each was complete with its forum, temples, courts of justice, gaols, baths, markets, and main drains. During the first century the builders evidently took a sanguine view of the resources and future of Britannia, and all their towns were projected to meet an increasing population. It was a period of hope.

The experts dispute the population of Roman Britain, and rival estimates vary between half a million and a million and a half. It seems certain that the army, the civil services, the townsfolk, the well-to-do, and their dependants amounted to three or four hundred thousand. To grow food for these, under the agricultural methods of the age, would have required on the land perhaps double their number. We may therefore assume a population of at least a million in the Romanised area. There may well have been more. But there are no signs that any large increase of population accompanied the Roman system. In more than two centuries of peace and order the inhabitants remained at about the same numbers as in the days of Cassivellaunus. This failure to foster and support a more numerous life spread disappointment and contraction throughout Roman Britain. The conquerors who so easily subdued and rallied the Britons to their method of social life brought with them no means, apart from stopping tribal war, of increasing the annual income derived from the productivity of the soil. The new society, with all its grace of structure, with its spice of elegance and luxury—baths, banquets, togas, schools, literature, and oratory—stood on no more sumptuous foundation than the agriculture of prehistoric times. The rude plenty in which the ancient Britons had dwelt was capable of supporting only to a moderate extent the imposing façade of Roman life. The cultivated ground was still for the most part confined to the lighter and more easily cultivated upland soils, which had for thousands of years been worked in a primitive fashion. The powerful Gallic plough on wheels was known in Britain, but it did not supplant the native implement, which could only nose along in shallow furrows. With a few exceptions, there was no large-scale attempt to clear the forests, drain the marshes, and cultivate the heavy clay soil of the valleys, in which so much fertility had been deposited. Such mining of lead and tin, such smelting, as had existed from times immemorial may have gained something from orderly administration; but there was no new science, no new thrust of power and knowledge in the material sphere. Thus the economic basis remained constant, and Britain became more genteel rather than more wealthy. The life of Britain continued upon a small scale, and in the main was stationary. The new edifice, so stately and admirable, was light and frail.

These conditions soon cast their shadows upon the boldly planned towns. The surrounding agricultural prosperity was not sufficient to support the hopes of their designers. There are several excavations which show that the original boundaries were never occupied, or that, having been at first occupied, portions of the town fell gradually into decay. There was not enough material well-being to make things go. Nevertheless men dwelt safely, and what property they had was secured by iron laws. Urban life in Britannia was a failure, not of existence, but of expansion. It ran on like the life of some cathedral city, some fading provincial town, sedate, restricted, even contracting, but not without grace and dignity.

We owe London to Rome. The military engineers of Claudius, the bureaucracy which directed the supply of the armies, the merchants who followed in their wake, brought it into a life not yet stilled. Trade followed the development of their road system. An extensive and well-planned city with mighty walls took the place of the wooden trading settlement of A.D. 61, and soon achieved a leading place in the life of the Roman province of Britain, superseding the old Belgic capital, Colchester, as the commercial centre. At the end of the third century money was coined in the London mint, and the city was the headquarters of the financial administration. In the later days of the province London seems to have been the centre of civil government, as York was of the military, although it never received the status of a *municipium*.

The efflorescence of Rome in Britain was found in its villa population all over the settled area. The villas of country gentlemen of modest station were built in the most delightful spots of a virgin countryside, amid primeval forests and the gushing of untamed streams. A very large number of comfortable dwellings, each with its lands around it, rose and thrived. At least five hundred have been explored in the southern counties. None is found farther north than Yorkshire or farther west than the Glamorgan sea-plain. The comparative unsuccess of urban life led the better-class Roman Britons to establish themselves in the country, and thus the villa system was the dominant feature of Roman Britain in its heyday. The villas retained their prosperity after the towns had already decayed. The towns were shrunken after the third century. The villas still flourished in the fourth, and in some cases lingered on into the darkening days of the fifth.

The need for strong defences at the time when the expansion of the Empire had practically reached its limits was met by the frontier policy of the Flavian emperors. Domitian was the first to build a continuous line of fortifications. About A.D. 89 the great earth rampart was constructed on the Black Sea, and another connecting the Rhine with the Danube. By the end of the first century a standard type of frontier barrier had been evolved. The work of Agricola in Northern Britain had been left unfinished at his hasty recall. No satisfactory line of defence had been erected, and the position which he had won in Scotland had to be gradually abandoned. The legions fell back on the line of the Stanegate, a road running eastwards from Carlisle. The years which followed revealed the weakness of the British frontier. The accession of Hadrian was marked by a serious disaster. The Ninth Legion disappears from history in combating an obscure rising of the tribes in Northern Britain. The defences were disorganised and the province was in danger. Hadrian came himself to Britain in 122, and the reorganisation of the frontier began.

During the next five years a military barrier was built between the Tyne and the Solway seventy-three miles long. It consisted of a stone rampart eight to ten feet thick, sustained by seventeen forts, garrisoned each by an auxiliary cohort, about eighty castles, and double that number of signal towers. In front of the wall was a 30-foot ditch, and behind it another ditch which seems to have been designed as a customs frontier and was probably controlled and staffed by the financial administration. The works needed a supporting garrison of about fourteen thousand men, not including some five thousand who, independent of the fighting units in the forts, were engaged in patrol work along the wall. The troops were provisioned by the local population, whose taxes were paid in wheat, and each fort contained granaries capable of holding a year's supply of food.

Twenty years later, in the reign of the Emperor Antoninus Pius, the Roman troops pushed northwards again over the ground of Agricola's conquests, and a new wall was built across the Forth-Clyde isthmus thirty-seven miles in length. The object was to control the tribes of the eastern and central Lowlands; but the Roman forces in Britain were not able to man the new defences without weakening their position on Hadrian's Wall and in the West. The middle years of the second century were troubled in the military area. Somewhere about the year 186 the Antonine Wall was abandoned, and the troops were concentrated on the original line of defence. Tribal revolts and Scottish raids continually assailed the northern frontier system, and in places the Wall and its supporting camps were utterly wrecked.

It was not until the Emperor Severus came to Britain in 208 and flung his energies into the task of reorganisation that stability was achieved. So great had been the destruction, so massive were his repairs, that in later times he was thought to have built the Wall, which in fact he only reconstructed. He died at York in 211; but for a hundred years there was peace along the Roman Wall.

We can measure the Roman activity in road-building by the milestones which are discovered from time to time, recording the name of the emperor under whose decree the work was done. These long, unswerving causeways stretched in bold lines across the Island. Ordinarily the road was made with a bottoming of large stones, often embedded in sand, covered with a surface of rammed gravel, the whole on an average eighteen inches thick. In special cases, or after much repairing, the formation extended to a 3-foot thickness. Over Blackstone Edge, where the road was laid upon peat, a 16-foot road-span was made of square blocks of millstone grit, with a kerb on either side and a line of large squared stones down the middle. Upon these the wheels of ancient carts going down the steep hill, braked by skid-pans, have made their grooves.[1]

The first half-century after the Claudian invasion was very active in road-building. In the second century we find most of the work concentrated upon the frontiers of the military districts. By the third century the road system was complete, and needed only to be kept in repair. It is true that for the period of Constantine no fewer than four milestones have been unearthed, which point to some fresh extension, but by 340 all new work was ended, and though repairs were carried out as long as possible no later milestones proclaim a forward movement. The same symptoms reproduced themselves in Gaul after the year 350. These pedestrian facts are one measure of the rise and decline of the Roman power.

If a native of Chester in Roman Britain could wake up to-day [2] he would find laws which were the direct fulfilment of many of those he had known. He would find in every village temples and priests of the new creed which in his day was winning victories everywhere. Indeed the facilities for Christian

[1] *An Economic Survey of Ancient Rome,* iii, 24.
[2] Written in 1939.

worship would appear to him to be far in excess of the number of devotees. Not without pride would he notice that his children were compelled to learn Latin if they wished to enter the most famous universities. He might encounter some serious difficulties in the pronunciation. He would find in the public libraries many of the masterpieces of ancient literature, printed on uncommonly cheap paper and in great numbers. He would find a settled government, and a sense of belonging to a worldwide empire. He could drink and bathe in the waters of Bath, or if this were too far he would find vapour baths and toilet conveniences in every city. He would find all his own problems of currency, land tenure, public morals and decorum presented in a somewhat different aspect, but still in lively dispute. He would have the same sense of belonging to a society which was threatened, and to an imperial rule which had passed its prime. He would have the same gathering fears of some sudden onslaught by barbarian forces armed with equal weapons to those of the local legions or auxiliaries. He would still fear the people across the North Sea, and still be taught that his frontiers were upon the Rhine. The most marked changes that would confront him would be the speed of communications and the volume of printed and broadcast matter. He might find both distressing. But against these he could set chloroform, antiseptics, and a more scientific knowledge of hygiene. He would have longer history books to read, containing worse tales than those of Tacitus and Dio. Facilities would be afforded to him for seeing "regions Cæsar never knew," from which he would probably return in sorrow and wonder. He would find himself hampered in every aspect of foreign travel, except that of speed. If he wished to journey to Rome, Constantinople, or Jerusalem, otherwise than by sea, a dozen frontiers would scrutinise his entry. He would be called upon to develop a large number of tribal and racial enmities to which he had formerly been a stranger. But the more he studied the accounts of what had happened since the third century the more satisfied he would be not to have been awakened at an earlier time.

     *   *   *   *   *

Carefully conserved, the resources of the Empire in men and material were probably sufficient to maintain the frontiers intact. But they were often wasted in war between rival emperors, and by the middle of the third century the Empire was politically in a state of chaos and financially ruined. Yet there was much vitality still, and from the Illyrian armies came a succession of great soldiers and administrators to restore the unity of the Empire and consolidate its defences. By the end of the century Rome seemed as powerful and stable as ever. But below the surface the foundations were cracking, and through the fissures new ideas and new institutions were thrusting themselves. The cities are everywhere in decline; trade, industry, and agriculture bend under the weight of taxation. Communications are less safe, and some provinces are infested with marauders, peasants who can no longer earn a living on the land. The Empire is gradually dissolving into units of a kind unknown to classical antiquity, which will some day be brought together in a new pattern, feudal and Christian. But before that can happen generations must pass, while the new absolutism struggles by main force to keep the roads open, the fields in cultivation, and the barbarian at bay.

Nevertheless the Roman Empire was an old system. Its sinews and arteries had borne the strain of all that the ancient world had endured. The Roman world, like an aged man, wished to dwell in peace and tranquillity and to enjoy in philosophic detachment the good gifts which life has to bestow upon the more fortunate classes. But new ideas disturbed the internal conservatism, and outside the carefully guarded frontiers vast masses of hungry, savage men surged and schemed.

The essence of the Roman peace was toleration of all religions and the acceptance of a universal system of government. Every generation after the middle of the second century saw an increasing weakening of the system and a gathering movement towards a uniform religion. Christianity asked again all the questions which the Roman world deemed answered for ever, and some that it had never thought of. Although the varieties of status, with all their grievous consequences, were accepted during these centuries, even by those who suffered from them most, as part of the law of nature, the institution of slavery, by which a third of Roman society was bound, could not withstand indefinitely the new dynamic thoughts which Christianity brought with it. The alternations between fanatic profligacy and avenging puritanism which marked the succession of the emperors, the contrast between the morals at the centre of power and those practised by wide communities in many subject lands, presented problems of ever-growing unrest. At the moment when mankind seemed to have solved a very large proportion of its secular difficulties and when a supreme Government offered unlimited freedom to spiritual experiment inexorable forces both within and without drove on the forward march. No rest; no stay. "For here have we no continuing city, but we seek one to come." Strange standards of destiny were unfurled, destructive of peace and order, but thrilling the hearts of men. Before the Roman system lay troubles immeasurable—squalor, slaughter, chaos itself, and the long night which was to fall upon the world.

From outside the uncouth barbarians smote upon the barriers. Here on the mainland were savage, fighting animals, joined together in a comradeship of arms, with the best fighting men and their progeny as leaders. In the rough-and-tumble of these communities, with all their crimes and bestialities, there was a more active principle of life than in the majestic achievements of the Roman Empire. We see these forces swelling like a flood against all the threatened dykes of the Roman world, not only brimming at the lip of the dam, but percolating insidiously, now by a breach, now in a mere ooze, while all the time men become conscious of the frailty of the structure itself. Floods of new untamed life burst ceaselessly from Asia, driving westward in a succession of waves. Against these there was no easy superiority of weapons. Cold steel and discipline and the slight capital surplus necessary to move and organise armies constituted the sole defences. If the superior virtue of the legion failed all fell. Certainly from the middle of the second century all these disruptive forces were plainly manifest. However, in Roman Britain men thought for many generations that they had answered the riddle of the Sphinx. They misconceived the meaning of her smile.

The Lost Island

NO one can understand history without continually relating the long periods which are constantly mentioned to the experiences of our own short lives. Five years is a lot. Twenty years is the horizon to most people. Fifty years is antiquity. To understand how the impact of destiny fell upon any generation of men one must first imagine their position and then apply the time-scale of our own lives. Thus nearly all changes were far less perceptible to those who lived through them from day to day than appears when the salient features of an epoch are extracted by the chronicler. We peer at these scenes through dim telescopes of research across a gulf of nearly two thousand years. We cannot doubt that the second and to some extent the third century of the Christian era, in contrast with all that had gone before and most that was to follow, were a Golden Age for Britain. But by the early part of the fourth century shadows had fallen upon this imperfect yet none the less tolerable society. By steady, persistent steps the sense of security departed from Roman Britain. Its citizens felt by daily experience a sense that the world-wide system of which they formed a partner province was in decline. They entered a period of alarm.

The spade of the archæologist, correcting and enlarging the study of historians, the discovery and scrutiny of excavations, ruins, stones, inscriptions, coins, and skeletons, the new yields of aerial photography, are telling a tale which none can doubt. Although the main impressions of the nineteenth century are not overthrown modern knowledge has become more true, more precise, and more profound. The emphasis placed by Victorian writers upon causes and events and their chronology has been altered, especially since the First World War. Their dramas have been modified or upset. A host of solid gradations and sharp-cut refinements is being marshalled in stubborn array. We walk with shorter paces, but on firmer footholds. Famous books which their writers after a lifetime's toil believed were final are now recognised as already obsolete, and new conclusions are drawn not so much from new standpoints as from new discoveries. Nevertheless the broad story holds, for it is founded in a dominating simplicity.

From the end of the third century, when Roman civilisation in Britain and the challenge to the supreme structure were equally at their height, inroads of barbarian peoples began, both from Europe and from the forlorn Island to the westward. The Scots, whom nowadays we should call the Irish, and the Picts from Scotland began to press on Hadrian's Wall, to turn both flanks of it by sea raids on a growing scale. At the same time the Saxons rowed in long-boats across the North Sea and lay heavy all along the east coast from Newcastle to Dover. From this time forth the British countryside dwelt under the same kind of menace of cruel, bloody, and sudden inroad from the sea as do modern nations from the air. Many proofs have been drawn from the soil in recent years. All point to the same conclusion. The villa life of Britain, upon which the edifice of Roman occupation was now built, was in jeopardy. We see the signs of fear spreading through the whole country. Besides the forts along the east and south coasts, and the system of galleys based upon them, a host of new precautions becomes evident. The walls of London were furnished with bastion towers, the stones for which were taken from dwelling-houses, now no longer required by a dwindling town-population. Here and there the broad Roman gateways of townships were narrowed to half their size with masonry, a lasting proof of the increasing insecurity of the times. All over the country hoards of coins have been found, hardly any of which are later than the year A.D. 400. Over this fertile, peaceful, ordered world lay the apprehension of constant peril.

Like other systems in decay, the Roman Empire continued to function for several generations after its vitality was sapped. For nearly a hundred years our Island was one of the scenes of conflict between a dying civilisation and lusty, famishing barbarism. Up to the year 300 Hadrian's Wall, with its garrisons, barred out the Northern savages, but thereafter a new front must be added. At the side of the "Duke of the Northern Marches" there must stand the "Count of the Saxon Shore." All round the eastern and southern coasts, from the Wash to Southampton Water, a line of large fortresses was laboriously built. Eight have been examined. Of these the chief was Richborough, known to the generation of the First World War as an invaluable ferry-port for the supply of the armies in France.

There is some dispute about the strategic conceptions upon which these strongholds were called into being. Many disparaging judgments have been passed upon a policy which is accused of seeking to protect four hundred miles of coastline from these eight points. Obviously these strictures are unjust. The new line of coastal fortresses could only have had any value or reason as bases for a British-Roman fleet.

Such a fleet, the Classis Britannica, had been maintained from the first century. Tiles with an Admiralty mark show that it had permanent stations at Dover and Lympne. But the whole coast was organised for defence, and for long periods these measures proved effective. Vegetius, writing in the fourth century on the art of war, mentions a special kind of light galley attached to the British fleet. These vessels, the hulls, sails, the men's clothes, and even faces, were painted sea-green, to make them invisible, and Vegetius tells us that in naval parlance they were called "the Painted Ones." As the Imperial and British sea-power gradually became unequal to the raiders the ramparts of the fortresses grew higher and their usefulness less. Flotilla defence by oared galleys working from bases fifty to a hundred miles apart could not contend indefinitely with raiding thrusts. Even a High Sea Fleet capable of keeping the sea for months at a time off the coasts of what are now called Holland, Germany, and Denmark, though a powerful deterrent, would have been too slow to deal with oared boats in calm weather.

The Roman Britons were lively and audacious members of the Empire. They took a particularist view, yet wished to have a hand in the game themselves. As time passed the Roman garrison in Britain steadily became more British, and towards the end of the third century it assumed a strong national character. While glorying in the name of citizens and Romans, and having no desire for independence, both province and army adopted a highly critical attitude towards the Imperial Government. Emperors who disregarded British opinion, or sacrificed British interests, above all those who could be accused of neglecting the defences of the province, were the objects of active resentment. A series of mutinies and revolts aggravated the growing dangers of the times. No one can suppose that the Roman military centres at Chester, York, or Caerleon-on-Usk threw up claimants for the Imperial diadem unsupported by a strong backing in local opinion. These were not merely mutinies of discontented soldiers. They were bold bids for control of the Roman Empire by legions only a few thousand strong, but expressing the mood, sentiments, and ambitions of the society in which they lived. They left the local scene for the supreme theatre, like players who wish to quit the provinces for the capital. Unhappily they took away with them at each stage important elements of the exiguous military forces needed to man the dykes.

*   *   *   *   *

The Emperor Diocletian has gone down to history principally as the persecutor of the early Christians, and the enormous work which he achieved in restoring the frontiers of the ancient world has remained under that shadow. His policy was to construct a composite Cæsarship. There were to be two Emperors and two Cæsars, he himself being the senior of the four. In due course the Emperors would retire in favour of the Cæsars, new ones would be appointed, and thus the succession would be preserved. The co-Emperor Maximian, sent to Gaul in 285, and responsible for Britannia, was deeply concerned by the raiding of the Saxon pirates. He strengthened the Channel fleet, and put at its head a sea officer from the Low Countries named Carausius. This man was tough, resolute, ambitious, and without scruple; from his base at Boulogne he encouraged the raiders to come and pillage, and then when they were laden with plunder he fell upon them with Roman-British flotillas, captured them by scores, and destroyed them without mercy. His success did not satisfy the British community; they accused him of having been in league with those he had destroyed. He explained that this was all part of his ambush; but the fact that he had retained all the spoil in his own hands told heavily against him. Maximian sought to bring him to execution, but Carausius, landing in Britain, declared himself Emperor, gained the Island garrison to his cause, and defeated Maximian in a sea battle. On this it was thought expedient to come to terms with the stubborn rebel, and in the year 287 Carausius was recognised as one of the Augusti in command of Britain and of Northern Gaul.

For six years this adventurer, possessing sea-power, reigned in our Island. He seems to have served its interests passably well. However, the Emperor Diocletian and his colleagues were only biding their time, and in the year 293 they cast away all pretence of friendship. One of the new Cæsars, Constantius Chlorus, besieged and took Boulogne, the principal Continental base of Carausius, who was soon assassinated by one of his officers. The new competitor sought to become Emperor in his stead. He did not gain the support of the British nation and the whole country fell into confusion. The Picts were not slow to seize their advantage. The Wall was pierced, and fire and sword wasted the Northern districts. Chlorus crossed the Channel as a deliverer. His colleague, with part of the force, landed near Portsmouth; he himself sailed up the Thames, and was received by London with gratitude and submission. He restored order. A gold medallion discovered at Arras in 1922 reveals him at the head of a fleet which had sailed up the Thames. He drove back the Northern invaders, and set to work to restore and improve the whole system of defence.

*   *   *   *   *

Continuous efforts were made by the Roman-British community to repel the inroads, and for two or three generations there were counter-strokes by flotillas of galleys, and hurried marchings of cohorts and of British auxiliaries towards the various thrusts of raid or invasion. But although the process of wearing down was spread over many years, and misery deepened by inches, we must recognise in the year 367 circumstances of supreme and murderous horror. In that fatal year the Picts, the Scots, and the Saxons seemed to work in combination. All fell together upon Britannia. The Imperial troops resisted manfully. The Duke of the Northern Marches and the Count of the Saxon Shore were killed in the battles. A wideopen breach was made in the defences, and murderous hordes poured in upon the fine world of country houses and homesteads. Everywhere they were blotted out. The ruins tell the tale. The splendid Mildenhall silver dinner service, now in the British Museum, is thought to have been buried at this time by its owners, when their villa was surprised by raiders. Evidently they did not live to dig it up again. The villa life of Britain only feebly recovered from the disaster. The towns were already declining. Now people took refuge in them. At least they had walls.

The pages of history reveal the repeated efforts made by the Imperial Government to protect Britannia. Again and again, in spite of revolts and ingratitude, officers and troops were sent to restore order or drive back the barbarians. After the disasters of 367 the Emperor Valentinian sent a general, Theodosius, with a considerable force to relieve the province. Theodosius achieved his task, and once again we find on the coastal fortifications the traces of a further strong reconstruction. Untaught however by continuing danger, the garrison and inhabitants of Britain in 383 yielded themselves willingly to a Spaniard, Magnus Maximus, who held the command in Britain and now declared himself Emperor. Scraping together all the troops he could find, and stripping the Wall and the fortresses of their already scanty defenders, Maximus hastened to Gaul, and defeated the Emperor Gratian near Paris. Gratian was murdered at Lyons by his troops, and Maximus became master of Gaul and Spain as well as Britain. For five years he struggled to defend his claim to these great dominions, but Theodosius, who had succeeded Gratian, at length defeated and slew him.

Meanwhile the Wall was pierced again, and Britain lay open to the raiders both from the North and from the sea. Seven years more were to pass before Theodosius could send his general, Stilicho, to the Island. This great soldier drove out the intruders and repaired the defences. The writings of Claudian, the court poet, describe in triumphant terms the liberation of Britain from its Saxon, Pictish, and Scottish assailants in the year 400. In celebrating the first consulship of Stilicho he tells how Britain has expressed her gratitude for her deliverance from the fear of these foes. This sentiment soon fades.

Stilicho had returned to Rome, and was in chief command when in the same year Alaric and the Visigoths invaded Italy. He was forced to recall a further part of the British garrison to defend the heart of the Empire. In 402 he defeated Alaric in the great battle of Pollentia, and drove him out of Italy. No sooner was this accomplished than a new barbarian invasion swept down upon him under Radagaisus. By 405 Stilicho had completely destroyed this second vast host. Italy was scarcely clear when a confederacy of Suevi, Vandals, Avars, and Burgundians broke through the Rhine frontiers and overran Northern Gaul. The indomitable Stilicho was preparing to meet this onslaught when the British army, complaining that the province was being neglected, mutinied. They set up a rival Emperor named Marcus, and on his speedy murder elected a Briton, Gratianus, in his stead. After his assassination four months later the soldiers chose another Briton, who bore the famous name of Constantine. Constantine, instead of protecting the Island, found himself compelled to defend upon the Continent the titles he had usurped. He drained Britain of troops, and, as Magnus Maximus had done, set forth for Boulogne to try his fortune. In the supreme theatre for three years, with varying success, he contended with Stilicho, and was finally captured and executed, as Maximus had been before him. None of the troops who had accompanied him ever returned to Britain. Thus in these fatal years the civilised parts of the Island were stripped of their defenders, both in order to aid the Empire and to strike against it.

By the beginning of the fifth century all the legions had gone on one errand or another, and to frantic appeals for aid the helpless Emperor Honorius could only send his valedictory message in 410, that "the cantons should take steps to defend themselves."

      *   *   *   *   *

The first glimpse we have of the British after the Roman Government had withdrawn its protection is afforded by the visit of St Germanus in 429. The Bishop came from Auxerre in order to uproot the Pelagian heresy, which in spite of other preoccupations our Christian Island had been able to evolve. This doctrine consisted in assigning an undue importance to free will, and cast a consequential slur upon the doctrine of original sin. It thus threatened to deprive mankind, from its very birth, of an essential part of our inheritance. The Bishop of Auxerre and another episcopal colleague arrived at St Albans, and we are assured that they soon convinced the doubters and eradicated the evil opinions to which they had incautiously hearkened. What kind of Britain did he find? He speaks of it as a land of wealth. There is treasure; there are flocks and herds; food is abundant; institutions, civil and religious, function; the country is prosperous, but at war. An invading army from the North or the East is approaching. It was an army said to be composed of Saxons, Picts, and Scots in ill-assorted and unholy alliance.

The Bishop had been a distinguished general in his prime. He organised the local forces. He reconnoitred the surrounding districts. He noticed in the line of the enemy's advance a valley surrounded by high hills. He took command, and lay in ambush for the ferocious heathen hordes. When the enemy were entangled in the defile, suddenly "The priests shouted a triple Alleluia at their foes. . . . The cry was taken up with one mighty shout and echoed from side to side of the enclosed valley; the enemy were smitten with terror, thinking that the rocks and the very sky were falling upon them; such was their fear that they could hardly run quickly enough. They threw away their arms in their disorderly flight, glad to escape naked; a river devoured many in their headlong fear, though in their advance they had crossed it in good order. The innocent army saw itself avenged, a spectator of a victory gained without exertion. The abandoned spoils were collected, . . . and the Britons triumphed over an enemy routed without loss of blood; the victory was won by faith and not by might. . . . So the Bishop returned to Auxerre, having settled the affairs of that most wealthy Island, and overcome their foes both spiritual and carnal, that is to say, both the Pelagians and Saxons." [1]

Another twelve years passed, and a Gaulish chronicler records this sombre note in A.D. 441 or 442: "The Britons in these days by all kinds of calamities and disasters are falling into the power of the Saxons." What had happened? Something more than the forays of the fourth century: the mass migration from North Germany had begun. Thereafter the darkness closes in.

Upon this darkness we have four windows, each obstructed by dim or coloured glass. We have the tract of Gildas the Wise, written, approximately, in A.D. 545, and therefore a hundred years after the curtain fell between Britannia and the Continent. Nearly two hundred years later the Venerable Bede, whose main theme was the history of the English Church, lets fall some precious scraps of information, outside his subject, about the settlement itself. A compilation known as the *Historia Britonum* contains some documents earlier than Bede. Finally, in the ninth century, and very likely at the direction of King Alfred, various annals preserved in different monasteries were put together as the *Anglo-Saxon Chronicle*. Checking these by each other, and by such certainties as archæology allows us to entertain, we have the following picture.

[1] Constantine of Lyons, a near contemporary biographer of St Germanus.

Imitating a common Roman practice, the dominant British chief about A.D. 450 sought to strengthen himself by bringing in a band of mercenaries from over the seas. They proved a trap. Once the road was open fresh fleet-loads made their way across and up the rivers, from the Humber perhaps as far round as Portsmouth. But the British resistance stiffened as the invaders got away from the coast, and their advance was brought to a standstill for nearly fifty years by a great battle won at Mount Badon. If now we draw a V-shaped line, one leg from Chester to Southampton, and the other back from Southampton to the Humber, we shall observe that the great bulk of pagan Saxon remains, and that place-names in *ing* or *ings*, usually evidence of early settlement, are to the east of this second line. Here then we have the England of about A.D. 500. The middle sector is the debatable land, and the West is still Britain.

So far this tale is confirmed, historically and geographically. Gildas could have heard the story of the mercenaries from old men whom he had known in his youth, and there is no real ground for doubting the statements of Nennius, a compiler probably of the ninth century, and Bede, who agree that the name of the deceived chief who invited these deadly foes was Vortigern. Hengist, a name frequently mentioned in Northern story, like a medieval mercenary was ready to sell his sword and his ships to anyone who would give him land on which to support his men; and what he took was the future kingdom of Kent.

Gildas has a tale to tell of this tragedy.

No sooner have they (the Britons) gone back to their land than the foul hosts of the Picts and Scots land promptly from their coracles. . . . These two races differ in part in their manners, but they agree in their lust for blood, and in their habit of covering their hang-dog faces with hair, instead of covering with clothing those parts of their bodies which demand it. They seize all the northern and outlying part of the country as far as to the Wall. Upon this Wall stands a timorous and unwarlike garrison. The wretched citizens are pulled down from the Wall and dashed to the ground by the hooked weapons of their naked foes. What shall I add? The citizens desert the high Wall and their towns, and take to a flight more desperate than any before. Again the enemy pursue them, and there is slaughter more cruel than ever. As lambs by butchers, so are our piteous citizens rent by their foes, till their manner of sojourning might be compared to that of wild beasts. For they maintained themselves by robbery for the sake of a little food. Thus calamities from outside were increased by native feuds; so frequent were these disasters that the country was stripped of food, save what could be procured in the chase.

Therefore again did the wretched remnants send a letter to Ætius, a powerful Roman—"To Ætius, three times Consul, the groans of the Britons": "The barbarians drive us to the sea, the sea drives us to the barbarians: between these two methods of death we are either massacred or drowned." But they got no help. Meantime dire famine compelled many to surrender to their spoilers. . . . But others would in no wise surrender, but kept on sallying from the mountains, caves, passes, and thick coppices. And then, for the first time, trusting not in man but in God, they slaughtered the foes who for so many years had been plundering their country. . . . For a time the boldness of our enemies was checked, but not the wickedness of our own countrymen: the enemy left our citizens, but our citizens did not leave their sins.

Nennius also tells us, what Gildas omits, the name of the British soldier who won the crowning mercy of Mount Badon, and that name takes us out of the mist of dimly remembered history into the daylight of romance. There looms, large, uncertain, dim but glittering, the legend of King Arthur and the Knights of the Round Table. Somewhere in the Island a great captain gathered the forces of Roman Britain and fought the barbarian invaders to the death. Around him, around his name and his deeds, shine all that romance and poetry can bestow. Twelve battles, all located in scenes untraceable, with foes unknown, except that they were heathen, are punctiliously set forth in the Latin of Nennius. Other authorities say, "No Arthur; at least, no proof of any Arthur." It was only when Geoffrey of Monmouth six hundred years later was praising the splendours of feudalism and martial aristocracy that chivalry, honour, the Christian faith, knights in steel and ladies bewitching, are enshrined in a glorious circle lit by victory. Later this would have been retold and embellished by the genius of Mallory, Spenser, and Tennyson. True or false, they have gained an immortal hold upon the thoughts of men. It is difficult to believe it was all an invention of a Welsh writer. If it was he must have been a marvellous inventor.

Modern research has not accepted the annihilation of Arthur. Timidly but resolutely the latest and best-informed writers unite to proclaim his reality. They cannot tell when in this dark period he lived, or where he held sway and fought his battles. They are ready to believe however that there was a great British warrior, who kept the light of civilisation burning against all the storms that beat, and that behind his sword there sheltered a faithful following of which the memory did not fail. All four groups of the Celtic tribes which dwelt in the tilted uplands of Britain cheered themselves with the Arthurian legend, and each claimed their own region as the scene of his exploits. From Cornwall to Cumberland a search for Arthur's realm or sphere has been pursued.

The reserve of modern assertions is sometimes pushed to extremes, in which the fear of being contradicted leads the writer to strip himself of almost all sense and meaning. One specimen of this method will suffice.

It is reasonably certain that a petty chieftain named Arthur did exist, probably in South Wales. It is possible that he may have held some military command uniting the tribal forces of the Celtic or highland zone or part of it against raiders and invaders (not all of them necessarily Teutonic). It is also possible that he may have engaged in all or some of the battles attributed to him; on the other hand, this attribution may belong to a later date.

This is not much to show after so much toil and learning. None the less, to have established a basis of fact for the story of Arthur is a service which should be respected. In this account we prefer to believe that the story with which Geoffrey delighted the fiction-loving Europe of the twelfth century is not all fancy.[1] If we could see exactly what happened we should find ourselves in the presence of a theme as well founded, as inspired, and as inalienable from the inheritance of mankind as the *Odyssey* or the Old Testament. It is all true, or it ought to be; and more and better besides. And wherever men are fighting against barbarism, tyranny, and massacre, for freedom, law, and honour, let them remember that the fame of their deeds, even though they themselves be exterminated, may perhaps be celebrated as long as the world rolls round. Let us then declare that King Arthur and his noble knights, guarding the Sacred Flame of Christianity and the theme of a world order, sustained by valour, physical strength, and good horses and armour, slaughtered innumerable hosts of foul barbarians and set decent folk an example for all time.

We are told he was Dux Bellorum. What could be more

[1] See Sir Frank Stenton, *Anglo-Saxon England* (1943), p. 3: "The silence of Gildas may suggest that the Arthur of history was a less imposing figure than the Arthur of legend. But it should not be allowed to remove him from the sphere of history, for Gildas was curiously reluctant to introduce personal names into his writing."

natural or more necessary than that a commander-in-chief should be accepted—a new Count of Britain, such as the Britons had appealed to Ætius to give them fifty years before? Once Arthur is recognised as the commander of a mobile field army, moving from one part of the country to another and uniting with local forces in each district, the disputes about the scenes of his actions explain themselves. Moreover the fourth century witnessed the rise of cavalry to the dominant position in the battlefield. The day of infantry had passed for a time, and the day of the legion had passed for ever. The Saxon invaders were infantry, fighting with sword and spear, and having little armour. Against such an enemy a small force of ordinary Roman cavalry might well prove invincible. If a chief like Arthur had gathered a band of mail-clad cavalry he could have moved freely about Britain, everywhere heading the local resistance to the invader and gaining repeated victories. The memory of Arthur carried with it the hope that a deliverer would return one day. The legend lived upon the increasing tribulations of the age. Arthur has been described as the last of the Romans. He understood Roman ideas, and used them for the good of the British people. "The heritage of Rome," Professor Collingwood says, "lives on in many shapes, but of the men who created that heritage Arthur was the last, and the story of Roman Britain ends with him."

Arthur's "twelfth battle," says Nennius, "was on Mount Badon, in which there fell in one day nine hundred and sixty men from the onslaught of Arthur only, and no one laid them low save he alone. And in all his battles he was victor. But they, when in all these battles they had been overthrown, sought help from Germany and increased without intermission."

All efforts to fix the battlefield of Mount Badon have failed. A hundred learned investigations have brought no results, but if, as seems most probable, it was fought in the Debatable Land to check the advance from the East, then the best claimant to the title is Liddington Camp, which looks down on Badbury, near Swindon. On the other hand, we are able to fix the date with unusual accuracy. Gildas speaks of it as having occurred forty-three years and a month from the date when he was writing, and he says that he remembers the date because it was that of his own birth. Now we know from his book that the King of North Wales, Maelgwyn, was still alive when he wrote, and the annals of Cambria tell us that he died of the plague in 547. Gildas thus wrote at the latest in this year, and the Battle of Mount Badon, forty-three years earlier, would have been fought in 503. We have also a cross-check in the Irish annals, which state that Gildas died in 569 or 570. His birth is therefore improbable before 490, and thus the date of the battle seems to be fixed between 490 and 503.

*   *   *   *   *

A broader question is keenly disputed. Did the invaders exterminate the native population, or did they superimpose themselves upon them and become to some extent blended with them? Here it is necessary to distinguish between the age of fierce forays in search of plunder and the age of settlement. Gildas is speaking of the former, and the scenes he describes were repeated in the Danish invasions three centuries later. But to the settler such raids are only occasional incidents in a life mainly occupied in subduing the soil, and in that engrossing task labour is as important as land. The evidence of place-names suggests that in Sussex extermination was the rule. Farther west there are grounds for thinking that a substantial British population survived, and the oldest West Saxon code of A.D. 694 makes careful provision for the rights of "Welshmen" of various degrees—substantial landowners, and "the King's Welshmen who ride his errands," his native gallopers in fact, who know the ancient track-ways. Even where self-interest did not preserve the native villagers as labourers on Saxon farms we may cherish the hope that somewhere a maiden's cry for pity, the appeal of beauty in distress, the lustful needs of an invading force, would create some bond between victor and vanquished. Thus the blood would be preserved, thus the rigours of subjugation would fade as generations passed away. The complete obliteration of an entire race over large areas is repulsive to the human mind. There should at least have been, in default of pity, a hearing for practical advantage or the natural temptations of sex. Thus serious writers contend that the Anglo-Saxon conquest was for the bulk of the British community mainly a change of masters. The rich were slaughtered; the brave and proud fell back in large numbers upon the Western mountains. Other numerous bands escaped betimes to Brittany, whence their remote posterity were one day to return.

The Saxon was moreover a valley-settler. His notion of an economic holding was a meadow for hay near the stream, the lower slopes under the plough, the upper slopes kept for pasture. But in many places a long time must have passed before these lower grounds could be cleared and drained, and while this work was in progress what did he live on but the produce of the upland British farms? It is more natural to suppose that he would keep his natives working as serfs on the land with which they were familiar until the valley was ready for sowing. Then the old British farms would go down to grass, and the whole population would cluster in the village by the stream or the spring. But the language of the valley-settlers, living in compact groups, would be dominant over that of the hill-cultivators, scattered in small and isolated holdings. The study of modern English place-names has shown that hill, wood, and stream names are often Celtic in origin, even in regions where the village names are Anglo-Saxon. In this way, without assuming any wholesale extermination, the disappearance of the British language can be explained even in areas where we know a British population to have survived. They had to learn the language of their masters: there was no need for their masters to learn theirs. Thus it came about that both Latin and British yielded to the speech of the newcomers so completely that hardly a trace of either is to be found in our earliest records.

There was no uniformity of practice in the Island. There is good reason to think that the newcomers in Kent settled down beside the old inhabitants, whose name, Cantiaci, they adopted. In Northumbria there are strong traces of Celtic law. In Hants and Wilts a broad belt of British names, from Liss to Deverill, seems to show the natives still cultivating their old fields on the downs, while the Saxon was clearing the valleys. There was no colour bar. In physical type the two races resembled each other; and the probabilities are that in many districts a substantial British element was incorporated in the Saxon stock.

The invaders themselves were not without their yearnings for settled security. Their hard laws, the rigours they endured, were but the results of the immense pressures behind them as the hordes of avid humanity spread westward from Central Asia. The warriors returning from a six months' foray liked to sprawl in lazy repose. Evidently they were not insensible to progressive promptings, but where, asked the chiefs and elders, could safety be found? In the fifth century, as the pressure from the East grew harder and as the annual raiding parties returned from Britain with plunder and tales of wealth there was created in the ruling minds a sense of the difficulty of getting to the island, and consequently of the security which would attend its occupation by a hardy and valiant race. Here, perhaps, in this wave-lapped Island men might settle down and enjoy the good things of life without the haunting fear of subjugation by a stronger hand, and without the immense daily sacrifices inseparable from military and tribal discipline on the mainland. To these savage swords Britain seemed a refuge. In the wake of the raiders there grew steadily the plan and system of settlement. Thus, with despair behind and hope before, the migration to Britain and its occupation grew from year to year.

* * * * *

Of all the tribes of the Germanic race none was more cruel than the Saxons. Their very name, which spread to the whole confederacy of Northern tribes, was supposed to be derived from the use of a weapon, the seax, a short one-handed sword. Although tradition and the Venerable Bede assign the conquest of Britain to the Angles, Jutes, and Saxons together, and although the various settlements have tribal peculiarities, it is probable that before their general exodus from Schleswig-Holstein the Saxons had virtually incorporated the other two strains.

The history books of our childhood attempted courageously to prescribe exact dates for all the main events. In 449 Hengist and Horsa, invited by Vortigern, founded the Jutish kingdom of Kent upon the corpses of its former inhabitants. In 477 Ella and his three sons arrived to continue the inroad. In 495 Cerdic and Cynric appeared. In 501 Port, the pirate, founded Portsmouth. In 514 the West Saxons Stuf and Wihtgar descended in their turn and put the Britons to flight. In 544 Wihtgar was killed. In 547 came Ida, founder of the kingdom of Northumberland. All that can be said about these dates is that they correspond broadly to the facts, and that these successive waves of invaders, bringing behind them settlers, descended on our unhappy shores.

Other authorities draw an alternative picture. "The bulk of the homesteads within the village," J. R. Green tells us,

> were those of its freemen or ceorls; but amongst these were the larger homes of eorls, or men distinguished among their fellows by noble blood, who were held in an hereditary reverence, and from whom the leaders of the village were chosen in war-time or rulers in times of peace. But the choice was a purely voluntary one, and the man of noble blood enjoyed no legal privilege amongst his fellows.[1]

If this were so we might thus early have realised the democratic ideal of "the association of us all through the leadership of the best." In the tribal conceptions of the Germanic nation lie, no doubt, many of those principles which are now admired, and which have formed a recognisable part of the message which the English-speaking peoples have given to the world. But the conquerors of Roman Britain, far from practising these ideals, introduced a whole scheme of society which was fundamentally sordid and vicious. The invaders brought into Britain a principle common to all Germanic tribes, namely, the use of the money power to regulate all the legal relations of men. If there was any equality it was equality within each social grade. If there was liberty it was mainly liberty for the rich. If there were rights they were primarily the rights of property. There was no crime committed which could not be compounded by a money payment. Except failure to answer a call to join an expedition, there was no offence more heinous than that of theft.

An elaborate tariff prescribed in shillings the "wergild" or exact value or worth of every man. An ætheling, or prince, was worth 1500 shillings, a shilling being the value of a cow in Kent, or of a sheep elsewhere; an eorl, or nobleman, 300

[1] *Short History of the English People,* p. 4.

shillings; a ceorl, now degraded to the word "churl," who was a yeoman farmer, was worth 100 shillings; a læt, or agricultural serf, 40–80 shillings, and a slave nothing. All these laws were logically and mathematically pushed to their extremes. If a ceorl killed an eorl he had to pay three times as much in compensation as if the eorl were the murderer. And these laws were applied to the families of all. The life of a slaughtered man could be compounded for cash. With money all was possible; without it only retribution or loss of liberty. However, the ætheling, valued at 1500 shillings, suffered in certain respects. The penalty for slander was the tearing out of the tongue. If an ætheling were guilty of this offence his tongue was worth five times that of an eorl and fifteen times as much as that of a common læt, and he could ransom it only on these terms. Thus the abuse of a humble tongue was cheap. Wergild at least, as Alfred said long afterwards, was better than the blood feud.

The foundation of the Germanic system was blood and kin. The family was the unit, the tribe was the whole. The great transition which we witness among the emigrants is the abandonment of blood and kin as the theme of their society and its replacement by local societies and lordship based on the ownership of land. This change arose, like so many of the lessons learned by men, from the grim needs of war. Fighting for life and foothold against men as hard pressed as themselves, each pioneering band fell inevitably into the hands of the bravest, most commanding, most fortunate war-leader. This was no longer a foray of a few months, or at the outside a year. Here were settlements to be founded, new lands to be reclaimed and cultivated, land which moreover offered to the deeper plough a virgin fertility. These must be guarded, and who could guard them except the bold chieftains who had gained them over the corpses of their former owners?

Thus the settlement in England was to modify the imported structure of Germanic life. The armed farmer-colonists found themselves forced to accept a stronger state authority owing to the stresses of continued military action. In Germany they had no kings. They developed them in Britain from leaders who claimed descent from the ancient gods. The position of the king continually increased in importance, and his supporters or companions gradually formed a new class in society, which carried with it the germ of feudalism, and was in the end to dominate all other conventions. But the lord was master; he must also be protector. He must stand by his people, must back them in the courts, feed them in time of famine, and they in return must work his land and follow him in war.

The king was at first only the war-leader made permanent; but, once set up, he had his own interests, his own needs, and his own mortal dangers. To make himself secure became his paramount desire. "To be thus is nothing, but to be safely thus . . ." But how was this to be achieved? Only by the king gathering round him a band of the most successful warriors and interesting them directly in the conquest and in the settlement. He had nothing to give them except land. There must be a hierarchy. The king must be surrounded by those who had shared his deeds and his bounty. The spoils of war were soon consumed, but the land remained for ever. Land there was in plenty, of varying quality and condition, but to give individual warriors a title to any particular tract was contrary to the whole tradition of the Germanic tribes. Now under the hard pressures of war and pioneering land increasingly became private property. Insensibly, at first, but with growing speed from the seventh century onwards, a landed aristocracy was created owing all they had to the king. While the resistance of the Britons was vigorously maintained, and the fortunes of the struggle swung this way and that way for nearly two hundred years, this new institution of personal leadership established in the divinely descended war-chief sank deeply into the fibre of the Anglo-Saxon invaders.

But with this movement towards a more coherent policy or structure of society there came also a welter of conflicting minor powers. Distances were usually prohibitive, and writing virtually unknown. Districts were separated from each other like islands in rough seas, and thus a host of kings and kinglets sprang into existence behind the fighting frontier of the intruding tribes. In marking the many root faults and vices which they possessed a high place must be assigned to their inability to combine. For a long time the Island presented only the spectacle of a chaos arising from the strife of small fiercely organised entities. Although from the time of the immigration the people south of the Humber were generally subject to a common overlord, they were never able to carry the evolution of kingship forward to a national throne. They remained marauders; but they had taken more pains to be sure of their booty.

Much has been written about the enervating character of Roman rule in Britain, and how the people were rendered lax and ineffectual by the modest comforts which it supplied. There is no doubt that Gildas, by his writings, imparted an impression, perhaps in this case well founded, of gross incompetence and fatuity in the society and administration which followed the decay of Roman power. But justice to this vanished epoch demands recognition of the fact that the Britons fought those who are now called the English for nearly two hundred and fifty years. For a hundred years they fought them under the ægis of Rome, with its world organisation; but for a hundred and fifty years they fought them alone. The conflict ebbed and flowed. British victories were gained, which once for a whole generation brought the conquest to a halt; and in the end the mountains which even the Romans had been unable to subdue proved an invincible citadel of the British race.

England

A RED sunset; a long night; a pale, misty dawn! But as the light grows it becomes apparent to remote posterity that everything was changed. Night had fallen on Britannia. Dawn rose on England, humble, poor, barbarous, degraded and divided, but alive. Britannia had been an active part of a world state; England was once again a barbarian island. It had been Christian, it was now heathen. Its inhabitants had rejoiced in well-planned cities, with temples, markets, academies. They had nourished craftsmen and merchants, professors of literature and rhetoric. For four hundred years there had been order and law, respect for property, and a widening culture. All had vanished. The buildings, such as they were, were of wood, not stone. The people had lost entirely the art of writing. Some miserable runic scribblings were the only means by which they could convey their thoughts or wishes to one another at a distance. Barbarism reigned in its rags, without even the stern military principles which had animated and preserved the Germanic tribes. The confusion and conflict of petty ruffians sometimes called kings racked the land. There was nothing worthy of the name of nationhood, or even of tribalism; yet this is a transition which the learned men of the nineteenth century banded themselves together to proclaim as an onward step in the march of mankind. We wake from an awful and, it might well have seemed, endless nightmare to a scene of utter prostration. Nor did the seeds of recovery spring from the savage hordes who had wrecked the Roman culture. They would certainly have continued to welter indefinitely in squalor, but for the fact that a new force was stirring beyond the seas which, moving slowly, fitfully, painfully, among the ruins of civilisation, reached at length by various paths the unhappy Island, to which, according to Procopius, the souls of the dead upon the mainland were ferried over by some uncouth Charon.

Christianity had not been established as the religion of the Empire during the first two centuries of the Roman occupation of Britain. It grew with many other cults in the large and easy tolerance of the Imperial system. There arose however a British Christian Church which sent its bishops to the early councils, and had, as we have seen, sufficient vitality to develop the Pelagian heresy from its own unaided heart-searchings. When the evil days overtook the land and the long struggle with the Saxons was fought out the British Church fell back with other survivors upon the western parts of the Island. Such was the gulf between the warring races that no attempt was made at any time by the British bishops to Christianise the invaders. Perhaps they were not given any chance of converting them. After an interval one of their leading luminaries, afterwards known as St David, accomplished the general conversion of what is now Wales. Apart from this British Christianity languished in its refuges, and might well have become moribund but for the appearance of a remarkable and charming personality.

St Patrick was a Roman Briton of good family dwelling probably in the Severn valley. His father was a Christian deacon, a Roman citizen, and a member of the municipal council. One day in the early fifth century there descended on the district a band of Irish raiders, burning and slaying. The young Patrick was carried off and sold into slavery in Ireland. Whether he dwelt in Connaught or in Ulster is disputed, and the evidence is contradictory. It may well be that both versions are true and that both provinces may claim the honour. For six years, wherever it was, he tended swine, and loneliness led him to seek comfort in religion. He was led by miraculous promptings to attempt escape. Although many miles separated him from the sea he made his way to a port, found a ship, and persuaded the captain to take him on board. After many wanderings we find him in one of the small islands off Marseilles, then a centre of the new monastic movement spreading westward from the Eastern Mediterranean. Later he consorted with Bishop Germanus of Auxerre. He conceived an earnest desire to return good for evil and spread the tidings he had learned among his former captors in Ireland. After fourteen years of careful training by the Bishop and self-preparation for what must have seemed a forlorn adventure Patrick sailed back in 432 to the wild regions which he had quitted. His success was speedy and undying. "He organised the Christianity already in existence; he converted kingdoms which were still pagan, especially in the West; he brought Ireland into connection with the Church of Western Europe, and made it formally part of universal Christendom." On a somewhat lower plane, although also held in perpetual memory, was the banishing of snakes and reptiles of all kinds from the Irish soil, for which from age to age his fame has been celebrated.

It was therefore in Ireland and not in Wales or England that the light of Christianity now burned and gleamed through the darkness. And it was from Ireland that the Gospel was carried to the North of Britain and for the first time cast its redeeming spell upon the Pictish invaders. Columba, born half a century after St Patrick's death, but an offspring of his Church, and imbued with his grace and fire, proved a new champion of the faith. From the monastery which he established in the island of Iona his disciples went forth to the British kingdom of Strathclyde, to the Pictish tribes of the

North, and to the Anglian kingdom of Northumbria. He is the founder of the Scottish Christian Church. Thus the message which St Patrick had carried to Ireland came back across the stormy waters and spread through wide regions. There was however a distinction in the form of Christianity which reached England through the mission of St Columba and that which was more generally accepted throughout the Christianised countries of Europe. It was monastic in its form, and it travelled from the East through Northern Ireland to its new home without touching at any moment the Roman centre. The Celtic churches therefore received a form of ecclesiastical government which was supported by the loosely knit communities of monks and preachers, and was not in these early decisive periods associated with the universal organisation of the Papacy.

*   *   *   *   *

In spite of the slow means of travel and scanty news, the Papacy had from an early stage followed with deep attention the results of St Columba's labours. Its interest was excited not only by the spread of the Gospel, but also by any straying from the true path into which new Christians might be betrayed. It saw with thankfulness an ardent Christian movement afoot in these remote Northern islands, and with concern that it was from the outset independent of the Papal throne. These were the days when it was the first care of the Bishop of Rome that all Christ's sheep should be gathered into one fold. Here in the North, where so much zeal and fervour were evident, the faith seemed to be awkwardly and above all separately planted.

For various reasons, including the spreading of the Gospel, it was decided in the closing decade of the sixth century that a guide and teacher should be sent to England to diffuse and stimulate the faith, to convert the heathen, and also to bring about an effective working union between British Christians and the main body of the Church. For this high task Pope Gregory, afterwards called "the Great," and the ecclesiastical statesmen gathered in Rome selected a trusty and cultured monk named Augustine. St Augustine, as he is known to history, began his mission in 596 under hopeful auspices. Kent had always been the part of the British Island most closely in contact with Europe, and in all its various phases the most advanced in culture. The King of Kent had married Bertha, a daughter of the Frankish king, the descendant of Clovis, now enthroned in Paris. Although her husband still worshipped Thor and Woden Queen Bertha had already begun to spread the truth through courtly circles. Her chaplain, an earnest and energetic Frank, was given full rein, and thus a powerful impulse came to the people of Kent, who were already in a receptive mood towards the dominant creed of Western Europe. St Augustine, when he landed in Kent, was therefore aware that much had been prepared beforehand. His arrival infused a mood of action. With the aid of the Frankish princess he converted King Ethelbert, who had for reasons of policy long meditated this step. Upon the ruins of the ancient British church of St Martin he refounded the Christian life of Canterbury, which was destined to become the centre and summit of religious England.

Ethelbert, as overlord of England, exercised an effective authority over the kingdoms of the South and West. His policy was at once skilful and ambitious; his conversion to Christianity, however sincere, was also in consonance with his secular aims. He was himself, as the only English Christian ruler, in a position where he might hold out the hand to the British princes, and, using the Christian faith as a bond of union, establish his supremacy over the whole country. This, no doubt, was also in accordance with the ideas which Augustine had carried from Rome. Thus at the opening of the seventh century Ethelbert and Augustine summoned a conference of the British Christian bishops. The place chosen in the Severn valley was on the frontier between the English and British domains, and far outside the bounds of the Kentish kingdom. Here, then, would be a chance of a general and lasting peace for both races, reconciled in the name of Christ; and of this settlement Ethelbert and his descendants could securely expect to be the heirs. We must regret that this hope, sustained by sagacious and benevolent politics, was not realised. It failed for two separate reasons: first, the sullen and jealous temper of the British bishops, and, secondly, the tactless arrogance of St Augustine.

There were two conferences, with an interval. The discussions were ostensibly confined to interesting but uncontroversial questions. There was the date of Easter, which is still debated, and also the form of the tonsure. Augustine urged the Roman custom of shaving only the top of the head. The British bishops had perhaps imitated the Druidical method of shaving from the centre to the ears, leaving a fringe on the forehead. It was a choice of the grotesque. These were matters which might well be capable of adjustment, but which conveniently offered ample pasture upon which the conferences could browse in public, while the vital issues were settling themselves in an atmosphere of goodwill, or being definitely compacted behind the scenes.

But the British bishops were found in no mood to throw themselves into the strong embraces of Rome. Why should they, who had so long defended the Faith against horrible cruelties and oppression, now receive their guidance from a Saxon Kentish king whose conversion was brand-new, and whose political designs, however inspiring, were none the less obvious? The second conference ended in a complete rupture.

When Augustine found himself in the presence of what he deemed to be unreasonable prejudice and deep-seated hostility, when he saw the few bishops who had been won over reproached by their brethren as backsliders and traitors, he fell back quite quickly upon threats. If British Christianity would not accept the fair offers now made the whole influence and prestige of Rome would be thrown against them upon the English side. The Saxon armies would be blessed and upheld by Rome and the unbroken traditions of the main Christian Church, and no sympathy would be felt for these long-faithful British Christians when they had their throats cut by the new English convert states. "If," the Saint exclaimed, "you will not have peace from your friends you shall have war from your foes." But this was no more than the British had faced for two hundred years. It was language they understood. The conference separated in enmity; the breach was irreparable. All further efforts by Rome through Ethelbert and the Kentish kingdom to establish even the slightest contact with Christian Britain were inexorably repulsed.

Augustine's mission therefore drew to a dignified but curtailed end. Except for the consecration of Mellitas as Bishop of the East Saxons in a church on the site of St Paul's, he had made little attempt to proselytise outside Kent. From the title loosely accorded him of "Apostle of the English" he enjoyed for many centuries the credit of having re-converted the once-famous Roman province of Britannia to the Christian faith; and this halo has shone about him until comparatively recent times.

* * * * *

Almost a generation passed before envoys from Rome began to penetrate into Northern England and rally its peoples to Christianity, and then it came about in the wake of political and dynastic developments. By a series of victories Redwald, King of the East Angles, had established a wide dominion over the lands of Central England from the Dee to the Humber. With Redwald's aid the crown of Northumbria was gained by an exiled prince, Edwin, who by his abilities won his way, step by step, to the foremost position in England. Even before the death of his ally Redwald, Edwin was recognised as over-lord of all the English kingdoms except Kent, and the isles of Anglesey and Man were also reduced by his ships. He not only established his personal primacy, but the confederation founded by him foreshadowed the kingdom of all England that was later to take shape under the kings of Mercia and Wessex. Edwin married a Christian princess of Kent, whose religion he had promised to respect. Consequently, in her train from Canterbury to Edwin's capital at York there rode in 625 the first Roman missionary to Northern England, Paulinus, an envoy who had first come to Britain in the days of St Augustine, twenty-four years before.

We have a picture agreeable and instructive of Edwin: "There was then a perfect peace in Britain wheresoever the dominion of King Edwin extended, and, as it is still prover-bially said, a woman with her new-born babe might walk throughout the Island from sea to sea without receiving any harm. That King took such care for the good of his nation that in several places where he had seen clear springs near the highways he caused stakes to be fixed with proper drinking-vessels hanging on them for the refreshment of travellers, nor durst any man touch them for any other purpose than that for which they were designed, either for the great fear they had of the King or for the affection which they bore him." He revived the Roman style: "Not only were his banners borne before him in battle, but even in peace when he rode about his cities, townships, or provinces with his thanes. A standard-bearer was always wont to go before him when he walked anywhere in the streets in the Roman fashion."

Such in his heyday was the prince to whom Paulinus resorted. Paulinus converted Edwin, and the ample kingdom of Northumbria, shaped like England itself in miniature, became Christian. But this blessed event brought with it swift and dire consequences. The overlordship of Northumbria was fiercely resented by King Penda of Mercia, or, as we should now say, of the Midlands. The drama unfolded with staggering changes of fortune. In 633 Penda, the heathen, made an unnatural alliance with Cadwallon, the Christian British King of North Wales, with the object of overthrowing the suzerainty of Edwin and breaking the Northumbrian power. Here for the first time noticed in history British and English fought side by side. Politics for once proved stronger than religion or race. In a savage battle near Doncaster Edwin was defeated and slain, and his head—not the last—was exhibited on the ramparts of captured York. It may be that York, long the home of a legion, still preserved Roman-British traditions which led them to welcome the British victors. This sudden destruction of the greatest king who had hitherto ruled in the Island brought in recoil an equally speedy vengeance. British Cadwallon had triumphed over Northumbria. Here at last was the chance, so long expected, of British vengeance upon their Saxon foes. Here was the faithful paying off of very old but very heavy debts. We might almost be seeing again the spirit of Boadicea.

But the inherent power of Northumbria was great. The name and fame of the slaughtered Edwin rang through the land. His successor, Oswald, of the house of Bernicia, which was one of the two provinces of the kingdom, had but to appear to find himself at the head of the newly Christianised and also infuriated Saxon warriors. Within a year of the death of

Edwin Oswald destroyed Cadwallon and his British forces in a hard battle which fell out along the line of the Roman Wall. This was the last pitched battle between the Britons and the Saxons; and it must be admitted that the Britons fared as badly in conduct as in fortune. They had joined with the heathen Saxon Midlands to avenge their wrongs, and had exploited an English movement towards the disunity of the land. They had shattered this bright hope of the Christianity they professed, and now they were themselves overthrown and cast aside. The long story of their struggle with the invaders ended thus in no fine way; but what is important to our tale is that it had ended at last.

The destruction of Cadwallon and the clearance from Northumbria of the wild Western Britons, whose atrocities had united all the Saxon forces in the North, was the prelude to the struggle with King Penda. He was regarded by the Saxon tribes as one who had brought boundless suffering and slaughter upon them through a shameful pact with the hereditary foe. Nevertheless he prospered for a while. He upheld the claims of Thor and Woden with all the strength of Mercia for seven years. He defeated, decapitated, and dismembered King Oswald, as he had destroyed his predecessor before him. But a younger brother of Oswald, Oswy by name, after a few years, settled the family account, and Penda fell by the sword he had drawn too often. Thus the power of Northumbria rose the stronger from the ordeal and eclipse through which its people had passed.

The failure of Ethelbert's attempt to make a Christian reunion of England and Britain left the direction of the immediate future with the Northumbrian Court. It was to York and not to Canterbury that Rome looked, and upon English, not British, armies that the hopes of organised Christendom were placed. When the disasters had overtaken Northumbria

Paulinus had hastened back by sea to Canterbury. Neither he nor Augustine was the kind of man to face the brutal warfare of those times. Carefully trained as they were in the doctrines, interests, and policy of the Papacy, they were not the stuff of which martyrs or evangelists are made. This British incursion was too rough. But the lieutenant of Paulinus, one James the Deacon, stuck to his post through the whole struggle, and preached and baptised continually in the midst of rapine and carnage. Still more important than his work was that of the Celtic mission to Northumbria under St Aidan. Much of Mercia and East Anglia, as well as Northumbria, was recovered to Christianity by the Celtic missionaries. Thus two streams of the Christian faith once more met in England, and the immediate future was to witness a struggle for supremacy between them.

With the defeat and death of Penda, and upon the surge of all the passions which had been loosed, Anglo-Saxon England was definitely rallied to the Christian faith. There was now no kingdom in which heathen practices prevailed. Indeed, apart from individuals, whose private adherence to Woden was overlooked, the whole Island was Christian. But this marvellous event, which might have brought in its train so many blessings, was marred by the new causes of division which now opened between the English and British peoples. To the ferocious British-English racial feud there was added a different view of Church government, which sundered the races almost as much as the difference between Christianity and heathenism. Henceforward the issue is no longer whether the Island shall be Christian or pagan, but whether the Roman or the Celtic view of Christianity shall prevail. These differences persisted across the centuries, much debated by the parties concerned.

The celebrated and largely successful attempt to solve them took place at the Synod of Whitby in 664. There the hinging issue was whether British Christianity should conform to the general life-plan of Christendom or whether it should be expressed by the monastic orders which had founded the Celtic Churches of the North. The issues hung in the balance, but in the end after much pious dissertation the decision was taken that the Church of Northumbria should be a definite part of the Church of Rome and of the Catholic system. Mercia soon afterwards conformed. Though the Celtic leader and his following retired in disgust to Iona, and the Irish clergy refused to submit, the importance of this event cannot be overrated. Instead of a religion controlled by the narrow views of abbots pursuing their strict rule of life in their various towns or remote resorts there was opened to every member of the English Church the broad vista of a world-state and universal communion. These events brought Northumbria to her zenith. In Britain for the first time there was achieved a unity of faith, morals, and Church government covering five-sixths of the Island. The decisive step had been taken in the spiritual sphere. The Island was now entirely Christian, and by far the greater and more powerful part was directly associated with the Papacy.

Rome had little reason to be satisfied with the mission of either Augustine or Paulinus. The Papacy realised that its efforts to guide and govern British Christianity through the kingdom of Kent had been misplaced. It now made a new plan, which illustrates the universal character of the Catholic Church. Two fresh emissaries were chosen in 668 to carry the light into the Northern mists, the first a native of Asia Minor, Theodore of Tarsus, the second an African named Hadrian from Carthage. These missionaries were of a stronger type than their precursors, and their character and integrity shone before all. When they arrived at Canterbury there were but three bishops from all England to greet them. When their work was finished the Anglican Church raised its mitred front in a majesty which has not yet been dimmed. Before he died in 690 Theodore had increased the number of bishoprics from seven to fourteen, and by his administrative skill he gave the Church a new cohesion. The Church has not canonised him as a saint. This remarkable Asiatic was the earliest of the statesmen of England, and guided her steps with fruitful wisdom.

*   *   *   *   *

There followed a long and intricate rivalry for leadership between the various Anglo-Saxon kings which occupied the seventh and eighth centuries. It was highly important to those whose span of life was cast in that period, but it left small marks on the subsequent course of histoiy. Let a few words suffice. The primacy of Northumbria was menaced and finally ended by the inherent geographical and physical weakness of its position. It was liable to be beset from every quarter, from the north by the Picts, on the west by the British kingdom of Strathclyde, in the south by Mercia, those jealous Midlands still smarting from the suppression of Penda and the punishments inflicted upon his adherents. These antagonisms were too much for Northumbria to bear, and although great efforts were made and amid the exhausting feuds of rival kings some wise chieftains occasionally prevailed, its collapse as the leading community in the Island was inevitable.

Northumbria was fortunate however in having in this twilight scene a chronicler, to whom we have already referred, whose words have descended to us out of the long silence of the past. Bede, a monk of high ability, working unknown in the recesses of the Church, now comes forward as the most effective and almost the only audible voice from the British islands in these dim times. Unlike Gildas, Bede wrote history. The gratitude of the Middle Ages bestowed on Gildas the title of "the Wise," and the name of "the Venerable Bede" still carries with it a proud renown. He alone attempts to paint for us, and, so far as he can, explain the spectacle of Anglo-Saxon England in its first phase: a Christian England, divided by tribal, territorial, dynastic, and personal feuds into what an Elizabethan antiquary called the Heptarchy, seven kingdoms of varying strength, all professing the Gospel of Christ, and striving over each other for mastery by force and fraud. For almost exactly a hundred years, from 731 to 829, there was a period of ceaseless warfare, conducted with cruelty and rapine under a single creed.

The leadership of Saxon England passed to Mercia. For nearly eighty years two Mercian kings asserted or maintained their ascendancy over all England south of the Humber. Ethelbald and Offa reigned each for forty years. Ethelbald had been an exile before he became an autocrat. As a fugitive he consorted with monks, hermits, and holy men. On attaining power he did not discard his Christian piety, but he found himself much oppressed by the temptations of the flesh. St Guthlac had comforted him in misfortune and poverty, but St Boniface was constrained to rebuke him for his immorality.

The moral sense had grown so strong in matters of sex that Churchmen could now brand a king as licentious. Boniface from Germany censured Ethelbald for the "twofold sin" which he committed in nunneries by using the advantages of his royal position to gain himself favours otherwise beyond his reach. The chronicles of this sovereign are scanty. He showed charity to the poor; he preserved law and order; in the South in 733 he raided Wessex; and in 740 he laid parts of Northumbria waste while its harassed chief was struggling with the Picts. After this last victory he took to styling himself "King of the Southern English" and "King of Britain." South of the Humber these claims were made good.

*　　*　　*　　*　　*

Ethelbald, having been at length murdered by his guards, was succeeded by a greater man. Little is known of Offa, who reigned for the second forty years, but the imprint of his power is visible not only throughout England but upon the Continent. Offa was the contemporary of Charlemagne. His policy interlaced with that of Europe; he was reputed to be the first "King of the English," and he had the first quarrel since Roman times with the mainland.

Charlemagne wished one of his sons to marry one of Offa's daughters. Here we have an important proof of the esteem in which the Englishman was held. Offa stipulated that his son must simultaneously marry a daughter of Charlemagne. The founder of the Holy Roman Empire appeared at first incensed at this assumption of equality, but after a while he found it expedient to renew his friendship with Offa. It seems that "the King of the English" had placed an embargo upon Continental merchandise, and the inconvenience of this retaliation speedily overcame all points of pride and sentiment. Very soon Offa was again the Emperor's "dearest brother," and Charlemagne is seen agreeing to arrange that there should be reciprocity of royal protection in both countries for merchants, "according to the ancient custom of trading." Apparently the commodities in question were "black stones," presumably coal, from France, in return for English cloaks. There were also questions of refugees and extradition. Charlemagne was interested in repatriating a Scot who ate meat in Lent. He sent presents of an ancient sword and silken mantles. Thus we see Offa admitted to equal rank with the greatest figure in Europe. It is evident that the Island Power must have counted for a great deal in these days. Monarchs of mighty empires do not make marriage contracts for their children and beat out the details of commercial treaties with persons of no consequence.

The advantage given by these two long reigns when everything was in flux had reinstated the Island again as a recognisable factor in the world. We know that Offa styled himself not only *rex Anglorum,* but also "King of the whole land of the English" (*rex totius Anglorum patriæ*). This expression *rex Anglorum* is rightly signalised by historians as a milestone in our history. Here was an English king who ruled over the greatest part of the Island, whose trade was important, and whose daughters were fit consorts for the sons of Charles the Great. We learn about Offa almost entirely through his impact on his neighbours. It is clear from their records that he suppressed the under-kings of the Severn valley, that he defeated the West Saxons in Oxfordshire and subjugated Berkshire, that he decapitated the King of East Anglia, that he was master of London, that he extirpated the monarchy which Hengist had founded in Kent, and put down a Kentish rising with extreme severity. Henceforth he gave his own orders in Kent. He captured their mint and inscribed his name upon the coins issued by the Archbishop of Canterbury. One of these coins tells its own quaint tale. It is a gold dinar, nicely copied from an Arabic die, and is stamped with the superscription *rex Offa.* The Canterbury mint evidently regarded the Arabic as mere ornamentation, and all men would have been shocked had they known that it declared "There is no God but one and Mahomet is his Prophet." Offa established a good understanding with the Pope. The Supreme Pontiff addressed him as *rex Anglorum.* The Papal envoys in 787 were joyfully received in the hall of Offa, and were comforted by his assurances of reverence for St Peter. These professions were implemented by a small annual tribute to the Papacy, part of it unwittingly paid in these same infidel coins which proclaimed an opposite creed.

In studying Offa we are like geologists who instead of finding a fossil find only the hollow shape in which a creature of unusual strength and size undoubtedly resided. Alcuin, one of the few recorders of this period at the Court of Charlemagne, addresses Offa in these terms: "You are a glory to Britain and a sword against its enemies." We have a tangible monument of Offa in the immense dyke which he caused to be built between converted Saxon England and the still unconquered British. The tables were now turned, and those who had never faltered in the old faith and had always maintained their independence had sunk in the estimation of men from the mere fact that they lived in barren mountainous lands, while their successful ravishers strode on in pomp and even dignity. This dyke, which runs over the hills and dales, leaving gaps for the impenetrable forests, from the mouth of the Severn to the neighbourhood of the Mersey, attests to our day the immense authority of the state over which Offa presided. When we reflect how grim was the struggle for life, and how the getting of enough food to keep body and soul together was the prime concern not only of families but of whole peoples, the fact that this extensive rampart could have been mainly the work of the lifetime and the will of a single man is startling. It conveys to us an idea of the magnitude and force of Offa's kingdom. Such works are not constructed except upon a foundation of effective political power. But "Offa's dyke" shows policy as well as man-power. In many sections it follows lines favourable to the British, and historians have concluded that it was a boundary rather than a fortification, and resulted from an agreement reached for common advantage. It was not a Roman wall, like those of Antonine and Hadrian, between savagery and civilisation, but rather the expression of a solemn treaty which for a long spell removed from Offa's problem the menace of a British incursion, and thus set him free with his back secure to parley and dispute with Europe.

*   *   *   *   *

Art and culture grew in the track of order. The English had brought with them from their Continental home a vigorous barbaric art and a primitive poetry. Once established in the Island, this art was profoundly affected by the Celtic genius for curve and colour, a genius suppressed by Roman provincialism, but breaking out again as soon as the Roman hand was removed. Christianity gave them a new range of subjects to adorn. The results are seen in such masterpieces as the Lindisfarne Gospels and the sculptured crosses of Northern England. A whole world of refinement and civilisation of which the monasteries were the home, and of which only fragments have come down to us, had come into being. Bede was universally honoured as the greatest scholar of his day. It is to his influence that the world owes the practice, adopted later, of reckoning the years from the birth of Christ. Aldhelm of Malmesbury was the most popular writer in Europe; of no author were more copies made in the monasteries of the Continent. Vernacular poetry flourished; in Wessex the first steps had been taken in the art of prose-writing. Another West Saxon, Boniface, from Crediton, near Exeter, was the Apostle of Germany. In the eighth century indeed England had claims to stand in the van of Western culture.

After the shapeless confusion of darker centuries, obscure to history and meaningless to almost all who lived through them, we now see a purpose steadily forming. England, with an independent character and personality, might scarcely yet be a part of a world civilisation as in Roman times, but there was a new England, closer than ever before to national unity, and with a native genius of her own. Henceforward an immortal spirit stood for all to see.

The Vikings

AFTER the fall of Imperial Rome the victorious barbarians were in their turn captivated and enthralled by the Gospel of Christ. Though no more successful in laying aside their sinful promptings than religious men and women are to-day, they had a common theme and inspiration. There was a bond which linked all the races of Europe. There was an international organisation which, standing erect in every country, was by far the most powerful, and indeed the only coherent surviving structure, and at the head of which the Bishop of Rome revived in a spiritual, or at least in an ecclesiastical form, the vanished authority of the Cæsars. The Christian Church became the sole sanctuary of learning and knowledge. It sheltered in its aisles and cloisters all the salvage of ancient days. It offered to men in their strife and error "the last solace of human woe, the last restraint of earthly power." Thus, while the light of pagan civilisation was by no means wholly extinguished, a new effulgence held, dazzled, and dominated the barbaric hordes, not only in our Island but throughout Europe. They were tamed and uplifted by the Christian revelation. Everywhere, from the Euphrates to the Boyne, old gods were forsworn, and a priest of Christ could travel far and wide, finding in every town an understanding brotherhood and a universal if sometimes austere hospitality.

Amid the turbulence and ignorance of the age of Roman decay all the intellectual elements at first found refuge in the Church, and afterwards exercised mastery from it. Here was the school of politicians. The virtual monopoly of learning and the art of writing made the Churchmen indispensable to the proud and violent chieftains of the day. The clerics became the civil servants, and often the statesmen, of every Court. They fell naturally, inevitably, into the place of the Roman magistrates whose garb they wore, and wear to-day. Triumphant barbarism yielded itself insensibly to a structure, reliance upon which was proved on numberless occasions to give success in the unending struggle for power. After the convulsions and disorders of the Dark Ages, when at last daylight fell again on the British Island, she awoke to a world also profoundly changed, but devoid neither of form nor majesty. There was even a gentler breeze in the air.

The fervour of the converted heathen brought in its train mischiefs which opened new calamities. The Church was bound by its spirit to inculcate mildness and mercy. It was led by zeal and by its interests to fortify in every way the structure of its own power. The humility and faith of the descendants of the invaders soon exposed them, in their human frailty, to an organised exploitation which during the sixth and seventh centuries led in many countries to an engrossment by the Church of treasure and lands out of all proportion to its capacity to control events. We see, then, Christendom pious but froward; spiritually united, but a prey to worldly feuds; in a state of grace, but by no means free from ambition.

Upon this revived, convalescent, loosely-knit society there now fell two blasting external assaults. The first came from the East. In Arabia Mahomet unfurled the martial and sacred standards of Islam. His celebrated escape from Mecca to Medina, called the Hejira, or emigration, from which the Moslem era dates, took place in 622. During the decades that followed, Mahomet and his successors, the Caliphs, made themselves masters of all Arabia, Persia, much of the Byzantine Empire, and the whole North African shore. At the be-

ginning of the next century, Islam crossed the Straits of Gibraltar and prevailed in Spain, whence it was not finally to be
dislodged for nearly eight hundred years. At one moment
France, too, seemed about to succumb, but the Arabs were
beaten back by Charles Martel, grandfather of Charlemagne,
in 732 at Poitiers. Thus, all the way from Mecca, the power
of Islam came almost to within striking distance of these islands.

For Britain, however, was reserved the second invading
wave. It came from the North. In Scandinavia the Vikings
fitted out their long-boats for sea. This double assault by Arab
infidels and Nordic pirates distracted the weakened life of
Europe for ten generations. It was not until the eleventh
century that the steel-clad feudalism of medieval Christendom,
itself consisting largely of the converted descendants of the
Vikings, assigned limits to the Arab conquests, and established
at the side of the Christian Church ample and effective military power.

*   *   *   *   *

Measure for measure, what the Saxon pirates had given to
the Britons was meted out to the English after the lapse of four
hundred years. In the eighth century a vehement manifestation
of conquering energy appeared in Scandinavia. Norway,
Sweden, and Denmark threw up bands of formidable fighting
men who, in addition to all their other martial qualities, were
the hardy rovers of the sea. The causes which led to this racial
ebullition were the spontaneous growth of their strength and
population, the thirst for adventure, and the complications of
dynastic quarrels. There was here no question of the Danes or
Norsemen being driven westward by new pressures from the
steppes of Asia. They moved of their own accord. Their
prowess was amazing. One current of marauding vigour struck
southwards from Sweden, and not only reached Constanti-

nople, but left behind it potent germs which across the centuries influenced European Russia. Another contingent sailed in their long-boats from Norway to the Mediterranean, harried all the shores of the inland sea, and were with difficulty repulsed by the Arab kingdoms of Spain and the north coast of Africa. The third far-ranging impulse carried the Scandinavian buccaneers to the British Isles, to Normandy, to Iceland, and presently across the Atlantic Ocean to the American continent.

The relations between the Danes and the Norwegians were tangled and varying. Sometimes they raided in collusion; sometimes they fought each other in desperate battles; but to Saxon England they presented themselves in the common guise of a merciless scourge. They were incredibly cruel. Though not cannibals, they were accustomed to cook their feasts of victory in cauldrons placed upon, or on spits stuck in, the bodies of their vanquished enemies. When, after a battle in Ireland between Northmen and Danes, the local Irish inhabitants— themselves none too particular—expressed horror at this disgusting habit, and, being neutral, asked them why they did it, they received the answer, "Why not? They would do it to us if they won." It was said of these Scandinavian hunters that they never wept for their sins, nor for the death of their friends. It is certain however that in many places where the raiding war-bands settled down they soon developed luxurious habits. They took baths. They wore silken robes. Their ships carried tents and beds for use on shore. Their war-chiefs in every land into which they penetrated practised polygamy, and in the East adopted quite readily the harem system. One conquering leader was credited with possessing no fewer than eight hundred concubines; but this was probably a Biblical illustration. When Limerick was captured from them in the year 936 the Irish were staggered by the beauty of the womenfolk already in the hands of the marauders, and by the mass of silks and embroideries with which they were decked. No doubt they recovered their poise before long.

*   *   *   *   *

The soul of the Vikings lay in the long-ship. They had evolved, and now, in the eighth and ninth centuries, carried to perfection, a vessel which by its shallow draught could sail far up rivers, or anchor in innumerable creeks and bays, and which by its beautiful lines and suppleness of construction could ride out the fiercest storms of the Atlantic Ocean.

We are singularly well informed about these ships. Half a dozen have been dug up almost intact. The most famous was unearthed at Gokstad, in Norway, in 1880, from a tumulus. It is almost complete, even to the cooking-pots and draught-boards of the sailors. It was remeasured with precision in 1944 in spite of other distractions. This ship was of the medium size, 76 feet 6 inches from stem to stern, 17 feet 6 inches beam, and drawing only 2 feet 9 inches amidships. She was clinker-built of sixteen strakes a side of solid oak planks, fastened with tree-nails and iron bolts, and caulked with cord of plaited animal-hair. Her planks fastened to the ribs with bast ties gave the framework great elasticity. She had a deck of loose unnailed boards, but no doubt her stores were contained in lockers which have perished. Her mast was stepped in a huge solid block, which, says Professor Collingwood (whose description I have revised to date), was so cunningly supported "that while the mast stands steady and firm there is no strain on the light elastic frame of the ship." She had sixteen oars a side, varying in length between 17 and 19 feet; the longer oars were used at the prow and stern, where the gunwale was higher above the water-line; they were all beautifully shaped, and passed through circular rowlocks cut in the main strake, which were neatly fitted with shutters that closed when the oars were shipped. Her rudder, stepped to the starboard quarter, was a large, short oar of cricket-bat shape, fitted with a movable tiller, and fastened to the ship by an ingenious contrivance which gave the blade full play. The mast, 40 feet high, had a long, heavy yard with a square sail. She could carry a smaller boat or dinghy, three of which were discovered with her. The Gokstad ship would carry a crew of fifty, and if necessary another thirty warriors or captives, in all weathers, for a month.

Such was the vessel which, in many different sizes, bore the Vikings to the plunder of the civilised world—to the assault of Constantinople, to the siege of Paris, to the foundation of Dublin, and the discovery of America. Its picture rises before us vivid and bright: the finely carved, dragon-shaped prow; the high, curving stern; the long row of shields, black and yellow alternately, ranged along the sides; the gleam of steel; the scent of murder. The long-ships in which the great ocean voyages were made were of somewhat stouter build, with a higher freeboard; but the Gokstad model was reproduced in 1892 and navigated by a Norwegian crew across the Atlantic in four weeks.

Yet this superb instrument of sea-power would have been useless without the men who handled it. All were volunteers. Parties were formed under leaders of marked ability. In the sagas we read of crews of "champions, or merry men": a ship's company picked no doubt from many applicants, "as good at the helm or oar as they were with the sword." There were strict regulations, or early "Articles of War," governing these crews once they had joined. Men were taken between the ages of sixteen and sixty, but none without a trial of his strength and activity. No feud or old quarrel must be taken up while afloat or on service. No woman was allowed on board. News was to be reported to the captain alone. All taken in war was to be brought to the pile or stake, and there sold and divided according to rule. This war booty was personal; that is to say, it was not part of the property which passed by Scandinavian law to a man's kindred. He was entitled to have it buried with him.

"With anything like equal numbers," says Oman, "the Vikings were always able to hold their own, but when the whole countryside had been raised, and the men of many shires came swarming up against the raiders, they had to beware lest they might be crushed by numbers." It was only when a fleet of very exceptional strength had come together that the Norsemen could dare to offer their opponents battle in the open field. Fighting was after all not so much their object as plunder, and when the land was rallied in overwhelming force the invaders took to their ships again and sailed off to renew their ravages in some yet intact province. They soon learned moreover to secure for themselves the power of rapid locomotion on land. When they came to shore they would sweep together all the horses of the neighbourhood and move themselves and their plunder on horseback across the land. It was with no intention of fighting as cavalry that they collected the horses, but only for swift marching. The first mention of this practice in England comes in the year 866, when "a great heathen army came to the land of the East Angles, and there was the army a-horse." [1]

When we reflect upon the brutal vices of these salt-water bandits, pirates as shameful as any whom the sea has borne, or recoil from their villainous destruction and cruel deeds, we must also remember the discipline, the fortitude, the comradeship and martial virtues which made them at this period beyond all challenge the most formidable and daring race in the world.

* * * * *

[1] *Anglo-Saxon Chronicle*, A.D. 866.

One summer's day, probably in 789, while "the innocent
English people, spread through their plains, were enjoying
themselves in tranquillity and yoking their oxen to the
plough," news was carried to the King's officer, the Reeve of
Dorchester, that three ships had arrived on the coast. The
Reeve "leapt on his horse and rode with a few men to the
harbour [probably Portland], thinking that they were merchants and not enemies. Giving his commands as one who had
authority, he ordered them to be sent to the King's town; but
they slew him on the spot and all who were with him." This
was a foretaste of the murderous struggle which, with many
changes of fortune, was to harry and devastate England for
two hundred and fifty years. It was the beginning of the Viking
Age.

In 793, on a January morning, the wealthy monastic settlement of Lindisfarne (or Holy Island), off the Northumbrian
coast, was suddenly attacked by a powerful fleet from Denmark. They sacked the place, devoured the cattle, killed many
of the monks, and sailed away with a rich booty in gold,
jewels, and sacred emblems, and all the monks who were likely
to fetch a good price in the European slave-market. This raid
had been planned with care and knowledge. It was executed
by complete surprise in the dead of winter before any aid from
the shore could reach the island. The news of the atrocity
travelled far and wide, not only in England but throughout
Europe, and the loud cry of the Church sounded a general
alarm. Alcuin, the Northumbrian, wrote home from the Court
of Charlemagne to condole with his countrymen:

> Lo, it is almost three hundred and fifty years that we and
> our forefathers have dwelt in this fair land, and never has such
> a horror before appeared in Britain, such as we have just suf-
> fered from the heathen. It was not thought possible that they

could have made such a voyage. Behold the church of St. Cuthbert sprinkled with the blood of the priests of Christ, robbed of all its ornaments. . . . In that place where, after the departure of Paulinus from York, the Christian faith had its beginning among us, there is the beginning of woe and calamity. . . . Portents of this woe came before it. . . . What signifies that rain of blood during Lent in the town of York?

When the next year the raiders returned and landed near Jarrow they were stoutly attacked while harassed by bad weather. Many were killed. Their "king" was captured and put to a cruel death, and the fugitives carried so grim a tale back to Denmark that for forty years the English coasts were unravaged. In this period the Vikings were little inclined for massed invasion or conquest, but, using their sea-power, made minor descents upon the east coast of Scotland and the Scottish islands. The monastic colonies which had hitherto found a safe retreat in these islands now found themselves as a particularly vulnerable prey. Their riches and their isolation left them the most attractive quarry of the sea-rovers. Iona was pillaged and destroyed in 802. The Irish religious establishments also presented attractive prizes to marauding greed, and from now onward their sufferings were unceasing. The vitality of the Church repaired the ruin with devoted zeal. The Vikings, having a large choice of action, allowed an interval of recovery before paying another visit. Iona was sacked thrice, and the monastery of Kildare no fewer than fourteen times.

Buccaneering had become a steady profession, and the Church was their perpetually replenished treasure-house. Charlemagne's historian, Eginhard, records that the ravages were continuous, and a new shadow of fear spread over Christendom. No effective measures were however taken, and the raiding business was so profitable that the taste for it spread throughout Scandinavia. "These merry, clean-limbed, stout-hearted gentlemen of the Northlands," as one of their Scottish eulogists describes them, sailed every year in greatly increasing numbers upon their forays, and returned triumphant and enriched. And their example inspired all audacious spirits and younger sons. Other fleets ranged more widely. They broke into the Mediterranean. Charlemagne, gazing through a window in a town near Narbonne, saw these sinister ships haunting the coast and uttered an impressive warning of the wrath to come.

* * * * *

It was not till 835 that the storm broke in fury, and fleets, sometimes of three or four hundred vessels, rowed up the rivers of England, France, and Russia in predatory enterprises on the greatest scale. For thirty years Southern England was constantly attacked. Paris was more than once besieged. Constantinople was assaulted. The harbour towns in Ireland were captured and held. Dublin was founded by the Vikings under Olaf. In many cases now the raiders settled upon the conquered territory. The Swedish element penetrated into the heart of Russia, ruling the river towns and holding the trade to ransom. The Norwegian Vikings, coming from a still more severe climate, found the Scottish islands good for settlement. They colonised the Shetlands, the Faroes, and Ireland. They reached Greenland and Stoneland (Labrador). They sailed up the St Lawrence. They discovered America; but they set little store by the achievement.

For a long time no permanent foothold was gained in Britain or France. It was not until 865, when resistance on the Continent had temporarily stiffened, that the great Danish invasion of Northumbria and Eastern England began.

Saxon England was at this time ripe for the sickle. The invaders broke in upon the whole eastern seaboard, once guarded by the "Count of the Saxon Shore," with its Imperial fortresses in ruins, buried already under the soil of centuries. No Roman galleys plied their oars upon the patrol courses. There was no Imperial Government to send a great commander or a legion to the rescue. But on all sides were abbeys and monasteries, churches, and even cathedrals, possessed in that starveling age of treasures of gold and silver, of jewels, and also large stores of food, wine, and such luxuries as were known. The pious English had accepted far too literally the idea of the absolution of sins as the consequence of monetary payment to the Church. Their sins were many, their repentances frequent, and the Church had thrived. Here were easy prizes for sharp swords to win.

To an undue subservience to the Church the English at this time added military mismanagement. Their system of defence was adapted to keeping the survivors of the ancient Britons in their barren mountain-lands or guarding the frontier against an incursion by a Saxon neighbour. The local noble, when called upon by his chief or king, could call upon the able-bodied cultivators of the soil to serve in their own district for about forty days. This service was grudgingly given, and when it was over the army dispersed without paying any serious regard to the enemies who might be afoot or the purposes for which the campaign had been undertaken. Now they found themselves in contact with a different type of enemy. The Danes and Norsemen had not only the advantages of surprise which sea-power so long imparted, but they showed both mobility and skill on land. They adopted the habit of fortifying their camps with almost Roman thoroughness. Their stratagems also have been highly praised. Among these "feigned flight" was foremost. Again and again we read that the English put the heathen army to rout, but at the end of the day the Danes held the field. On one occasion their leader, who was besieging a town, declared himself to be dying and begged the bishop of the place to give him Christian burial. The worthy Churchman rejoiced in the conversion and acceded to the request, but when the body of the deceased Viking was brought into the town for Christian burial it suddenly appeared that the attendants were armed warriors of proved quality, disguised in mourning, who without more ado set to work on sack and slaughter. There are many informing sidelights of this kind upon the manners and customs of the Vikings. They were, in fact, the most audacious and treacherous type of pirate and shark that had ever yet appeared, and, owing to the very defective organisation of the Saxons and the conditions of the period, they achieved a fuller realisation of their desires than any of those who have emulated their proficiency—and there have been many.

      *   *   *   *   *

In Viking legend at this period none was more famous than Ragnar Lodbrok, or "Hairy-breeches." He was born in Norway, but was connected with the ruling family of Denmark. He was a raider from his youth. "West over seas" was his motto. His prow had ranged from the Orkneys to the White Sea. In 845 he led a Viking fleet up the Seine and attacked Paris. The onslaught was repulsed, and plague took an unforeseeable revenge upon the buccaneers. He turned his mobile arms against Northumbria. Here again fate was adverse. According to Scandinavian story, he was captured by King Ælle of Northumbria, and cast into a snake-pit to die. Amid the coiling mass of loathsome adders he sang to the end his death-song. Ragnar had four sons, and as he lay among the venomous reptiles he uttered a potent threat: "The little pigs would grunt now if they knew how it fares with the old boar." The skalds tell us how his sons received the news. Bjorn "Ironside" gripped his spear shaft so hard that the print of his fingers remained stamped upon it. Hvitserk was playing chess, but he clenched his fingers upon a pawn so tightly that the blood started from under his nails. Sigurd "Snake-eye" was trimming his nails with a knife, and kept on paring until he cut into the bone. But the fourth son was the one who counted. Ivar, "the Boneless," demanded the precise details of his father's execution, and his face "became red, blue, and pale by turns, and his skin appeared puffed up by anger." [1]

A form of vengeance was prescribed by which sons should requite the killer of their fathers. It was known as the "Blood-red Eagle." The flesh and ribs of the killer must be cut and sawn out in an aquiline pattern, and then the dutiful son with his own hands would tear out the palpitating lungs. This was the doom which in legend overtook King Ælle. But the actual consequences to England were serious. Ivar "the Boneless" was a warrior of command and guile. He was the master-mind behind the Scandinavian invasion of England in the last quarter of the ninth century. He it was who planned the great campaigns by which East Anglia, Deira in Northumbria, and Mercia were conquered. Hitherto he had been fighting in Ireland, but he now appeared in 866 in East Anglia. In the spring of 867 his powerful army, organised on the basis of ships' companies, but now all mounted not for fighting but for locomotion, rode north along the old Roman road and was ferried across the Humber.

He laid siege to York. And now—too late—the Northumbrians, who had been divided in their loyalties between two rival kings, forgot their feuds and united in one final effort. They attacked the Danish army before York. At first they were successful; the heathens were driven back upon the city walls. The defenders sallied out, and in the confusion the Vikings

[1] From *The Vikings and their Voyages*, by A. MacCallum Scott, "The Universal History of the World," ed. J. A. Hammerton, vol. iv.

defeated them all with grievous slaughter, killing both their kings and destroying completely their power of resistance. This was the end of Northumbria. The North of England never recovered its ascendancy.

As Hodgkin has put it:

> The schools and monasteries dwindled into obscurity or nothingness; and the kingdom which had produced Bede and Alcuin, which had left the great stone crosses as masterpieces of Anglican art, and as evidences of Anglican poetry the poems of Cædmon and the Vision of the Rood, sank back in the generation following the defeat of the year 867 sank back into the old life of obscure barbarism. . . . A dynasty was broken, a religion was half smothered, and a culture was barbarised.[1]

Simeon of Durham, writing a hundred and fifty years after this disastrous battle at York, confirms these lamentations:

> The army raided here and there and filled every place with bloodshed and sorrow. Far and wide it destroyed the churches and monasteries with fire and sword. When it departed from a place it left nothing standing but roofless walls. So great was the destruction that at the present day one can scarcely see anything left of these places, nor any sign of their former greatness.[2]

But Ivar's object was nothing less than the conquest of Mercia, which, as all men knew, had for nearly a hundred years represented the strength of England. Ivar lay before Nottingham. The King of Mercia called for help from Wessex. The old King of Wessex was dead, but his two sons, Ethelred and

[1] *History of the Anglo-Saxons*, vol. ii, p. 525.
[2] Quoted in Hodgkin, vol. II, p. 524.

Alfred, answered the appeal. They marched to his aid, and offered to join him in his attack upon the besiegers' lines; but the Mercians flinched, and preferred a parley. Ivar warred with policy as well as arms. He had not harmed churches at York and Ripon. He was content to set up a vassal king, one Egbert, in Northumbria, and after ending the campaign of 868 by a treaty which left him master of Nottingham he spent the winter fortifying himself in York.

While the Danes in their formidable attempt at conquest spread out from East Anglia, subdued Mercia, and ravaged Northumbria, the King of Wessex and his brother Alfred quietly built up their strength. Their fortunes turned on balances so delicate and precarious that even the slightest addition to their burdens must have been fatal. It was therefore a deliverance when Ivar, after breaking the Treaty of Nottingham and subjecting King Edmund of East Anglia to martyrdom, suddenly quitted England for ever. The annals of Ulster explain that Olaf and Ivar, the two kings of the Northmen, came again to Dublin in 870 from Scotland, and "a very great spoil of captives, English, British, and Pictish, was carried away to Ireland." But then there is this final entry: "872. Ivar, King of the Northmen of all Ireland and Britain, ended his life." He had conquered Mercia and East Anglia. He had captured the major stronghold of the kingdom of Strathclyde, Dumbarton. Laden with loot and seemingly invincible, he settled in Dublin, and died there peacefully two years later. The pious chroniclers report that he "slept in Christ." Thus it may be that he had the best of both worlds.

*   *   *   *   *

The Danish raiders now stayed longer every year. In the summer the fleets came over to plunder and destroy, but each year the tendency was to dally in a more genial and more verdant land. At last the warrior's absence on the raids became long enough and the conditions of his conquest sure enough for him to bring over his wife and family. Thus again behind piracy and rapine there grew the process of settlement. But these settlements of the Danes differed from those of the Saxons; they were the encampment of armies, and their boundaries were the fighting fronts sustained by a series of fortified towns. Stamford, Nottingham, Lincoln, Derby, Leicester were the bases of the new invading force. Behind their frontier lines the soldiers of one decade were to become the colonists and landowners of the next. The Danish settlement in England was essentially military. They cut their way with their swords, and then planted themselves deeply in the soil. The warrior type of farmer asserted from the first a status different from the ordinary agriculturist. Without any coherent national organisation to repel from the land on which they had settled the ever-unknowable descents from the seas, the Saxons, now for four centuries entitled to be deemed the owners of the soil, very nearly succumbed completely to the Danish inroads. That they did not was due—as almost every critical turn of historic fortune has been due—to the sudden apparition in an era of confusion and decay of one of the great figures of history.

Alfred the Great

THE story of Alfred is made known to us in some detail in the pages of Asser, a monk of St David's, who became Bishop of Sherborne. The Bishop dwells naturally upon the religious and moral qualities of his hero; but we must also remember that, in spite of ill-health, he was renowned as a hunter, and that his father had taken him to Rome as a boy, so that he had a lively comprehension of the great world. Alfred began as second-in-command to his elder brother, the King. There were no jealousies between them, but a marked difference of temperament. Ethelred inclined to the religious view that faith and prayer were the prime agencies by which the heathen would be overcome. Alfred, though also devout, laid the emphasis upon policy and arms.

In earlier years the overlordship of Mercia had never been popular, and her kings had made the serious mistake of quarrelling with the See of Canterbury. When, in 825, the Mercian army, invading Wessex, was overthrown by Alfred's grandfather, King Egbert, at Ellandun, near Swindon, all the South and East made haste to come to terms with the victor, and the union of Kent, the seat of the Primate, with Wessex, now the leading English kingdom, created a solid Southern block. This, which had been the aim of West Saxon policy for many generations, was achieved just in time to encounter the invasion from the North. And Wessex was strategically strong, with sharp ridges facing north, and none of those long, slow rivers up which the Danes used to steer their long-ships into the heart of Mercia. Wessex had moreover developed a local organisation

which gave her exceptional resiliency under attack: the alderman at the head of the shire could act on his own account. The
advantages of this system were later to be proved. Definite
districts, each under an accepted commander, or governor, for
civil and military purposes, constituted a great advance on
the ancient tribal kingdoms, or the merely personal union of
tribes under a single king. When the dynasties of Kent, Northumbria, and Mercia had disappeared all eyes turned to Wessex, where there was a royal house going back without a break
to the first years of the Saxon settlement.

The Danes had occupied London, not then the English capital, but a town in the kingdom of Mercia, and their army had
fortified itself at Reading. Moving forward, they met the forces
of the West Saxons on the Berkshire downs, and here, in
January 871, was fought the Battle of Ashdown. Both sides
divided their forces into two commands. Ethelred tarried long
at his devotions. The Vikings, with their brightly painted
shields and banners, their finery and golden bracelets, made
the West Saxons seem modest by contrast. As they slowly ap-
proached they clashed their shields and weapons and raised
long, repeated, and defiant war-cries. Although archery was
not much in use, missiles began to fly. The King was still at his
prayers. God came first, he declared to those who warned him
that the battle must soon be joined. "But Alfred," according to
Bishop Asser, who had the account from "truthful eye-
witnesses,"

> seeing the heathen had come quickly on to the field and were
> ready for battle . . . could bear the attacks of the enemy no
> longer, and he had to choose between withdrawing altogether
> or beginning the battle without waiting for his brother. At last,
> like a wild boar, he led the Christian forces boldly against the
> army of the enemy . . . in spite of the fact that the King
> had not yet arrived. And so, relying on God's counsel and

trusting to His help, he closed the shield-wall in due order and thereupon moved his standards against the enemy.[1]

The fight was long and hard. King Ethelred, his spiritual duty done, soon joined his brother. "The heathens," said the Bishop, "had seized the higher ground, and the Christians had to advance uphill. There was in that place a single stunted thorn-tree which we have seen with our own eyes. Round about this tree, then, the opposing ranks met in conflict, with a great shouting from all men—one side bent on evil, the other side fighting for life and their loved ones and their native land." At last the Danes gave way, and, hotly pursued, fled back to Reading. They fled till nightfall; they fled through the night and the next day, and the whole breadth of Ashdown— meaning the Berkshire hills—was strewn with their corpses, among which were found the body of one of the Viking kings and five of his jarls.

The results of this victory did not break the power of the Danish army; in a fortnight they were again in the field. But the Battle of Ashdown justly takes its place among historic encounters because of the greatness of the issue. If the West Saxons had been beaten all England would have sunk into heathen anarchy. Since they were victorious the hope still burned for a civilised Christian existence in this Island. This was the first time the invaders had been beaten in the field. The last of the Saxon kingdoms had withstood the assault upon it. Alfred had made the Saxons feel confidence in themselves again. They could hold their own in open fight. The story of this conflict at Ashdown was for generations a treasured memory of the Saxon writers. It was Alfred's first battle.

All through the year 871 the two armies waged deadly war. King Ethelred soon fell sick and died. Although he had young

[1] Hodgkin, vol. ii, pp. 544–545.

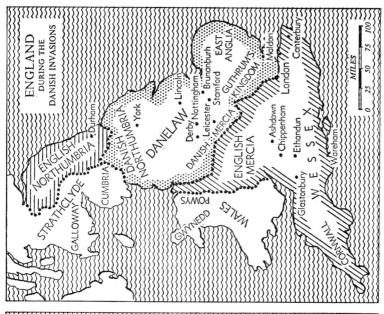

SAXON ENGLAND
IN THE
EIGHTH CENTURY

STRATHCLYDE
GALLOWAY
LOTHIAN
Lindisfarne
NORTHUMBRIA
CUMBRIA
DIERA
York

NORTH WALES

MERCIA

EAST
ANGLIA

ESSEX
London
Canterbury
KENT
W E S S E X
Winchester
SUSSEX
Glastonbury

WEST WALES

0   25   50   75   100
MILES

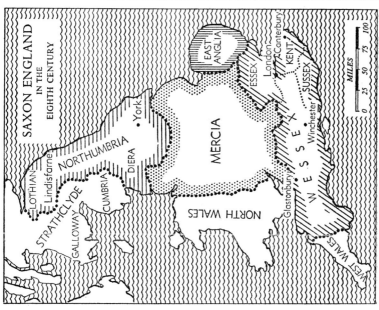

ENGLAND
DURING THE
DANISH INVASIONS

STRATHCLYDE
GALLOWAY
CUMBRIA
ENGLISH
NORTHUMBRIA
Durham
DANISH
NORTHUMBRIA
York
DANELAW
Lincoln
Derby · Nottingham
Leicester · Stamford
DANISH MERCIA
Brunanburh
EAST
ANGLIA
GUTHRUM'S
KINGDOM

GWYNEDD
POWYS
WALES

ENGLISH
MERCIA

Ashdown
Chippenham
Ethandun
Glastonbury
W E S S E X
Wareham

London
Maldon
Canterbury
W E S S E X

CORNWALL

0   25   50   75   100
MILES

· 107 ·

children there was no doubt who his successor must be. At twenty-four Alfred became King, and entered upon a desperate inheritance. To and fro the fighting swayed, with varying fortunes. The Danes were strongly reinforced from overseas; "the summer army," as it was called, "innumerable," "eager to fight against the army of the West Saxons," arrived to join them. Seven or eight battles were fought, and we are told the Danes usually held the field. At Wilton, in the summer, about a month after Alfred had assumed the crown, he sustained a definite defeat in the heart of his own country. His numbers had been worn down by death and desertion, and once again in the field the Vikings' ruse of a feigned retreat was successful.

On the morrow of this misfortune Alfred thought it best to come to terms while he still had an army. We do not know the conditions, but there is no doubt that a heavy payment was among them. "The Saxons made peace with the heathen on the condition that they should depart from them, and this they did," declares the *Chronicle* laconically. But as they took three or four months before retiring upon London it seems that they waited for the Danegeld to be paid. Nevertheless Alfred and his Saxons had in all this fighting convinced the Vikings of their redoubtable force. By this inglorious treaty and stubborn campaign Alfred secured five years in which to consolidate his power.

The reasons which led the Danes to make a truce with Alfred are hard to analyse at this date. They were certainly convinced that only by prolonged and bloody fighting could they master the West Saxons. Both sides liked war, and this had been ding-dong: there was little to show but scars and corpses on either side. But Alfred had always counted upon the invaders dividing, and the stresses at work within the heathen army justified his policy.

Still maintaining their grip on London, the Danes moved

back to the Midlands, which were now in complete submission. "The Mercians made peace with the army." Their king Burgred in 874 was driven overseas, and died in piety under the Papal compassion in Rome. "After his expulsion," says Asser, "the heathen subjected the whole kingdom of the Mercians to their lordship." They set up a local puppet, in a fashion which has often been imitated since, after he had given hostages and taken an oath "that he would not obstruct their wishes, and would be obedient in everything."

*   *   *   *   *

But now in the last quarter of the century a subtle, profound change came over the "Great Heathen Army." Alfred and the men of Wessex had proved too stubborn a foe for easy subjugation. Some of the Danes wished to settle on the lands they already held; the rest were for continuing the war at a suitable moment till the whole country was conquered. Perhaps these two bodies acted in concert, the former providing a sure and solid base, the latter becoming an expeditionary force. Thus, after mauling the kingdom of Strathclyde and carrying off the stock and implements of agriculture nearly half of the sea-pirates settled themselves in Northumbria and East Anglia. Henceforward they began "to till the ground for a livelihood." Here was a great change. We must remember their discipline and organisation. The ships' companies, acting together, had hitherto fought ashore as soldiers. All their organisation of settlements was military. The sailors had turned soldiers, and the soldiers had turned yeomen. They preserved that spirit of independence, regulated only by comradeship and discipline for vital purposes, which was the life of the long-ship.

The whole of the East of England thus received a class of cultivator who, except for purposes of common defence, owed allegiance to none; who had won his land with the sword, and was loyal only to the army organisation which enabled him to keep it. From Yorkshire to Norfolk this sturdy, upstanding stock took root. As time passed they forgot the sea; they forgot the army; they thought only of the land—their own land. They liked the life. Although they were sufficiently skilful agriculturists, there was nothing they could teach the older inhabitants; they brought no new implements or methods, but they were resolved to learn.

They were not dependent wholly upon their own labour. They must have exploited the former possessors and their serfs. The distribution of the land was made around a unit which could support a family. What eight oxen could plough in a certain time under prescribed conditions, much disputed by students, became the measure of the holding. They worked hard themselves, but obviously they used the local people too.

Thus the Danish differs in many ways from the Saxon settlement four hundred years earlier. There was no idea of exterminating the older population. The two languages were not very different; the way of life, the methods of cultivation, very much the same. The colonists—for such they had now become —brought their families from Scandinavia, but also it is certain that they established human and natural relations with the expropriated English. The blood-stream of these vigorous individualists, proud and successful men of the sword, mingled henceforward in the Island race. A vivifying, potent, lasting, and resurgent quality was added to the breed. As modern steel is hardened by the alloy of special metals in comparatively small quantities, this strong strain of individualism, based upon land-ownership, was afterwards to play a persistent part, not only in the blood but in the politics of England. When in the reign of Henry II, after much disorder, great laws were made and royal courts of justice were opened descendants of these hardy farmers—not only "sokemen" or independent peasants, but much smaller folk—were found in a state of high assertiveness. The tribulations of another three hundred years had not destroyed their original firmness of character nor their deep attachment to the conquered soil. All through English history this strain continues to play a gleaming part.

The reformed and placated pirate-mariners brought with them many Danish customs. They had a different notation, which they would have been alarmed to hear described as the "duodecimal system." They thought in twelves instead of tens, and in our own day in certain parts of East Anglia the expression "the long hundred" (*i.e.*, 120) is heard on market-days.

They had a different view of social justice from that entertained by the manorialised Saxons. Their customary laws as they gradually took shape were an undoubted improvement upon the Saxon theme.

> With East Anglia we enter the region within which Danish influence endured. Long before the Norman Conquest it had developed a distinctive form of rural society, which preserved many Scandinavian features, and in which the free man of peasant condition was holding his own successfully against the contemporary drift towards manorialism.[1]

Scandinavian England reared a free peasant population which the burdens of taxation and defence had made difficult in Wessex and English Mercia. And this population related itself so closely to the original invaders that students seek in the Domesday Book of the eleventh century for the means of estimating the size of the Viking armies in the ninth. We shall see presently the equitable, deferential terms which even after their final victory the Anglo-Saxon monarchs proffered to the districts settled by the Danes, known as the Danelaw. It remained only for conversion to Christianity to mingle these races inextricably in the soul and body of a nation. These con-

[1] F. Stenton, *The Danes in England*, 1927, p. 13.

siderations may aptly fill the five years' breathing-space which Alfred had gained by courageous fighting and politic Danegeld. In this interval Halfdene, the Viking king, departed like Ivar from the scene. The tortured, plundered Church requited his atrocities by declaring that God punished him in the long run by madness and a smell which made his presence unendurable to his fellows.

At Lindisfarne, in Dane-ravaged Northumbria, a pathetic tale is told. The ruined monks quitted their devastated, polluted sanctuary and carried on their shoulders the body of St Cuthbert and the bones of St Aidan. After seven years of pilgrimage by land and sea they established themselves in a new patrimony of St Cuthbert as Chester-le-Street. The veneration felt throughout the North for St Cuthbert brought such wealth to his see that in 995 its bishops began to build a new cathedral on the rock at Durham. Thither St Cuthbert's bones were taken, and so great was his prestige that until the nineteenth century the Bishops of Durham were Prince-Bishops, exercising immense power in North-Eastern England.

*　　*　　*　　*　　*

Alfred's dear-bought truce was over. Guthrum, the new war-leader of the mobile and martial part of the heathen army, had formed a large design for the subjugation of Wessex. He operated by sea and land. The land army marched to Wareham, close to Portland Bill, where the sea army joined him in Poole harbour. In this region they fortified themselves, and proceeded to attack Alfred's kingdom by raid and storm from every quarter. The prudent King sought peace and offered an indemnity. At the same time it seems probable that he had hemmed in the land army very closely at Wareham. The Danes took the gold, and "swore upon the Holy Ring" they would depart and keep a faithful peace. With a treachery to which all adjectives are unequal they suddenly darted away and seized Exeter. Alfred, mounting his infantry, followed after, but arrived too late. "They were in the fortress, where they could not be come at." But let all heathen beware of breaking oaths! A frightful tempest smote the sea army. They sought to join their comrades by sea. They were smitten in the neighbourhood of Swanage by the elements, which in those days were believed to be personally directed by the Almighty. A hundred and twenty ships were sunk, and upwards of five thousand of these perjured marauders perished as they deserved. Thus the whole careful plan fell to pieces, and Alfred, watching and besetting Exeter, found his enemies in the summer of 877 in the mood for a new peace. They swore it with oaths of still more compliant solemnity, and they kept it for about five months.

Then in January 878 occurred the most surprising reversal of Alfred's fortunes. His headquarters and Court lay at Chippenham, in Wiltshire. It was Twelfth Night, and the Saxons, who in these days of torment refreshed and fortified themselves by celebrating the feasts of the Church, were off their guard, engaged in pious exercises, or perhaps even drunk. Down swept the ravaging foe. The whole army of Wessex, sole guarantee of England south of the Thames, was dashed into confusion. Many were killed. The most part stole away to their houses. A strong contingent fled overseas. Refugees arrived with futile appeals at the Court of France. Only a handful of officers and personal attendants hid themselves with Alfred in the marshes and forests of Somerset and the Isle of Athelney which rose from the quags. This was the darkest hour of Alfred's fortunes. It was some months before he could even start a guerrilla. He led "with thanes and vassals an unquiet life in great tribulation. . . . For he had nothing wherewith to supply his wants except what in frequent sallies he could seize either stealthily or openly, both from the heathen and from the Christians who had submitted to their rule." He lived as Robin Hood did in Sherwood Forest long afterwards.

This is the moment when those gleaming toys of history were fashioned for the children of every age. We see the warrior-king disguised as a minstrel harping in the Danish camps. We see him acting as a kitchen-boy to a Saxon housewife. The celebrated story of Alfred and the Cakes first appears in a late edition of Bishop Asser's Life. It runs: "It happened one day that the countrywoman, who was the wife of the cowherd with whom King Alfred was staying, was going to bake bread, and the King was sitting by the fireside making ready his bow and arrows and other weapons. A moment came when the woman saw that her bread was burning; she rushed up and removed it from the fire, upbraiding the undaunted King with these words (recorded, strangely, in the original in Latin hexameters): 'Alack, man, why have you not turned over the bread when you see that it is burning, especially as you so much like eating it hot.' The misguided woman little thought that she was talking to King Alfred, who had fought so vigorously against the heathens and won so many victories over them." Low were the fortunes of the once ruthless English. Pent in their mountains, the lineal descendants of the Ancient Britons, slatternly, forlorn, but unconquered, may well have grinned.

The leaders of the Danish army felt sure at this time that mastery was in their hands. To the people of Wessex it seemed that all was over. Their forces were dispersed, the country overrun; their King, if alive, was a fugitive in hiding. It is the supreme proof of Alfred's quality that he was able in such a plight to exercise his full authority and keep contact with his subjects.

Towards the end of Lent the Danes suffered an unexpected misfortune. The crews of twenty-three ships, after committing many atrocities in Wales, sailed to Devon and marched to the attack of one of Alfred's strongholds on Exmoor. The place was difficult to assail, but

> in besetting it they thought that the King's thanes would soon give way to hunger and thirst . . . since the fortress had no supply of water.
>
> The Christians, before they endured any such distress, by the inspiration of heaven judged it to be better either to suffer death or to gain the victory. Accordingly at daybreak they suddenly rushed forth against the heathen, and at the first attack they laid low most of the enemy, including their king. A few only by flight escaped to their ships.[1]

Eight hundred Danes were killed, and the spoils of the victory included an enchanted banner called the Raven, of which it was said that the three daughters of Ragnar Lodbrok had woven it in a single day, and that "in every battle in which that banner went before them the raven in the middle of the design seemed to flutter as though it were alive if they were going to have the victory." On this occasion it did not flutter, but hung listlessly in its silken folds. The event proved that it was impossible for the Danes to win under these conditions.

Alfred, cheered by this news and striving to take the field again, continued a brigand warfare against the enemy while sending his messengers to summon the "fyrd," or local militia, for the end of May. There was a general response; the King was loved and admired. The news that he was alive and active caused widespread joy. All the fighting men came back. After all, the country was in peril of subjugation, the King was a hero, and they could always go home again. The troops of Somerset, Wiltshire, and Hampshire concentrated near Selwood. A point was chosen near where the three shires met, and we can see from this the burdens which lay upon Alfred's tac-

[1] Quoted in Hodgkin, *loc. cit.*, vol. ii, pp. 565–566.

tics. Nevertheless here again was an army: "and when they saw the King they received him like one risen from the dead, after so great tribulations, and they were filled with great joy."

Battle must be sought before they lost interest. The Danes still lay upon their plunder at Chippenham. Alfred advanced to Ethandun, now Edington, and on the bare downs was fought the largest and culminating battle of Alfred's wars. All was staked. All hung in the scales of fate. On both sides the warriors dismounted; the horses were sent to the rear. The shield-walls were formed, the masses clashed against each other, and for hours they fought with sword and axe. But the heathen had lost the favour of God through their violated oath, and eventually from this or other causes they fled from the cruel and clanging field. This time Alfred's pursuit was fruitful. Guthrum, king of the Viking army, so lately master of the one unconquered English kingdom, found himself penned in his camp. Bishop Asser says, "the heathen, terrified by hunger, cold, and fear, and at the last full of despair, begged for peace." They offered to give without return as many hostages as Alfred should care to pick and to depart forthwith.

But Alfred had had longer ends in view. It is strange that he should have wished to convert these savage foes. Baptism as a penalty of defeat might lose its spiritual quality. The workings of the spirit are mysterious, but we must still wonder how the hearts of these hard-bitten swordsmen and pirates could be changed in a single day. Indeed these mass conversions had become almost a matter of form for defeated Viking armies. It is reported that one old veteran declared he had been through this washing twenty times, and complained that the alb with which he was supplied was by no means up to the average standard. But Alfred meant to make a lasting peace with Guthrum. He had him and his army in his power. He could have starved them into surrender and slaughtered them to a man. He wished instead to divide the land with them, and that the two races, in spite of fearful injuries given and received, should dwell together in amity. He received Guthrum with thirty prominent buccaneers in his camp. He stood godfather to Guthrum; he raised him from the font; he entertained him for twelve days; he presented him and his warriors with costly gifts; he called him his son.

This sublime power to rise above the whole force of circumstances, to remain unbiased by the extremes of victory or defeat, to persevere in the teeth of disaster, to greet returning fortune with a cool eye, to have faith in men after repeated betrayals, raises Alfred far above the turmoil of barbaric wars to his pinnacle of deathless glory.

* * * * *

Fourteen years intervened between the victory of Ethandun and any serious Danish attack. In spite of much uneasiness and disturbance, by the standards of those days there was peace. Alfred worked ceaselessly to strengthen his realm. He had been content that the Danes should settle in East Anglia, but he cultivated the best relations with the harassed kingdom of Mercia, which had become tributary to the Danes, though still largely unoccupied by them. In 886 he married his eldest daughter to the regent, Ethelred, who was striving to bear the burden abandoned to him by the fugitive king, Burhred. There had already been several inter-marriages in the Mercian and Wessex royal families, and this set the final seal upon the co-operation of the South and the Midlands.

The first result of this new unity was the recovery of London in 886. London had long been the emporium of Christian England. Ancient Rome had seen in this bridgehead of the Thames, at the convergence of all the roads and sea routes, the greatest commercial and military centre in the Island. Now the City was set on the road to becoming the national capital. We read in the *Chronicle:* "King Alfred restored London, and all the English—those of them who were free from Danish bondage—turned to him, and he then entrusted the borough to the keeping of the ealdorman Ethelred." It would seem that heavy fighting and much slaughter attended the regaining of London, but of this nothing has been recorded. We know little more than the bare fact, and that Alfred after the victory made the citizens organise an effective defence force and put their walls in the highest order.

King Alfred's main effort was to restore the defences and raise the efficiency of the West Saxon force. He reorganised the "fyrd," dividing it into two classes which practised a rotation of service. Though his armies might be smaller, Alfred's peasant soldiers were encouraged not to desert on a long campaign, because they knew that their land was being looked after by the half of the militia that had stayed at home. The modesty of his reforms shows us the enormous difficulties which he had to overcome, and proves that even in that time of mortal peril it was almost impossible to keep the English under arms. The King fortified the whole country by boroughs, running down the Channel and then across to the Severn estuary and so back by the Thames valley, assigning to each a contributory district to man the walls and keep the fortifications in repair. He saw too the vision of English sea-power. To be safe in an island it was necessary to command the sea. He made great departures in ship design, and hoped to beat the Viking numbers by fewer ships of much larger size. These conclusions have only recently become antiquated.

Then King Alfred commanded to be built against the Danish warships longships which were well-nigh twice as long as the others. Some had sixty oars, some more. They were both swifter and steadier, and also higher than the others. They were shaped neither as the Frisian nor as the Danish, but as it seemed to himself that they might be most useful.[1]

But the big ships were beyond the skill of their inexperienced seamen to handle. In an action when nine of them fought six pirate vessels several were run ashore "most awkwardly," says the *Chronicle,* and only two of the enemy fell into Alfred's hands, to afford him the limited satisfaction of hanging their crews at Winchester. Still, the beginning of the English Navy must always be linked with King Alfred.

In spite of the disorders a definite treaty was achieved after the reconquest of London in 886. Significance attaches to the terms in which the contracting parties are described. On Alfred's side there are "the counsellors of the English nation," on Guthrum's "the people who dwell in East Anglia." The organisation of the Danelaw, based entirely upon the army and the subjugated inhabitants, had not yet assumed the form of a State. The English, on the other hand, had already reached the position of "King and Witan"; and none did more to enforce the idea than Alfred himself. The treaty defined a political boundary running up the Thames, up the Lea, along the Lea to its source, then straight to Bedford, and after by the Ouse to Watling Street, beyond which no agreement was made. This line followed no natural frontiers. It recognised a war front. It was drawn in No Man's Land.

The second part of the treaty is curious and instructive. Both sides were familiar with the idea of "wergeld." In order to deal with the ceaseless murders and physical injuries which the anarchic conditions had produced, a scale for compensation or revenge must at all cost be agreed. Nothing would stop the Danes from killing and robbing the English, and *vice versa;*

[1] Quoted in Hodgkins, vol. II, p. 584.

but if there was to be any cessation of war a tariff must be agreed. Both Danish and English independent peasants were accordingly valued at 200 silver shillings each, and men of higher rank were assigned a wergeld of 8½ marks of pure gold. In accepting this clause of the treaty Guthrum was in fact undertaking not to discriminate in wergelds between his English and his Danish subjects. Alfred had gained an important point, which is evidence of the reality of his power.

* * * * *

King Alfred's Book of Laws, or Dooms, as set out in the existing laws of Kent, Wessex, and Mercia, attempted to blend the Mosaic code with Christian principles and old Germanic customs. He inverted the Golden Rule. Instead of "Do unto others as you would that they should do unto you," he adopted the less ambitious principle, "What ye will that other men should *not* do to you, that do ye not to other men," with the comment, "By bearing this precept in mind a judge can do justice to all men; he needs no other law-books. Let him think of himself as the plaintiff, and consider what judgment would satisfy him." The King, in his preamble, explained modestly that "I have not dared to presume to set down in writing many laws of my own, for I cannot tell what will meet with the approval of our successors." The Laws of Alfred, continually amplified by his successors, grew into that body of customary law administered by the shire and hundred courts which, under the name of the Laws of St Edward (the Confessor), the Norman kings undertook to respect, and out of which, with much manipulation by feudal lawyers, the Common Law was founded.

The King encouraged by all his means religion and learning. Above all he sought the spread of education. His rescript to the Bishop of Worcester has been preserved:

I would have you informed that it has come into my re-
membrance what wise men there formerly were among the
English race, both of the sacred orders and the secular; and
what happy times those were throughout the English race, and
how the kings who had the government of the folk in those
days obeyed God and His Ministers; and they on the one hand
maintained their peace and morality and their authority within
their borders, while at the same time they enlarged their territory abroad; and how they prospered both in war and in wisdom, . . . how foreigners came to this land for wisdom and
instruction. . . . So clean was it fallen away in the English
race that there were very few on this side Humber who could
understand their Mass-books in English, or translate a letter
from Latin into English; and I ween that there were not many
beyond the Humber.[1]

He sought to reform the monastic life, which in the general
confusion had grossly degenerated.

If anyone takes a nun from a convent without the King's or
the bishop's leave he shall pay 120 shillings, half to the King,
half to the bishop. . . . If she lives longer than he who ab-
ducted her, she shall inherit nothing of his property. If she
bears a child it shall inherit no more of the property than its
mother.[2]

Lastly in this survey comes Alfred's study of history. He it
was who set on foot the compiling of the *Saxon Chronicle*. The
fact that the early entries are fragmentary gives confidence that
the compilers did not draw on their imagination. From King
Alfred's time they are exact, often abundant, and sometimes
written with historic grasp and eloquence.

[1] Quoted in Hodgkin, *History of the Anglo-Saxons*, p. 609.
[2] *Ibid.*, p. 612.

We discern across the centuries a commanding and versatile intelligence, wielding with equal force the sword of war and of justice; using in defence arms and policy; cherishing religion, learning, and art in the midst of adversity and danger; welding together a nation, and seeking always across the feuds and hatreds of the age a peace which would smile upon the land.

This King, it was said, was a wonder for wise men. "From his cradle he was filled with the love of wisdom above all things," wrote Asser. The Christian culture of his Court sharply contrasted with the feckless barbarism of Viking life. The older race was to tame the warriors and teach them the arts of peace, and show them the value of a settled common existence. We are watching the birth of a nation. The result of Alfred's work was the future mingling of Saxon and Dane in a common Christian England.

In the grim time of Norman overlordship the figure of the great Alfred was a beacon-light, the bright symbol of Saxon achievement, the hero of the race. The ruler who had taught them courage and self-reliance in the eternal Danish wars, who had sustained them with his national and religious faith, who had given them laws and good governance and chronicled their heroic deeds, was celebrated in legend and song as Alfred the Great.

*   *   *   *   *

One final war awaited Alfred. It was a crisis in the Viking story. In 885 they had rowed up the Seine with hundreds of ships and an army of forty thousand men. With every device known to war they laid siege to Paris, and for more than a year battered at its walls. They were hampered by a fortified bridge which the Franks had thrown across the river. They dragged their long-ships overland to the higher reaches and laid waste the land; but they could not take Paris. Count Odo, a warrior prince, defended it against these shameless pirates, and far and wide the demand was made that the King of the Franks should come to the rescue of his capital. Charles the Great had not transmitted his qualities to his children. The nicknames which they received as their monuments sufficiently attest their degeneracy. Charles the Bald was dead, and Charles the Fat reigned in his stead. This wretched invalid was at length forced to gather a considerable army and proceed with it to the aid of Paris. His operations were ineffectual, but the city held firm under its resolute governor. The Viking attack flagged and finally collapsed. All the records are confused. We hear at this time of other battles which they fought with Germanic armies, in one of which the dyke was filled with their corpses. Evidently their thrust in all directions in Western Europe encountered resistance, which, though inefficient, was more than they could overcome. For six years they ravaged the interior of Northern France. Famine followed in their footsteps. The fairest regions had been devoured; where could they turn? Thus they began again to look to England: something might have had time to grow there in the interval. On the Continent their standards were declining, but perhaps again the Island might be their prey. "It was," says Hodgkin in his admirable account, "a hungry monster which turned to England for food as well as plunder." A group of pagan ruffians and pirates had gained possession of an effective military and naval machine, but they faced a mass of formidable veterans whom they had to feed and manage, and for whom they must provide killings. Such men make plans, and certainly their descent upon England was one of the most carefully considered and elaborately prepared villainies of that dark time.

Guthrum died in 891, and the pact which he had sworn with Alfred, and loosely kept, ended. Suddenly in the autumn of 892 a hostile armada of two hundred and fifty ships appeared off Lympne, carrying "the Great Heathen Army" that had ravaged France to the invasion of England. They disembarked and fortified themselves at Appledore, on the edge of the forest. They were followed by eighty ships conveying a second force of baffled raiders from the Continent, who sailed up the Thames and established themselves on its southern bank at Milton, near Sittingbourne. Thus Kent was to be attacked from both sides. This immense concerted assault confronted Alfred with his third struggle for life. The English, as we may call them—for the Mercians and West Saxons stood together—had secured fourteen years of unquiet peace in which to develop their defences. Many of the Southern towns were fortified; they were "burhs." The "fyrd" had been improved in organisation, though its essential weaknesses had not been removed. There had been a re-gathering of wealth and food; there was a settled administration, and the allegiance of all was given to King Alfred. Unlike Charlemagne, he had a valiant son. At twenty-two Edward could lead his father's armies to the field. The Mercians also had produced an Ethelred, who was a fit companion to the West Saxon prince. The King, in ill-health, is not often seen in this phase at the head of armies; we have glimpses of him, but the great episodes of the war were centred, as they should be, upon the young leaders.

The English beat the Vikings in this third war. Owning the command of the sea, the invaders gripped the Kentish peninsula from the north and south. Alfred had tried to buy them off, and certainly delayed their full attack. He persuaded Hæsten, the Viking leader, at least to have his two young sons baptised. He gave Hæsten much money, and oaths of peace were interchanged, only to be broken. Meanwhile the Danes raided mercilessly, and Alfred tried to rouse England to action. In 893 a third expedition composed of the Danish veterans who had settled in Northumbria and East Anglia sailed round the south coast, and, landing, laid siege to Exeter. But now the young leaders struck hard. Apparently they had a strong mounted force, not indeed what we should call cavalry, but possessing swiftness of movement. They fell upon a column of the raiders near the modern Aldershot, routed them, and pursued them for twenty miles till they were glad to swim the Thames and shelter behind the Colne. Unhappily, the army of the young princes was not strong enough to resume the attack, and also it had run out of provisions. The pursuit therefore had to be abandoned and the enemy escaped.

The Danes had fortified themselves at Benfleet, on the Thames below London, and it is said that their earthworks can be traced to this day. Thence, after recovering from their defeat, they sallied forth to plunder, leaving a moderate garrison in their stronghold. This the princes now assaulted. It had very rarely been possible in these wars to storm a well-fortified place; but Alfred's son and his son-in-law with a strong army from London fell upon Benfleet and "put the army to flight, stormed the fort, and took all that there was within, goods as well as women and children, and brought all to London. And all the ships they either broke in pieces or burnt or brought to London or Rochester." Such are the words of the *Saxon Chronicle.* When in the nineteenth century a railway was being made across this ground the charred fragments of the ships and numbers of skeletons were unearthed upon the site of Benfleet. In the captured stronghold the victors found Hæsten's wife and his two sons. These were precious hostages, and King Alfred was much criticised at the time, and also later, because he restored them to Hæsten. He sent back his wife on broad grounds of humanity. As for the two sons, they had been baptised; he was godfather to one of them, and Ethelred of Mercia to the other. They were therefore Christian brethren, and the King protected them from the consequences of their father's wrongful war. The ninth century found it very hard to understand this behaviour when the kingdom was fighting desperately against brutal marauders, but that is one of the reasons why in the after-time the King is called "Alfred the Great." The war went on, but so far as the records show Hæsten never fought again. It may be that mercy and chivalry were not in vain.

In this cruel war the Vikings used their three armies: the grand army that Hæsten had brought from the Continent, the army which had landed near Lympne, and the third from the Danelaw. But in the end they were fairly beaten in full and long fight by the Christians from Mercia, Wessex, and Wales.

One other incident deserves to be noticed. The *Saxon Chronicle* says:

> Before the winter [the winter of A.D. 894–5] the Danes . . . towed their ships up the Thames and then up the Lea . . . and made a fort twenty miles above Lunden burh. . . . In the autumn [895] the King camped close to the burh while they reaped their corn, so that the Danes might not deprive them of the crop. Then one day the King rode up by the river, and looked at a place where it might be obstructed, so that they could not bring their ships out. . . . He made two forts on the two sides of the river; . . . then the army perceived that they could not bring their ships out. Therefore they left them and went across country, . . . and the men of Lunden burh fetched the ships, and all that they could not take away they broke up, and all that were worth taking they brought into Lunden burh.

In 896 the war petered out, and the Vikings, whose strength seemed at this time to be in decline, dispersed, some settling in the Danelaw, some going back to France. "By God's mercy," exclaims the *Chronicle,* in summing up the war, "the [Danish] army had not too much afflicted the English people." Alfred had well defended the Island home. He had by policy and arms preserved the Christian civilisation in England. He had built up the strength of that mighty South which has ever since sustained much of the weight of Britain, and later of her Empire. He had liberated London, and happily he left behind him descendants who, for several generations, as we shall see, carried his work forward with valour and success.

* * * * *

Alfred died in 899, but the struggle with the Vikings had yet to pass through strangely contrasted phases. Alfred's blood gave the English a series of great rulers, and while his inspiration held victory did not quit the Christian ranks. In his son Edward, who was immediately acclaimed King, the armies had already found a redoubtable leader. A quarrel arose between Edward and his cousin, Ethelwald, who fled to the Danelaw and aroused the Vikings of Northumbria and East Anglia to a renewed inroad upon his native land. In 904 Ethelwald and the Danish king crossed the upper reaches of the Thames at Cricklade and ravaged part of Wiltshire. Edward in retaliation ordered the invasion of East Anglia, with an army formed of the men of Kent and London. They devastated Middle Anglia; but the Kentish contingent, being slow to withdraw, was overtaken and brought to battle by the infuriated Danes. The Danes were victorious, and made a great slaughter; but, as fate would have it, both Eric, the Danish king, and the renegade Ethelwald perished on the field, and the new king, Guthrum II, made peace with Edward on the basis of Alfred's treaty of 886, but with additions which show that the situation had changed. It is now assumed that the Danes are Christians and will pay their tithes, while the parish priest is to be fined if he misleads his flock as to the time of a feast-day or a festival.

In 910 this treaty was broken by the Danes, and the war was renewed in Mercia. The main forces of Wessex and Kent had already been sent by Edward, who was with the fleet, to the aid of the Mercians, and in heavy fighting at Tettenhall, in Staffordshire, the Danes were decisively defeated.

This English victory was a milestone in the long conflict. The Danish armies in Northumbria never recovered from the battle, and the Danish Midlands and East Anglia thus lay open to English conquest. Up to this point Mercia and Wessex had been the defenders, often reduced to the most grievous straits. But now the tide had turned. Fear camped with the Danes.

Edward's sister had been, as we have seen, married to Earl Ethelred of Mercia. Ethelred died in 911, and his widow, Ethelfleda, succeeded and surpassed him. In those savage times the emergence of a woman ruler was enough to betoken her possession of extraordinary qualities. Edward the Elder, as he was afterwards called, and his sister, "the Lady of the Mercians," conducted the national war in common, and carried its success to heights which Alfred never knew. The policy of the two kingdoms, thus knit by blood and need, marched in perfect harmony, and the next onslaught of the Danes was met with confident alacrity and soon broken. The victors then set themselves deliberately to the complete conquest of the Danelaw and its Five Boroughs. This task occupied the next ten years, brother and sister advancing in concert upon their respective lines, and fortifying towns they took at every stage. In 918, when Edward stormed Tempsford, near Bedford, and King Guthrum was killed, the whole resistance of East Anglia collapsed, and all the Danish leaders submitted to Edward as their protector and lord. They were granted in return their estates and the right to live according to their Danish customs. At the same time "the Lady of the Mercians" conquered Leicester, and received even from York offers of submission. In this hour of success Ethelfleda died, and Edward, hastening to Tamworth, was invited by the nobles of Mercia to occupy the vacant throne.

Alfred's son was now undisputed King of all England south of the Humber, and the British princes of North and South Wales hastened to offer their perpetual allegiance. Driving northwards in the next two years, Edward built forts at Manchester, at Thelwall in Cheshire, and at Bakewell in the Peak Country. The Danes of Northumbria saw their end approaching. It seemed as if a broad and lasting unity was about to be reached. Edward the Elder reigned five years more in triumphant peace, and when he died in 925 his authority and his gifts passed to a third remarkable sovereign, capable in every way of carrying on the work of his father and grandfather.

The Saxon Dusk

ATHELSTAN, the third of the great West Saxon kings, sought at first, in accordance with the traditions of his house, peaceful relations with the unconquered parts of the Danelaw; but upon disputes arising he marched into Yorkshire in 926, and there established himself. Northumbria submitted; the Kings of the Scots and of Strathclyde acknowledged him as their "father and lord," and the Welsh princes agreed to pay tribute. There was another uneasy interlude; then in 933 came a campaign against the Scots, and in 937 a general rebellion and renewed war, organised by all the hitherto defeated characters in the drama. The whole of North Britain—Celtic, Danish, and Norwegian, pagan and Christian—together presented a hostile front under Constantine, King of the Scots, and Olaf of Dublin, with Viking reinforcements from Norway. On this occasion neither life nor time was wasted in manœuvres. The fight that followed is recorded for us in an Icelandic saga and an English poem. According to the saga-man, Athelstan challenged his foes to meet him in a pitched battle, and to this they blithely agreed. The English king even suggested the place where all should be put to the test. The armies, very large for those impoverished times, took up their stations as if for the Olympic Games, and much parleying accompanied the process. Tempers rose high as these masses of manhood flaunted their shields and blades at one another and flung their gibes across a narrow space; and there was presently a fierce clash between the Northumbrian and the Icelandic Vikings on the one hand and a part of the English army on the other. In this, although the Northumbrian commander fled, the English were worsted. But on the following day the real trial of strength was staged. The rival hosts paraded in all the pomp of war, and then in hearty goodwill fell on with spear, axe, and sword. All day long the battle raged.

The original victory-song on Brunanburh opens to us a view of the Anglo-Saxon mind, with its primitive imagery and war-delight. "Here Athelstan King, of earls the lord, the giver of the bracelets of the nobles, and his brother also, Edmund the Ætheling, an age-long glory won by slaughter in battle, with the edges of swords, at Brunanburh. The wall of shields they cleaved, they hewed the battle shafts with hammered weapons, the foe flinched . . . the Scottish people and the ship-fleet. . . . The field was coloured with the warriors' blood! After that the sun on high, . . . the greatest star, glided over the earth, God's candle bright! till the noble creature hastened to her setting. There lay soldiers, many with darts struck down, Northern men over their shields shot. So were the Scotch; weary of battle, they had had their fill! They left behind them, to feast on carrion, the dusty-coated raven with horned beak, the black-coated eagle with white tail, the greedy battle-hawk, and the grey beast, the wolf in the wood."

The victory of the English was overwhelming. Constantine, "the perjured" as the victors claimed, fled back to the North, and Olaf retired with his remnants to Dublin. Thus did King Alfred's grandson, the valiant Athelstan, become one of the first sovereigns of Western Europe. He styled himself on coin and charter *Rex totius Britanniæ.*

These claims were accepted upon the Continent. His three sisters were wedded respectively to the Carolingian king, Charles the Simple, to the Capetian, Hugh the Great, and to Otto the Saxon, a future Holy Roman Emperor. He even installed a Norwegian prince, who swore allegiance and was

baptised as his vassal at York. Here again one might hope that
a decision in the long quarrel had been reached; yet it persisted;
and when Athelstan died, two years after Brunanburh, and
was succeeded by his half-brother, a youth of eighteen, the
beaten forces welled up once more against him. Edmund, in
the spirit of his race, held his own. He reigned only six years,
but when he died in 946 he had not ceded an inch or an ell.
Edmund was succeeded by his brother Edred, the youngest son
of Alfred's son Edward the Elder. He too maintained the realm
against all comers, and, beating them down by force of arms,
seemed to have quenched for ever the rebellious fires of
Northumbria.

* * * * *

Historians select the year 954 as the end of the first great
episode in the Viking history of England. A hundred and
twenty years had passed since the impact of the Vikings had
smitten the Island. For forty years English Christian society
had struggled for life. For eighty years five warrior kings—
Alfred, Edward, Athelstan, Edmund, and Edred—defeated
the invaders. The English rule was now restored, though in a
form changed by the passage of time, over the whole country.
Yet underneath it there had grown up, deeply rooted in the
soil, a Danish settlement covering the great eastern plain, in
which Danish blood and Danish customs survived under the
authority of the English king.

In the brilliant and peaceful reign of Edgar all this long
building had reached its culmination. The reconquest of England was accompanied step by step by a conscious administrative reconstruction which has governed the development of
English institutions from that day to this. The shires were re-
organised, each with its sheriff or reeve, a royal officer directly
responsible to the Crown. The hundreds, subdivisions of the
shire, were created, and the towns prepared for defence. An

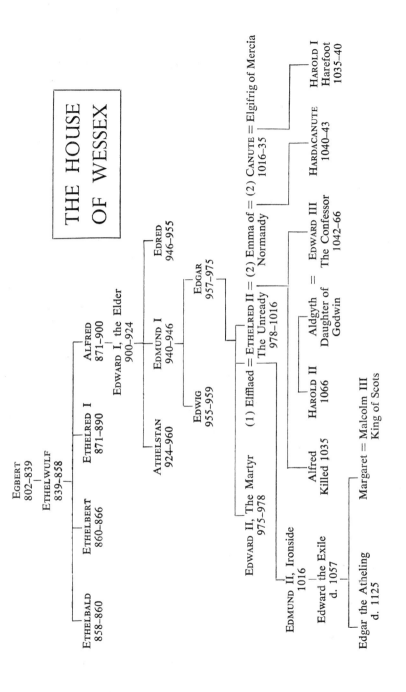

THE HOUSE OF WESSEX

EGBERT
802–839

ETHELWULF
839–858

ETHELBALD
858–860

ETHELBERT
860–866

ETHELRED I
871–890

ALFRED
871–900

EDWARD I, the Elder
900–924

ATHELSTAN
924–960

EDMUND I
940–946

EDRED
946–955

EDWIG
955–959

EDGAR
957–975

EDWARD II, The Martyr
975–978

(1) Elflaed = ETHELRED II = (2) Emma of
The Unready
978–1016

(2) CANUTE = Elgifrig of Mercia
1016–35

EMMA of
Normandy

EDMUND II, Ironside
1016

Edward the Exile
d. 1057

Alfred
Killed 1035

HAROLD II
1066

Aldgyth
Daughter of
Godwin

EDWARD III
The Confessor
1042–66

HARDACANUTE
1040–43

HAROLD I
Harefoot
1035–40

Edgar the Atheling
d. 1125

Margaret = Malcolm III
King of Scots

elaborate system of shire, hundred, and burgh courts maintained law and order and pursued criminals. Taxation was reassessed. Finally, with this military and political revival marched a great re-birth of monastic life and learning and the beginning of our native English literature. The movement was slow and English in origin, but advanced with great strides from the middle of the century as it came in contact with the religious revival on the Continent. The work of Dunstan, Archbishop of Canterbury, and his younger contemporaries, Oswald, Bishop of Worcester, and Æthelwold, Bishop of Winchester, was to revive the strict observance of religion within the monasteries, and thereby indirectly to reform the Episcopate as more and more monks were elected to bishoprics. Another and happy, if incidental, result was to promote learning and the production of splendid illuminated manuscripts which were much in demand in contemporary Europe. Many of these, designed for the religious instruction of the laity, were written in English. The Catholic Homilies of Ælfric, Abbot of Eynsham, mark, we are told, the first achievement of English as a literary language—the earliest vernacular to reach this eminence in the whole of Europe. From whatever point of view we regard it, the tenth century is a decisive step forward in the destinies of England. Despite the catastrophic decline of the monarchy which followed the death of Edgar, this organisation and English culture were so firmly rooted as to survive two foreign conquests in less than a century.

It must have seemed to contemporaries that with the magnificent coronation at Bath in 973, on which all coronation orders since have been based, the seal was set on the unity of the realm. Everywhere the courts are sitting regularly, in shire and borough and hundred; there is one coinage, and one system of weights and measures. The arts of building and decoration are reviving; learning begins to flourish again in the

Church; there is a literary language, a King's English, which all educated men write. Civilisation had been restored to the Island. But now the political fabric which nurtured it was about to be overthrown. Hitherto strong men armed had kept the house. Now a child, a weakling, a vacillator, a faithless, feckless creature, succeeded to the warrior throne. Twenty-five years of peace lapped the land, and the English, so magnificent in stress and danger, so invincible under valiant leadership, relaxed under its softening influences. We have reached the days of Ethelred the Unready. But this expression, which conveys a truth, means literally Ethelred the Ill-counselled, or Ethelred the "Redeless."

In 980 serious raids began again. Chester was ravaged from Ireland. The people of Southampton were massacred by marauders from Scandinavia or Denmark. Thanet, Cornwall, and Devon all suffered butchery and pillage. We have an epic poem upon "The Battle of Maldon," fought in 991. The Danes were drawn up on Northey Island, east of Maldon, with the English facing them from the south bank of the Blackwater estuary. The battle turned upon the causeway joining Northey to the mainland, which was flooded at high tide. The Vikings bargained in their characteristic fashion: "Send quickly rings for your safety; it is better for you to buy off with tribute this storm of spears than that we should share the bitter war. . . . We will with gold set up a truce. . . . We will go abroad with the tribute, and sail the sea, and be at peace with you." [1]

But Byrhtnoth, alderman of Essex, replied: "Hearest thou, rover, what this people saith? They will give you in tribute spears, and deadly darts, and old swords. . . . Here stands an earl not mean, with his company, who will defend this land, Æthelred's home, my prince's folk and field. The heathen shall fall in the war. Too shameful it seems to me that ye should go

[1] Kendrick's *History of the Vikings*, p. 259.

· *135* ·

abroad with our tribute, unfought with, now that ye have come thus far into our land. Not so lightly shall ye come by the treasure: point and edge shall first make atonement, grim war-play, before we pay tribute." [1]

These high words were not made good by the event. As the tide was running out while these taunts were being exchanged the causeway was now exposed and the English naïvely agreed to let the Vikings cross and form on the south bank in order that the battle might be fairly drawn. No sooner had it begun than the English were worsted. Many of Byrhtnoth's men took to flight, but a group of his thanes, knowing that all was lost, fought on to the death. Then followed the most shameful period of Danegeld.

We have seen that Alfred in his day had never hesitated to use money as well as arms. Ethelred used money instead of arms. He used it in ever-increasing quantities, with ever-diminishing returns. He paid as a bribe in 991 ten thousand pounds of silver, with rations for the invaders. In 994, with sixteen thousand pounds, he gained not only a brief respite, but the baptism of the raider, Olaf, thrown in as a compliment. In 1002 he bought a further truce for twenty-four thousand pounds of silver, but on this occasion he was himself to break it. In their ruin and decay the English had taken large numbers of Danish mercenaries into their service. Ethelred suspected these dangerous helpers of a plot against his life. Panic-stricken, he planned the slaughter of all Danes in the south of England, whether in his pay or living peaceably on the land. This atrocious design was executed in 1002 on St Brice's Day. Among the victims was Gunnhild, the wife of Pallig, one of the chief Vikings, and sister of Sweyn, King of Denmark. Sweyn swore implacable revenge, and for two years executed it upon the wretched Islanders. Exeter, Wilton, Norwich, and

[1] *Ibid.*

Thetford all record massacres, which show how widely the retaliation was applied. The fury of the avenger was not slaked by blood. It was baffled, but only for a space, by famine. The Danish army could no longer subsist in the ruined land, and departed in 1005 to Denmark. But the annals of 1006 show that Sweyn was back again, ravaging Kent, sacking Reading and Wallingford. At last Ethelred, for thirty-six thousand pounds of silver, the equivalent of three or four years' national income, bought another short-lived truce.

A desperate effort was now made to build a fleet. In the energy of despair which had once inflamed the Carthaginians to their last effort an immense number of vessels were constructed by the poor, broken people, starving and pillaged to the bone. The new fleet was assembled at Sandwich in 1009. "But," says the *Chronicle,* "we had not the good fortune nor the worthiness that the ship-force could be of any use to this land." Its leaders quarrelled. Some ships were sunk in the fighting; others were lost in a storm, and the rest were shamefully abandoned by the naval commanders. "And then afterwards the people who were in the ships brought them to London, and they let the whole nation's toil thus lightly pass away." There is the record of a final payment to the Vikings in 1012. This time forty-eight thousand pounds' weight of silver was exacted, and the oppressors enforced the collection by the sack of Canterbury, holding Archbishop Alphege to ransom, and finally killing him at Greenwich because he refused to coerce his flock to raise the money. The *Chronicle* states: "All these calamities fell upon us through evil counsel, because tribute was not offered to them at the right time, nor yet were they resisted; but, when they had done the most evil, then was peace made with them. And notwithstanding all this peace and tribute they went everywhere in companies, harried our wretched people, and slew them."

It is vain to recount further the catalogue of miseries. In earlier ages such horrors remain unknown because unrecorded. Just enough flickering light plays upon this infernal scene to give us the sense of its utter desolation and hopeless wretchedness and cruelty. It suffices to note that in 1013 Sweyn, accompanied by his youngest son, Canute, came again to England, subdued the Yorkshire Danes and the five boroughs in the Danelaw, was accepted as overlord of Northumbria and Danish Mercia, sacked Oxford and Winchester in a punitive foray, and, though repulsed from London, was proclaimed King of England, while Ethelred fled for refuge to the Duke of Normandy, whose sister he had married. On these triumphs Sweyn died at the beginning of 1014. There was another respite. The English turned again to Ethelred, "declaring that no lord was dearer to them than their natural lord, if he would but rule them better than he had done before."

But soon the young Danish prince, Canute, set forth to claim the English crown. At this moment the flame of Alfred's line rose again in Ethelred's son, Edmund—Edmund Ironside, as he soon was called. At twenty he was famous. Although declared a rebel by his father, and acting in complete disobedience to him, he gathered forces, and in a brilliant campaign struck a succession of heavy blows. He gained battles, he relieved London, he contended with every form of treachery; the hearts of all men went out to him. New forces sprang from the ruined land. Ethelred died, and Edmund, last hope of the English, was acclaimed King. In spite of all odds and a heavy defeat he was strong enough to make a partition of the realm, and then set himself to rally his forces for the renewal of the struggle; but in 1016, at twenty-two years of age, Edmund Ironside died, and the whole realm abandoned itself to despair.

The ecclesiastical aristocracy which played so great a part

in politics dwelt long upon the prophecies of coming woe ascribed to St. Dunstan. At Southampton, even while Edmund lived, the lay and spiritual chiefs of England agreed to abandon the descendants of Ethelred for ever and recognise Canute as King. All resistance, moral and military, collapsed before the Dane. The family of Ethelred was excised from the royal line, and the last sons of the house of Wessex fled into exile. The young Danish prince received this general and abject submission in a good spirit, although a number of bloody acts were required to attain and secure his position. He made good his promise to fulfill the duties of a king both in spiritual and temporal affairs to the whole country. The English magnates agreed to buy off the Danish army with a huge indemnity, and the new King, in "an oath of his soul," endorsed by his chiefs, bound himself to rule for all. Such was the compact solemnly signed by the English and Danish leaders. "The kingly house," as Ranke put it, "whose right and pre-eminence was connected with the earliest settlements, which had completed the union of the realm and delivered it from the worst distress, was at a moment of moral deterioration and disaster excluded by the spiritual and temporal chiefs, of Anglo-Saxon and Danish origin." [1]

*   *   *   *   *

There were three principles upon which sovereignty could be erected: conquest, which none could dispute; hereditary right, which was greatly respected; and election, which was a kind of compromise between the two. It was upon this last basis that Canute began his reign. It is possible that the early English ideal of kingship and just government in Alfred and Canute was affected by the example of Trajan. This emperor was a favourite of Pope Gregory, who had sent the first missionaries. There is evidence that stories of Trajan's virtue were read aloud in the English church service. Canute may also

[1] *History of England*, vol. i, p. 25.

have studied, and certainly he reproduced, the poise of the Emperor Augustus. Everyone knows the lesson he administered to his flatterers when he sat on the seashore and forbade the tide to come in. He made a point of submitting himself to the laws whereby he ruled. He even in his military capacity subjected himself to the regulations of his own household troops. At the earliest moment he disbanded his great Danish army and trusted himself broadly to the loyalty of the humbled English. He married Emma of Normandy, the widow of Ethelred, and so forestalled any action by the Duke of Normandy on behalf of her descendants by Ethelred.

Canute became the ruling sovereign of the North, and was reckoned as having five or six kingdoms under him. He was already King of Denmark when he conquered England, and he made good his claim to be King of Norway. Scotland offered him its homage. The Viking power, although already undermined, still stretched across the world, ranging from Norway to North America, and through the Baltic to the East. But of all his realms Canute chose England for his home and capital. He liked, we are told, the Anglo-Saxon way of life. He wished to be considered the "successor of Edgar," whose seventeen years of peace still shone by contrast with succeeding times. He ruled according to the laws, and he made it known that these were to be administered in austere detachment from his executive authority.

He built churches, he professed high devotion to the Christian faith and to the Papal diadem. He honoured the memory of St Edmund and St Alphege, whom his fellow-countrymen had murdered, and brought their relics with pious pomp to Canterbury. From Rome, as a pilgrim, in 1027, he wrote a letter to his subjects couched in exalted and generous terms, promising to administer equal justice, and laying particular emphasis upon the payment of Church dues. His daughter was married to the Emperor Conrad's eldest son, who ultimately carried his empire across Schleswig to the banks of the Eider. These remarkable achievements, under the blessing of God and the smiles of fortune, were in large measure due to his own personal qualities. Here again we see the power of a great man to bring order out of ceaseless broils and command harmony and unity to be his servants, and how the lack of such men has to be paid for by the inestimable suffering of the many.

Some early records of Canute throw a vivid light upon his character and moods. "When he entered monasteries, and was received with great honour, he proceeded humbly; keeping his eyes fixed with a wonderful reverence on the ground, and, shedding tears copiously—nay, I may say, in rivers—he devoutly sought the intervention of the Saints. But when it came to making his royal oblations, oh! how often did he fix his weeping eyes upon the earth! How often did he beat that noble breast! What sighs he gave! How often he prayed that he might not be unworthy of clemency from on high!" [1]

But this from a saga two centuries later is in a different vein:

"When King Canute and Earl Ulf had played a while the King made a false move, at which the Earl took a knight from the King; but the King set the piece again upon the board, and told the Earl to make another move; but the Earl grew angry, threw over the chess-board, stood up, and went away. The King said, 'Run away, Ulf the Fearful.' The Earl turned round at the door and said, '. . . Thou didst not call me Ulf the Fearful at Helge River, when I hastened to thy help while the Swedes were beating thee like a dog.' The Earl then went out,

[1] From the *Encomium Emma Regina,* in Langebek, *Scriptores Rerum Danicarum* (1773).

and went to bed. . . . The morning after, while the King was putting on his clothes, he said to his foot-boy, 'Go thou to Earl Ulf and kill him.'

"The lad went, was away a while, and then came back.

"The King said, 'Hast thou killed the Earl?'

" 'I did not kill him, for he was gone to Saint Lucius' church.'

"There was a man called Ivar White, a Norwegian by birth, who was the King's court-man and chamberlain. The King said to him, 'Go thou and kill the Earl.'

"Ivar went to the church, and in at the choir, and thrust his sword through the Earl, who died on the spot. Then Ivar went to the King, with the bloody sword in his hand.

"The King said, 'Hast thou killed the Earl?'

" 'I have killed him,' says he.

" 'Thou didst well.'

"After the Earl was killed the monks closed the church and locked the doors. When that was told the King he sent a message to the monks, ordering them to open the church and sing High Mass. They did as the King ordered; and when the King came to the church he bestowed on it great property, so that it had a large domain, by which that place was raised very high; and those lands have since always belonged to it." [1]

* * * * *

Meanwhile across the waters of the English Channel a new military power was growing up. The Viking settlement founded in Normandy in the early years of the tenth century had become the most vigorous military state in France. In less than a hundred years the sea-rovers had transformed themselves into a feudal society. Such records as exist are overlaid by legend. We do not even know whether Rollo, the traditional founder of the Norman state, was a Norwegian, a Dane, or a

[1] From the *Heimskringla* of Snorre Sturlason.

Swede. Norman history begins with the Treaty of Saint-Clair-sur-Epte, made by Rollo with Charles the Simple, King of the West Franks, which affirmed the suzerainty of the King of France and defined the boundaries of the Duchy of Normandy.

In Normandy a class of knights and nobles arose who held their lands in return for military service, and sublet to inferior tenants upon the same basis. The Normans, with their craving for legality and logic, framed a general scheme of society, from which there soon emerged an excellent army. Order was strenuously enforced. No one but the Duke might build castles or fortify himself. The Court or "Curia" of the Duke consisted of his household officials, of dignitaries of the Church, and of the more important tenants, who owed him not only military service but also personal attendance at Court. Here the administration was centred. Respect for the decisions and interests of the Duke was maintained throughout Normandy by the Vicomtes, who were not merely collectors of taxes from the ducal estates, but also, in effect, prefects, in close touch with the Curia, superintending districts like English counties. The Dukes of Normany created relations with the Church which became a model for medieval Europe. They were the protectors and patrons of the monasteries in their domains. They welcomed the religious revival of the tenth century, and secured the favour and support of its leaders. But they made sure that bishops and abbots were ducal appointments.

It was from this virile and well-organised land that the future rulers of England were to come. Between the years 1028 and 1035 the Viking instincts of Duke Robert of Normandy turned him seriously to plans of invasion. His death and his failure to leave a legitimate heir suspended the project, but only for a while.

The figure of Emma, sister of Robert of Normandy, looms large in English history at this time. Ethelred had originally married her from a reasonable desire to supplement his failing armaments by a blood-tie with the most vigorous military state in Europe. Canute married her to give him a united England. Of her qualities and conduct little is known. Nevertheless few women have stood at the centre of such remarkable converging forces. In fact Emma had two husbands and two sons who were Kings of England.

In 1035 Canute died, and his empire with him. He left three sons, two by Elgiva of Northampton and one, Hardicanute, by Emma. These sons were ignorant and boorish Vikings, and many thoughts were turned to the representatives of the old West Saxon line, Alfred and Edward, sons of Ethelred and Emma, then living in exile in Normandy. The elder, Alfred, "the innocent Prince" as the chronicler calls him, hastened to England in 1036, ostensibly to visit his again-widowed mother, the ex-Queen Emma. A Wessex earl, Godwin, was the leader of the Danish party in England. He possessed great abilities and exercised the highest political influence. The venturesome Alfred was arrested and his personal attendants slaughtered. The unfortunate prince himself was blinded, and in this condition soon ended his days in the monastery at Ely. The guilt of this crime was generally ascribed to Godwin. The succession being thus simplified, Canute's sons divided the paternal inheritance. Sweyn reigned in Norway for a spell, but his two brothers who ruled England were short-lived, and within six years the throne of England was again vacant.

Godwin continued to be the leading figure in the land, and was now master of its affairs. There was still living in exile in Normandy Edward, the remaining son of Ethelred and Emma, younger brother of the ill-starred Alfred. In these days of reviving anarchy all men's minds turned to the search for some stable institution. This could only be found in monarchy, and the illustrious line of Alfred the Great possessed unequalled claims and titles. It was the Saxon monarchy which for five or six generations had provided the spearhead of resistance to the Danes. The West Saxon line was the oldest in Europe. Two generations back the house of Capet were lords of little more than Paris and the Ile de France, and the Norman dukes were Viking rovers. A sense of sanctity and awe still attached to any who could claim descent from the Great King, and beyond him to Egypt and immemorial antiquity. Godwin saw that he could consolidate his power and combine both English and Danish support by making Edward King. He bargained with the exile, threatening unless his terms were met to put a nephew of Canute on the throne. Of these the first was the restriction of Norman influence in England. Edward made no difficulty; he was welcomed home and crowned; and for the next twenty-four years, with one brief interval, England was mainly governed by Godwin and his sons. "He had been to such an extent exalted," says the *Chronicle* of Florence of Worcester, "as if he had ruled the King and all England."

Edward was a quiet, pious person without liking for war or much aptitude for administration. His Norman upbringing made him the willing though gentle agent of Norman influence, so far as Earl Godwin would allow. Norman prelates appeared in the English Church, Norman clerks in the royal household, and Norman landowners in the English shires. To make all smooth Edward was obliged to marry Godwin's young and handsome daughter, but we are assured by contemporary writers that this union was no more than formal. According to tradition the King was a kindly, weak, chubby albino. Some later writers profess to discern a latent energy in a few of his dealings with the formidable group of Anglo-Danish warriors that surrounded him. Nevertheless his main interest in life was religious, and as he grew older his outlook was increasingly that of a monk. In these harsh times he played much the same part as Henry VI, whose nature was similar, during the Wars of the Roses. His saintliness brought him as the years passed by a reward in the veneration of his people, who forgave him his weakness for the sake of his virtues.

Meanwhile the Godwin family maintained their dictatorship under the Crown. Nepotism in those days was not merely the favouring of a man's own family; it was almost the only way in which a ruler could procure trustworthy lieutenants. The family tie, though frequently failing, gave at least the assurance of a certain identity of interest. Statistics had not been collected, but there was a general impression in these primitive times that a man could trust his brother, or his wife's brother, or his son, better than a stranger. We must not therefore hasten to condemn Earl Godwin because he parcelled out the English realm among his relations; neither must we marvel that other ambitious magnates found a deep cause of complaint in this distribution of power and favour. For some years a bitter intrigue was carried on between Norman and Saxo-Danish influences at the English Court.

A crisis came in the year 1051, when the Norman party at Court succeeded in driving Godwin into exile. During Godwin's absence William of Normandy is said to have paid an official visit to the Confessor in England in quest of the succession to the Crown. Very likely King Edward promised that William should be his heir. But in the following year Godwin returned, backed by a force raised in Flanders, and with the active help of his son Harold. Together father and son obliged King Edward to take them back into power. Many of the principal Norman agents in the country were expelled, and the authority of the Godwin family was felt again throughout the land. The territories that they directly controlled stretched south of a line from the Wash to the Bristol Channel.

Seven months after his restoration Godwin died, in 1053. Since Canute first raised him to eminence he had been thirty-five years in public life. Harold, his eldest surviving son, succeeded to his father's great estates. He now filled his part to the full, and for the next thirteen adventurous years was the virtual ruler of England. In spite of the antagonism of rival Anglo-Danish earls, and the opposition of the Norman elements still attached to the Confessor's Court, the Godwins, father and son, maintained their rule under what we should now call a constitutional monarchy. A brother of Harold's became Earl of Mercia, and a third son of Godwin, Tostig, who courted the Normans, and was high in the favour of King Edward, received the Earldom of Northumbria, dispossessing the earls of those regions. But there was now no unity within the house of Godwin. Harold and Tostig soon became bitter foes. All Harold's competence, vigour, and shrewdness were needed to preserve the unity of the realm. Even so, as we shall see, the rift between the brothers left the land a prey to foreign ambitions.

*   *   *   *   *

The condition of England at the close of the reign of Edward the Confessor was one of widespread political weakness. Illuminated manuscripts, sculpture, metalwork and architecture of much artistic merit were still produced, religious life flourished, and a basis of sound law and administration remained, but the virtues and vigour of Alfred's posterity were exhausted and the Saxon monarchy itself was in decline. A strain of feeble princes, most of whom were short-lived, had died without children. Even the descendants of the prolific Ethelred the Unready died out with strange rapidity, and at this moment only a sickly boy and his sister and the aged sovereign represented the warrior dynasty which had beaten the Vikings and reconquered the Danelaw. The great earls were becoming independent in the provinces.

Though England was still the only state in Europe with a royal treasury to which sheriffs all over the country had to account, royal control over the sheriffs had grown lax. The King lived largely upon his private estates and governed as best he could through his household. The remaining powers of the monarchy were in practice severely restricted by a little group of Anglo-Danish notables. The main basis of support for the English kings had always been this select Council, never more than sixty, who in a vague manner regarded themselves as the representatives of the whole country. It was in fact a committee of courtiers, the greater thanes, and ecclesiastics. But at this time this assembly of "wise men" in no way embodied the life of the nation. It weakened the royal executive without adding any strength of its own. Its character and quality suffered in the general decay. It tended to fall into the hands of the great families. As the central power declined a host of local chieftains disputed and intrigued in every county, pursuing private and family aims and knowing no interest but their own. Feuds and disturbances were rife. The people, too, were hampered not only by the many conflicting petty authorities, but by the deep division of custom between the Saxon and the Danish districts. Absurd anomalies and contradictions obstructed the administration of justice. The system of land-tenure varied from complete manorial conditions in Wessex to the free communities of the Danelaw in the North and East. There was no defined relation between Lordship and Land. A thane owed service to the King as a personal duty, and not in respect of lands he held. The Island had come to count for little on the Continent, and had lost the thread of its own progress. The defences, both of the coast and of the towns, were neglected. To the coming conquerors the whole system, social, moral, political, and military, seemed effete.

The figure of Edward the Confessor comes down to us faint, misty, frail. The medieval legend, carefully fostered by the Church, whose devoted servant he was, surpassed the man. The lights of Saxon England were going out, and in the gathering darkness a gentle, grey-beard prophet foretold the end. When on his death-bed Edward spoke of a time of evil that was coming upon the land his inspired mutterings struck terror into the hearers. Only Archbishop Stigand, who had been Godwin's stalwart, remained unmoved, and whispered in Harold's ear that age and sickness had robbed the monarch of his wits. Thus on January 5, 1066, ended the line of the Saxon kings. The national sentiment of the English, soon to be conquered, combined in the bitter period that lay before them with the gratitude of the Church to circle the royal memory with a halo. As the years rolled by his spirit became the object of popular worship. His shrine at Westminster was a centre of pilgrimage. Canonised in 1161, he lived for centuries in the memories of the Saxon folk. The Normans also had an interest in his fame. For them he was the King by whose wisdom the crown had been left, or so they claimed, to their Duke. Hence both sides blessed his memory, and until England appropriated St George during the Hundred Years War St Edward the Confessor was the kingdom's patron saint. St George proved undoubtedly more suitable to the Islanders' needs, moods, and character.

BOOK TWO

THE MAKING OF THE NATION

The Norman Invasion

ENGLAND, distracted by faction and rivalry at home, had for a long time lain under rapacious glare from overseas. The Scandinavians sought to revive the empire of Canute. The Normans claimed that their Duke held his cousin Edward's promise of the throne. William of Normandy had a virile origin and a hard career. The prize was large enough for the separate ambitions of both the hungry Powers. Their simultaneous action in the opening stages was an advantage to be shared in common.

*   *   *   *   *

One morning Duke Robert of Normandy, the fourth descendant of Rollo, was riding towards his capital town, Falaise, when he saw Arlette, daughter of a tanner, washing linen in a stream. His love was instantly fired. He carried her to his castle, and, although already married to a lady of quality, lived with her for the rest of his days. To this romantic but irregular union there was born in 1027 a son, William, afterwards famous.

Duke Robert died when William was only seven, and in those harsh times a minor's hold upon his inheritance was precarious. The great nobles who were his guardians came one by one to violent ends, and rival ambitions stirred throughout Normandy. Were they to be ruled by a bastard? Was the grandson of a tanner to be the liege lord of the many warrior families? The taint of bastardy clung, and sank deep into William's nature. It embittered and hardened him. When, many years afterwards, he besieged the town of Alençon the citizens imprudently hung out hides upon the walls, shouting, "Hides for the tanner!" William repaid this taunt by devastating the town, and mutilating or flaying alive its chief inhabitants.

It was the declared policy of King Henry of France to recognise and preserve the minor upon the ducal throne. He became his feudal guardian and overlord. But for this the boy could hardly have survived. In 1047, when he was twenty, a formidable conspiracy was organised against him, and at the outset of the revolt he narrowly missed destruction. The confederates proposed to divide the duchy among themselves, conferring on one of their number, to whom they took an oath, the nominal title of Duke. William was hunting in the heart of the disaffected country. His seizure was planned, but his fool broke in upon him with a timely warning to fly for his life. By daybreak he had ridden forty miles, and was for the moment safe in loyal Falaise. Knowing that his own strength could not suffice, he rode on ceaselessly to appeal for help to his overlord, the King of France. This was not denied. King Henry took the field. William gathered together his loyal barons and retainers. At the Battle of Val-ès-Dunes, fought entirely on both sides by cavalry, the rebels were routed, and thenceforward, for the first time, William's position as Duke of Normandy was secure.

There was room enough within the existing social system for feuds, and in some fiefs even private wars, but when the state fell into the hands of strong overlords these were kept within bounds, which did not prevent the rapid growth of a martial society, international both in its secular and military principles. The sense of affinity to the liege lord at every stage in the hierarchy, the association of the land with fighting power, the acceptance of the Papal authority in spiritual matters, united the steel-clad knights and nobles over an ever-widening area of

Europe. To the full acceptance of the universal Christian Church was added the conception of a warrior aristocracy, animated by ideas of chivalry, and knit together in a system of military service based upon the holding of land. This institution was accompanied by the rise of mail-clad cavalry to a dominant position in war, and new forces were created which could not only conquer but rule.

In no part of the feudal world was the fighting quality of the new organisation carried to a higher pitch than among the Normans. William was a master of war, and thereby gave his small duchy some of the prestige which England had enjoyed thirty years before under the firm and clear-sighted government of Canute. He and his knights now looked out upon the world with fearless and adventurous eyes. Good reasons for gazing across the Channel were added to the natural ambitions of warlike men. William, like his father, was in close touch with the Saxon Court, and had watched every move on the part of the supporters of the Anglo-Danish party, headed by Godwin and his son Harold.

Fate played startlingly into the hands of the Norman Duke. On some visit of inspection, probably in 1064, Harold was driven by the winds on to the French coast. The Count of Ponthieu, who held sway there, looked upon all shipwrecked mariners and their gear as treasure-trove. He held Harold to ransom for what he was worth, which was much. The contacts between the Norman and English Courts were at this time close and friendly, and Duke William asked for the release of King Edward's thane, acting at first by civil request, and later by armed commands. The Count of Ponthieu reluctantly relinquished his windfall, and conducted Harold to the Norman Court. A friendship sprang up between William and Harold. Politics apart, they liked each other well. We see them, falcon on wrist, in sport; Harold taking the field with

William against the Bretons, or rendering skilful service in hazardous broils. He was honoured and knighted by William. But the Duke looked forward to his future succession to the English crown. Here indeed was the prize to be won. Harold had one small streak of royal blood on his mother's side; but William, through his father, had a more pointed or at least less cloudy claim to the Island throne. This claim he was resolved to assert. He saw the power which Harold wielded under Edward the Confessor, and how easily he might convert it into sovereignty if he happened to be on the spot when the Confessor died. He invited Harold to make a pact with him whereby he himself should become King of England, and Harold Earl of the whole splendid province of Wessex, being assured thereof and linked to the King by marriage with William's daughter.

All this story is told with irresistible charm in the tapestry chronicle of the reign commonly attributed to William's wife, Queen Matilda, but actually designed by English artists under the guidance of his half-brother, Odo, Bishop of Bayeux. It is of course the Norman version, and was for generations proclaimed by their historians as a full justification—and already even in those days aggressors needed justifications—of William's invasion of England. The Saxons contended that this was mere Norman propaganda, and there is the usual conflict of evidence. It is probable however that Harold swore a solemn oath to William to renounce all rights or designs upon the English crown, and it is likely that if he had not done so he might never have seen either crown or England again.

The feudal significance of this oath making Harold William's man was enhanced by a trick novel to those times, yet adapted to their mentality. Under the altar or table upon which Harold swore there was concealed a sacred relic, said by some later writers to have been some of the bones of St Edmund.

An oath thus reinforced had a triple sanctity, well recognised throughout Christendom. It was a super-oath; and the obligation, although taken unbeknown, was none the less binding upon Harold. Nevertheless it cannot be said that the bargain between the two men was unreasonable, and Harold probably at the time saw good prospects in it for himself.

By this time William had consolidated his position at home. He had destroyed the revolting armies of his rivals and ambitious relations, he had stabilised his western frontier against Brittany, and in the south-west he had conquered Maine from the most powerful of the ruling houses of Northern France, the Angevins. He had forced the powers in Paris who had protected his youth to respect his manhood; and by his marriage with Matilda, daughter of the Count of Flanders, he had acquired a useful ally on his eastern flank.

Meanwhile Harold, liberated, was conducting the government of England with genuine acceptance and increasing success. At length, in January 1066, Edward the Confessor died, absolved, we trust, from such worldly sins as he had been tempted to commit. With his dying breath, in spite of his alleged promise to William, he is supposed to have commended Harold, his young, valiant counsellor and guide, as the best choice for the crown which the Witan, or Council could make. At any rate, Harold, at the beginning of the fateful year 1066, was blithely accepted by London, the Midlands, and the South, and crowned King with all solemnity in Westminster Abbey.

This event opened again the gates of war. There had been a precedent in France of a non-royal personage, Hugh Capet, becoming King; but this had been strongly resented by the nobility, whose pride, common ideas, and sentiments were increasingly giving the law to Western Europe. Every aspiring thane who heard the news of Harold's elevation was conscious of an affront, and also of the wide ranges open to ability and the sword. Moreover, the entire structure of the feudal world rested upon the sanctity of oaths. Against the breakers of oaths the censures both of chivalry and the Church were combined with blasting force. It was a further misfortune for Harold that Stigand, the Archbishop of Canterbury, had himself received the pallium from a schismatic Pope. Rome therefore could not recognise Harold as King.

At this very moment the Almighty, reaching down from His heavenly sphere, made an ambiguous gesture. The tailed comet or "hairy star" which appeared at the time of Harold's coronation is now identified by astronomers as Halley's Comet, which had previously heralded the Nativity of Our Lord; and it is evident that this example of divine economy in the movements for mundane purposes of celestial bodies might have been turned by deft interpretation to Harold's advantage. But the conquerors have told the tale, and in their eyes this portent conveyed to men the approaching downfall of a sacrilegious upstart.

Two rival projects of invasion were speedily prepared. The first was from Scandinavia. The successors of Canute in Norway determined to revive their traditions of English sovereignty. An expedition was already being organised when Tostig, Harold's exiled and revengeful half-brother, ousted from his Earldom of Northumbria, arrived with full accounts of the crisis in the Island and of the weak state of the defences. King Harold Hardrada set forth to conquer the English crown. He sailed at first to the Orkneys, gathering recruits from the Scottish isles and from the Isle of Man. With Tostig he wended towards the north-east coast of England with a large fleet and army in the late summer of 1066.

Harold of England was thus faced with a double invasion from the north-east and from the south. In September 1066 he heard that a Norwegian fleet, with Hardrada and Tostig on board, had sailed up the Humber, beaten the local levies under Earls Edwin and Morcar, and encamped near York at Stamford Bridge. He now showed the fighting qualities he possessed. The news reached him in London, where he was waiting to see which invasion would strike him first, and where. At the head of his Danish household troops he hastened northwards up the Roman road to York, calling out the local levies as he went. His rapidity of movement took the Northern invaders completely by surprise. Within five days of the defeat of Edwin and Morcar Harold reached York, and the same day marched to confront the Norwegian army ten miles from the city.

The battle began. The Englishmen charged, but at first the Norsemen, though without their armour, kept their battle array. After a while, deceived by what proved to be a feint, the common ruse of those days, they opened up their shield rampart and advanced from all sides. This was the moment for which Harold had waited. The greatest crash of weapons arose. Hardrada was hit by an arrow in the throat, and Tostig, assuming the command, took his stand by the banner "Landravager." In this pause Harold offered his brother peace, and also quarter to all Norsemen who were still alive; but "the Norsemen called out all of them together that they would rather fall, one across the other, than accept of quarter from the Englishmen." [1] Harold's valiant house-carls, themselves of Viking blood, charged home, and with a war shout the battle began again. At this moment a force left on board ship arrived to succour the invaders. They, unlike their comrades, were clad in proof, but, breathless and exhausted from their hurried march, they cast aside their ring-mail, threw in their lot with their hard-pressed friends, and nearly all were killed. The victorious Harold buried Hardrada in the seven feet of English earth he had scornfully promised him, but he spared his son

[1] From the *Heimskringla Saga,* by Snorre Sturlason.

Olaf and let him go in peace with his surviving adherents. Tostig paid for his restless malice with his life. Though the Battle of Stamford Bridge has been overshadowed by Hastings it has a claim to be regarded as one of the decisive contests of English history. Never again was a Scandinavian army able seriously to threaten the power of an English king or the unity of the realm.

At the moment of victory news reached the King from the South that "William the Bastard" had landed at Pevensey.

*   *   *   *   *

William the Conqueror's invasion of England was planned like a business enterprise. The resources of Normandy were obviously unequal to the task; but the Duke's name was famous throughout the feudal world, and the idea of seizing and dividing England commended itself to the martial nobility of many lands. The barons of Normandy at the Council of Lillebonne refused to countenance the enterprise officially. It was the Duke's venture, and not that of Normandy. But the bulk of them hastened to subscribe their quota of knights and ships. Brittany sent a large contingent. It must be remembered that some of the best stocks from Roman Britain had found refuge there, establishing a strong blood strain which had preserved a continuity with the Classic Age and with the British race. But all France was deeply interested. Mercenaries came from Flanders, and even from beyond the Alps; Normans from South Italy and Spain, nobles and knights, answered the advertisement. The shares in this enterprise were represented by knights or ships, and it was plainly engaged that the lands of the slaughtered English would be divided in proportion to the contributions, subject of course to a bonus for good work in the field. During the summer of 1066 this great gathering of audacious buccaneers, land-hungry, war-hungry, assembled in a merry company around St Valery, at the mouth of the

Somme. Ships had been built in all the French ports from the spring onwards, and by the beginning of August nearly seven hundred vessels and about seven thousand men, of whom the majority were persons of rank and quality, were ready to follow the renowned Duke and share the lands and wealth of England.

But the winds were contrary. For six whole weeks there was no day when the south wind blew. The heterogeneous army, bound by no tie of feudal allegiance, patriotism, or moral theme, began to bicker and grumble. Only William's repute as a managing director and the rich pillage to be expected held them together. At length extreme measures had to be taken with the weather. The bones of St Edmund were brought from the church of St Valery and carried with military and religious pomp along the seashore. This proved effective, for the very next day the wind changed, not indeed to the south, but to the south-west. William thought this sufficient, and gave the signal. The whole fleet put to sea, with all their stores, weapons, coats of mail, and great numbers of horses. Special arrangements were made to keep the fleet together, the rendezvous being at the mouth of the Somme, and the Duke by night having a lamp of special brilliancy upon his masthead. The next morning all steered towards the English coast. The Duke, who had a faster vessel, soon found himself alone in mid-Channel. He hove to and breakfasted with his staff "as if he had been in his own hall." Wine was not lacking, and after the meal he expressed himself in enthusiastic terms upon his great undertaking and the prizes and profit it would bring to all engaged therein.

On September 28 the fleet hove in sight, and all came safely to anchor in Pevensey Bay. There was no opposition to the landing. The local "fyrd" had been called out this year four times already to watch the coast, and having, in true English style, come to the conclusion that the danger was past because it had not yet arrived had gone back to their homes. William landed, as the tale goes, and fell flat on his face as he stepped out of the boat. "See," he said, turning the omen into a favourable channel, "I have taken England with both my hands." He occupied himself with organising his army, raiding for supplies in Sussex, and building some defensive works for the protection of his fleet and base. Thus a fortnight passed.

Meanwhile Harold and his house-carls, sadly depleted by the slaughter of Stamford Bridge, jingled down Watling Street on their ponies, marching night and day to London. They covered the two hundred miles in seven days. In London the King gathered all the forces he could, and most of the principal persons in Wessex and Kent hastened to join his standard, bringing their retainers and local militia with them. Remaining only five days in London, Harold marched out towards Pevensey, and in the evening of October 13 took up his position upon the slope of a hill which barred the direct march upon the capital.

The military opinion of those as of these days has criticised his staking all upon an immediate battle. The loyalty of the Northern earls, Edwin and Morcar, was doubtful. They were hastening south with a substantial reinforcement, but he could not be sure which side they would join. In the event they "withdrew themselves from the conflict." Some have suggested that he should have used the tactics which eleven hundred years before Cassivellaunus had employed against Cæsar. But these critics overlook the fact that whereas the Roman army consisted only of infantry, and the British only of charioteers and horsemen, Duke William's was essentially a cavalry force assisted by archers, while Harold had nothing but foot-soldiers who used horses only as transport. It is one thing for mounted forces to hover round and harry an infantry army, and the opposite for bands of foot-soldiers to use these tactics against cavalry. King Harold had great confidence in his redoubtable axe-men, and it was in good heart that he formed his shield-wall on the morning of October 14. There is a great dispute about the numbers engaged. Some modern authorities suppose the battle was fought by five or six thousand Norman knights and men-at-arms, with a few thousand archers, against eight to ten thousand axe- and spear-men, and the numbers on both sides may have been fewer. However it may be, at the first streak of dawn William set out from his camp at Pevensey, resolved to put all to the test; and Harold, eight miles away, awaited him in resolute array.

As the battle began Ivo Taillefer, the minstrel knight who had claimed the right to make the first attack, advanced up the hill on horseback, throwing his lance and sword into the air and catching them before the astonished English. He then charged deep into the English ranks, and was slain. The cavalry charges of William's mail-clad knights, cumbersome in manœuvre, beat in vain upon the dense, ordered masses of the English. Neither the arrow hail nor the assaults of the horsemen could prevail against them. William's left wing of cavalry was thrown into disorder, and retreated rapidly down the hill. On this the troops on Harold's right, who were mainly the local "fyrd," broke their ranks in eager pursuit. William, in the centre, turned his disciplined squadrons upon them and cut them to pieces. The Normans then re-formed their ranks and began a second series of charges upon the English masses, subjecting them in the intervals to severe archery. It has often been remarked that this part of the action resembles the after-noon at Waterloo, when Ney's cavalry exhausted themselves upon the British squares, torn by artillery in the intervals. In both cases the tortured infantry stood unbroken. Never, it was said, had the Norman knights met foot-soldiers of this stubbornness. They were utterly unable to break through the shield-walls, and they suffered serious losses from deft blows of the axe-men, or from javelins, or clubs hurled from the ranks behind. But the arrow showers took a cruel toll. So closely were the English wedged that the wounded could not be removed, and the dead scarcely found room in which to sink upon the ground.

The autumn afternoon was far spent before any result had been achieved, and it was then that William adopted the time-honoured ruse of a feigned retreat. He had seen how readily Harold's right had quitted their positions in pursuit after the first repulse of the Normans. He now organised a sham retreat in apparent disorder, while keeping a powerful force in his own hands. The house-carls around Harold preserved their discipline and kept their ranks, but the sense of relief to the less trained forces after these hours of combat was such that seeing their enemy in flight proved irresistible. They surged forward on the impulse of victory, and when half-way down the hill were savagely slaughtered by William's horsemen. There remained, as the dusk grew, only the valiant bodyguard who fought round the King and his standard. His brothers, Gyrth and Leofwine, had already been killed. William now directed his archers to shoot high into the air, so that the arrows would fall behind the shield-wall, and one of these pierced Harold in the right eye, inflicting a mortal wound. He fell at the foot of the royal standard, unconquerable except by death, which does not count in honour. The hard-fought battle was now decided. The last formed body of troops was broken, though by no means overwhelmed. They withdrew into the woods behind, and William, who had fought in the foremost ranks and had three horses killed under him, could claim the victory. Nevertheless the pursuit was heavily checked. There is a sudden deep ditch on the reverse slope of the hill of

Hastings, into which large numbers of Norman horsemen fell, and in which they were butchered by the infuriated English lurking in the wood.

The dead king's naked body, wrapped only in a robe of purple, was hidden among the rocks of the bay. His mother in vain offered the weight of the body in gold for permission to bury him in holy ground. The Norman Duke's answer was that Harold would be more fittingly laid upon the Saxon shore which he had given his life to defend. The body was later transferred to Waltham Abbey, which he had founded. Although here the English once again accepted conquest and bowed in a new destiny, yet ever must the name of Harold be honoured in the Island for which he and his famous house-carls fought indomitably to the end.

William the Conqueror

THE invading army had camped upon the battlefield. Duke William knew that his work was but begun. For more than a year he had been directly planning to invade England and claim the English throne. Now he had, within a month of landing, annihilated the only organised Saxon army and killed his rival. But the internal cleavages which had riven the Island in recent years added new dangers to the task of conquest. The very disunity which had made assault successful made subjugation lengthy. Saxon lords in the North and in the West might carry on endless local struggles and cut communications with the Continent. Cautiously the advance began upon London.

William was a prime exponent of the doctrine, so well known in this civilised age as "frightfulness" [1]—of mass terrorism through the spectacle of bloody and merciless examples. Now, with a compact force of Normans, French, and Bretons, he advanced through Kent upon the capital, and at first no native came to his camp to do him homage. The people of Romney had killed a band of Norman knights. Vengeance fell upon them. The news spread through the country, and the folk flocked "like flies settling on a wound" to make their submission and avoid a similar fate. The tale of these events bit deep into the hearts of the people.

When William arrived near London he marched round the

[1] Written early in 1939.

city by a circuitous route, isolating it by a belt of cruel desolation. From Southwark he moved to Wallingford, and thence through the Chilterns to Berkhamsted, where the leading Saxon notables and clergy came meekly to his tent to offer him the crown. On Christmas Day Aldred, Archbishop of York, crowned him King of England at Westminster. He rapidly established his power over all England south of the Humber. Within two years of the conquest Duchess Matilda, who ruled Normandy in William's absence, came across the sea to her coronation at Westminster on Whit Sunday 1068, and later in the year a son, Henry, symbol and portent of dynastic stability, was born on English soil.

The North still remained under its Saxon lords, Edwin and Morcar, unsubdued and defiant. The King gathered an army and marched towards them. The track of William in the North was marked for generations upon the countryside and in the memories of the survivors and their descendants. From coast to coast the whole region was laid desolate, and hunted men took refuge in the wooded valleys of Yorkshire, to die of famine and exposure, or to sell themselves into slavery for food. For long years after tales were told of the "waste" and of the rotting bodies of the famine-stricken by the roadside. At Christmas 1069 William wintered at York, and, the feasting over, continued the man-hunt. Only one town in England had not yet been subjected to the Conqueror's will—Chester. Across England in the depth of the winter of 1070 he marched his army. The town surrendered at the summons, and submitted to the building of a castle.

England north of the Humber was now in Norman control. The great Earldom of Richmond was created, possessing broad estates in Yorkshire and in the adjacent counties as well. The Bishopric of Durham was reorganised, with wide powers of local government. It was now clear that Normandy had the force and spirit to absorb all Saxon England; but whether William would retain the whole of his conquests unchallenged from without was not settled till his closing years. The period of English subjugation was hazardous. For at least twenty years after the invasion the Normans were an army camped in a hostile country, holding the population down by the castles at key points. The Saxon resistance died hard. Legends and chroniclers have painted for us the last stand of Hereward the Wake in the broad wastes of the fens round Ely. Not until five years after Hastings, in 1071, was Hereward put down. In his cause had fallen many of the Saxon thanage, the only class from whose ranks new leaders could spring. The building of Ely Castle symbolised the end of their order.

Other internal oppositions arose. In 1075 a serious revolt of disaffected Norman knights broke out in the Midlands, East Anglia and on the Welsh border, and one surviving Saxon leader, Waltheof, who had made his peace with William, joined them. The King in Normandy must hasten back to crush the rebels. The Saxon population supported the Conqueror against chaos. The "fyrd" took the field. Vengeance was reserved for Waltheof alone, and his execution upon a hill outside Winchester is told in moving scenes by the Saxon-hearted monkish chroniclers of the time. Medieval legend ascribed the fate of William in his later years to the guilt of this execution. It marked also the final submission of England. Norman castles guarded the towns, Norman lords held the land, and Norman churches protected men's souls. All England had a master, the conquest was complete, and the work of reconstruction began.

Woe to the conquered! Here were the Normans entrenched on English soil, masters of the land and the fullness thereof. An armed warrior from Anjou or Maine or Brittany, or even from beyond the Alps and the Pyrenees, took possession of manor and county, according to his rank and prowess, and set to work to make himself secure. Everywhere castles arose. These were not at first the massive stone structures of a later century; they were simply fortified military posts consisting of an earthen rampart and a stockade, and a central keep made of logs. From these strongpoints horsemen sallied forth to rule and exploit the neighbourhood; above them all, at the summit, sat William, active and ruthless, delighting in his work, requiring punctual service from his adherents, and paying good spoil to all who did their duty.

In their early days the Normans borrowed no manners and few customs from the Islanders. The only culture was French. Surviving Saxon notables sent their sons to the monasteries of France for education. The English repeated the experience of the Ancient Britons; all who could learnt French, as formerly the contemporaries of Boadicea had learnt Latin. At first the conquerors, who despised the uncouth English as louts and boors, ruled by the force of sharpened steel. But very soon in true Norman fashion they intermarried with the free population and identified themselves with their English past.

William's work in England is the more remarkable from the fact that all the time as Duke of Normandy he was involved in endless intrigues and conflicts with the King of France. Though England was a more valuable possession than Normandy, William and his sons were always more closely interested in their continental lands. The French kings, for their part, placed in the forefront of their policy the weakening of these Dukes of Normandy, now grown so powerful, and whose frontiers were little more than twenty miles from Paris. Hence arose a struggle that was solved only when King John lost Normandy in 1203. Meanwhile, years passed. Queen Matilda was a capable regent at Rouen, but plagued by the turbulence of her sons. The eldest, Robert, a Crusading knight, reckless and spendthrift, with his father's love of fighting and adventure but without his ruthless genius or solid practical aims, resented William's persistent hold on life and impatiently claimed his Norman inheritance. Many a time the father was called across the Channel to chastise rebellious towns and forestall the conspiracies of his son with the French Court. Robert, driven from his father's lands, found refuge in King Philip's castle of Gerberoi. William marched implacably upon him. Beneath the walls two men, visor down, met in single combat, father and son. Robert wounded his father in the hand and unhorsed him, and would indeed have killed him but for a timely rescue by an Englishman, one Tokig of Wallingford, who remounted the overthrown conqueror. Both were sobered by this chance encounter, and for a time there was reconciliation.

Matilda died, and with increasing years William became fiercer in mood. Stung to fury by the forays of the French, he crossed the frontier, spreading fire and ruin till he reached the gate of Mantes. His Normans surprised the town, and amid the horrors of the sack fire broke out. As William rode through the streets his horse stumbled among the burning ashes and he was thrown against the pommel of the saddle. He was carried in agony to the priory of St Gervase at Rouen. There, high above the town, he lay, through the summer heat of 1087, fighting his grievous injury. When death drew near his sons William and Henry came to him. William, whose one virtue had been filial fidelity, was named to succeed the Conqueror in England. The graceless Robert would rule in Normandy at last. For the youngest, Henry, there was nothing by five thousand pounds of silver, and the prophecy that he would one day reign over a united Anglo-Norman nation. This proved no empty blessing.

Fear fell upon the Conqueror's subjects when it was known that he was dying. What troubles would follow the end of a strong ruler? On Thursday, September 9, 1087, as the early bells of Rouen Cathedral echoed over the hills, William and his authority died. The caitiff attendants stripped the body and plundered the chamber where he lay. The clergy of Rouen bore him to the church of St Stephen at Caen, which he had founded. Even his final journey was disturbed. In the graveyard one Ascelin cried out that his father had been deprived by the dead Duke of this plot of ground, and before all the concourse demanded justice from the startled priests. For the price of sixty shillings the Conqueror came thus humbly to his grave. But his work lived. Says the chronicler:

"He was a very stern and violent man, so that no one dared do anything contrary to his will. He had earls in his fetters, who acted against his will. He expelled bishops from their sees, and abbots from their abbacies, and put thanes in prison, and finally he did not spare his own brother, who was called Odo; he was a very powerful bishop in Normandy and was the foremost man next the king, and had an earldom in England. He [the King] put him in prison. Amongst other things the good security he made in this country is not to be forgotten—so that any honest man could travel over his kingdom without injury with his bosom full of gold: and no one dared strike another, however much wrong he had done him. And if any man had intercourse with a woman against her will, he was forthwith castrated.

"He ruled over England, and by his cunning it was so investigated that there was not one hide of land in England that he did not know who owned it, and what it was worth, and then set it down in his record. Wales was in his power, and he built castles there, and he entirely controlled that race. In the same way, he also subdued Scotland to himself, because of his great strength. The land of Normandy was his by natural inheritance, and he ruled over the county called Maine: and if he could have lived two years more, he would have conquered

Ireland by his prudence and without any weapons. Certainly in his time people had much oppression and very many injuries."

At this point the chronicler breaks into verse:

He had castles built
And poor men hard oppressed.
The king was so very stark
And deprived his underlings of many a mark
Of gold and more hundreds of pounds of silver,
That he took by weight and with great injustice
From his people with little need for such a deed.
Into avarice did he fall
And loved greediness above all,
He made great protection for the game
And imposed laws for the same.
That who so slew hart or hind
Should be made blind.

He preserved the harts and boars
And loved the stags as much
As if he were their father . . .[1]

*   *   *   *   *

The Normans introduced into England their system of land tenure based upon military service. A military caste was imposed from above. A revolution not only in warfare, but also in the upper reaches of society, had taken place. William aimed first at securing an effective and compact army, and the terms of knight-service and the quota of men due from each of his greater subjects interested him more than the social relationships prevailing on the lands they held. The Normans, a

[1] *Anglo-Saxon Chronicle,* in *English Historical Documents,* vol. ii. (Eyre and Spottiswoode, 1953.)

small minority, had destroyed the Saxon governing class and had thrust an alien domination upon England. But the mass of the inhabitants were only indirectly affected by the change, and the feudal superstructure was for many years as unsure as it was impressive. There were interminable controversies among the new masters of the country about the titles to their lands, and how these fitted the customs and laws of Anglo-Saxon England. The bishoprics and abbeys were especially loud in their complaints, and royal legates repeatedly summoned great assemblies of the shire courts to settle these disputes. Finally in 1086 a vast sworn inquiry was made into the whole wealth of the King's feudal vassals, from whom he derived a large part of his own income. The inquest or description, as it was called, was carried through with a degree of minuteness and regularity unique in that age and unequalled for centuries after. The history of many an English village begins with an entry in Domesday Book. The result of this famous survey showed that the underlying structure of England and its peasant life were little changed by the shock of the invasion.

But the holding of the great Domesday inquest marks a crisis. The Norman garrison in England was threatened from abroad by other claimants. The rulers of Scandinavia still yearned for the Island once the west of their empire. They had supported the rising in the North in 1069, and again in 1085, they threatened to intervene with greater vigour. A fleet was fitted out, and though it never sailed, because its leader was murdered, William took precautions. It became necessary that all feudal controversies arising out of the Conquest should be speedily settled, and it was under the shadow of this menace that Domesday Book was compiled. In 1086 William called together at Salisbury "all the land-holding men of any account throughout England whosoever men they were." The King had need of an assurance of loyalty from all his feudal tenants of substance, and this substantial body bound itself together by oath and fealty to his person.

The Norman achievement in England was not merely military in character. Although knight-service governed the holding of property and produced a new aristocracy, much was preserved of Saxon England. The Normans were administrators and lawyers rather than legislators. Their centre of government was the royal Curia, the final court of appeal and the instrument of supervision; here were preserved and developed the financial and secretarial methods of the Anglo-Saxon kingdom. The whole system of Saxon local government, also of immense usefulness for the future—the counties, the sheriffs, and the courts—survived, and through this the King maintained his widespread contacts with the country. In fact the Conqueror himself by these means collected the information for Domesday. Not only the courts, but also the dues and taxes such as Danegeld, were preserved for the sake of the Norman revenues. The local militia raised by the counties survived the Conquest, and proved serviceable to William and his successors. Thus in the future government of England both Norman and Saxon institutions were unconsciously but profoundly blended.

In some respects all this was a sudden acceleration of the drift toward the manorial system, a process which had already gone a long way in Anglo-Saxon England, and certainly in Wessex. But even in Wessex the idea still persisted that the tie of lord and man was primarily personal, so that a free man could go from one lord to another and transfer his land with him. The essence of Norman feudalism, on the other hand, was that the land remained under the lord, whatever the man might do. Thus the landed pyramid rose up tier by tier to the King, until every acre in the country could be registered as held of somebody by some form of service. But besides the services which the man owed to the lord in arms there was the service of attending the courts of the hundred and the county, which were—apart from various exemptions—courts of the King, administering old customary law. The survival of the hundred, the county court and the sheriff makes the great difference between English and Continental feudalism. In England the King is everywhere—in Northumberland as in Middlesex; a crime anywhere is a breach of his peace; if he wants to know anything he tells his officer, the sheriff, to impanel a jury and find out, or, in later days, to send some respectable persons to Westminster and tell him. But perhaps when they got to Westminster they told him that he was badly advised, and that they would not pay any taxes till he mended his ways. Far ahead we see the seventeenth-century constitutional issue. There were in Norman days no great mercantile towns in England, except London. If William had not preserved the counties and hundreds as living and active units, there would have been no body of resistance or counter-poise to the central Government, save in the great baronial families.

In the Norman settlement lay the germ of a constitutional opposition, with the effect if not the design of controlling the Government, not breaking it up. The seat of this potential opposition was found in the counties, among the smaller nobility and their untitled descendants, Justices of the Peace and knights of the shire. They were naturally for the Crown and a quiet life. Hence after centuries they rallied to the Tudor sovereigns; and in another age to the Parliament against the Crown itself. Whatever else changed they were always *there*. And the reason why they were there is that William found the old West Saxon organisation, which they alone could administer, exceedingly convenient. He did not mean to be treated as he had treated the King of France. He had seen, and profited by seeing, the mischief of a country divided into great provinces. The little provinces of England, with the King's officers at the head of each, gave him exactly the balance of power he needed for all purposes of law and finance, but were at the same time incapable of rebelling as units. The old English nobility disappeared after the Battle of Hastings. But all over Domesday Book the opinion of what we should later call the gentry of the shire is quoted as decisive. This is the class—people of some consideration in the neighbourhood, with leisure to go to the sheriff's court and thereafter to Westminster. Out of this in the process of time the Pyms and Hampdens arose.

The Conquest was the supreme achievement of the Norman race. It linked the history of England anew to Europe, and prevented for ever a drift into the narrower orbit of a Scandinavian empire. Henceforward English history marched with that of races and lands south of the Channel.

*   *   *   *   *

The effect of the Conquest on the Church was no less broad and enlivening. The bishoprics and abbeys and other high posts, were now as a matter of course given to Normans, and insular customs supplanted by the newest fashions from abroad. The age of the Conquest coincided with the many-sided reforms of the Church and advances in Papal power initiated by Hildebrand who became Pope as Gregory VII in 1073. Under its new leaders England was brought into the van of this movement. New abbeys sprang up all over the country which attested the piety of the conquerors, though few of the new houses attained to the wealth or standing of the older foundations. These monasteries and bishoprics were the chief centres of religion and learning until after a century they were gradually eclipsed by the rise of the universities. But the new Churchmen were even less disposed than the nobles to draw any deep line across history at the Norman Conquest. Slowly but surely the Frenchmen came to venerate the old English saints and English shrines, and the continuity of religious life with the age of Dunstan was maintained. Under Lanfranc and Anselm, successively Archbishops of Canterbury, the Church was ruled by two of the greatest men of the age, and through them derived incalculable benefits.

In his expedition of 1066 William had received the full support of the Pope, and his standards were blessed by orthodoxy. He was known to be a zealous ecclesiastical reformer, and the Saxon Church was thought to be insular and obstinate. Peter's Pence had not been regularly paid since the Danish invasions. Stigand, blessed only by the schismatic Benedict IX, held both Winchester and Canterbury in plurality. In face of such abuses William stood forth, the faithful son of the Church. Once the secular conquest had been made secure he turned to the religious sphere. The key appointment was the Archbishopric of Canterbury. In 1070 the Saxon Stigand was deposed and succeeded by Lanfranc. A Lombard of high administrative ability, Lanfranc had been trained in the famous North Italian schools and at the Norman Abbey of Bec, of which he became Abbot, and he rapidly infused new life into the English Church. In a series of councils such as had not been held in England since the days of Theodore organisation and discipline were reformed. Older sees were transplanted from villages to towns —Crediton to Exeter, and Selsey to Chichester. New episcopal seats were established, and by 1087 the masons were at work on seven new cathedrals. At the same time the monastic movement, which had sprung from the Abbey of Cluny, began to spread in England. The English Church was rescued by the Conquest from the backwater in which it had languished, and came once again into contact with the wider European life of the Christian Church and its heritage of learning.

The spirit of the long-vanished Roman Empire, revived by

the Catholic Church, returned once more to our Island, bringing with it three dominant ideas. First, a Europe in which
nationalism or even the conception of nationality had no place,
but where one general theme of conduct and law united the
triumphant martial classes upon a plane far above race. Secondly, the idea of monarchy, in the sense that Kings were the
expression of the class hierarchy over which they presided and
the arbiters of its frequently conflicting interests. Thirdly, there
stood triumphant the Catholic Church, combining in a strange
fashion Roman imperialism and Christian ethics, pervaded by
the social and military system of the age, jealous for its own
interests and authority, but still preserving all that was left of
learning and art.

Growth Amid Turmoil

THE first generation after the Norman Conquest formed a period when the victorious army and caste were settling themselves upon the lands they had gained, and forcing Saxon England, where the tie between a man and his lord was mainly personal, into the feudal pattern, where it primarily rested on landholding. Under William the Conqueror this process had been harsh and thorough. Under his son William, dubbed Rufus, the Red, it was not less harsh, but also capricious. Moreover, the accession of the Conqueror's second surviving son to the throne of England did not pass without dispute. William I's decision to divide his English from his Norman lands brought new troubles in its train. The greater barons possessed property on both sides of the Channel. They therefore now owed feudal allegiance to two soverign lords, and not unnaturally they sought to play one against the other. Both Duke Robert and William II were dissatisfied with the division, and their brotherly ties did not mitigate their covetous desires. During the thirteen years of the reign of William the Anglo-Norman realms were vexed by fratricidal strife and successive baronial revolts. The Saxon inhabitants of England, fearful of a relapse into the chaos of pre-Conquest days, stood by the King against all rebels. The "fyrd" obeyed every summons, and supported him in the field as it had his father in 1075. Thus he was able finally to bring Cumberland and Westmorland into the kingdom. The feckless Robert, who had plagued the Conqueror so long, eventually departed in a fit of gallantry on the First Crusade, leaving Normandy pawned to Rufus for the loan of 10,000 marks.

*   *   *   *   *

The Crusading spirit had for some time stirred the minds of men all over western Europe. The Christian kingdoms of Spain had led the way with their holy wars against the Arabs. Now, towards the end of the eleventh century, a new enemy of Christendom appeared fifteen hundred miles to the east. The Seljuk Turks were pressing hard upon the Byzantine Empire in Asia Minor, and harassing devout pilgrims from Europe through Syria to the Holy Land. The Byzantine Emperor appealed to the West for help, and in 1095 Pope Urban II, who had long dreamt of recovering Jerusalem for Christendom, called on the chivalry of Europe to take the Cross. The response was immediate, overwhelming, and at first disastrous. An itinerant monk named Peter the Hermit took up the cry to arms. So powerful was his preaching that in 1096 an enthusiastic but undisciplined train of twenty thousand men, most of them peasants unskilled in war, set off from Cologne for the East under his leadership. Few of them ever reached the Holy Land. After marching through Hungary and the Balkans, the majority perished by Turkish arrows amid the mountains of Asia Minor.

The so-called "People's Crusade" thus collapsed. But by now the magnates of Europe had rallied to the Cause. Four armies, each numbering perhaps ten thousand men, and led by some of the greatest nobles of the age, among them Godfrey de Bouillon, converged on Constantinople from France, Germany, Italy and the Low Countries. The Byzantine Emperor was embarrassed. He had hoped for manageable mercenaries as reinforcements from the West. Instead, he found camped around his capital four powerful and ambitious hosts.

The march of the Crusaders through his dominions into the Turkish-held lands was marred by intrigue and by grievous disputes. But there was hard fighting too. A way was hacked through Asia Minor; and Antioch, once a great bastion of the Christian faith, which the Turks had taken, was besieged and captured in 1098. The Crusaders were cheered and succoured by the arrival off the Syrian coast of a fleet manned by Englishmen and commanded by an English prince, Edgar the Atheling, great-nephew of Edward the Confessor. Thus by a strange turn of fortune the displaced heir of the Saxon royal line joined hands with Robert of Normandy, the displaced heir of William the Conqueror.

Aided by divisions among the Turkish princes and by jealousy between the Turks and the Sultans of Egypt the Crusaders pressed forward. On June 7, 1099, they reached their long-sought goal and encamped about Jerusalem, then in Egyptian hands. On July 14 the City fell to their assault. Godfrey de Bouillon, refusing to wear a crown in Christ's Holy City, was acclaimed ruler, with the title of "Defender of the Holy Sepulchre." Victory was made secure by the defeat at the Battle of Ascalon of a relieving army from Egypt. Many of the principal Crusaders thereupon went home, but for nearly a century a mixed international body of knights, all commonly called Franks, ruled over a string of Christian principalities in Palestine and along the coast of Syria. Western Christendom, so long the victim of invaders, had at last struck back and won its first great footing in the Eastern world.

*   *   *   *   *

At home Rufus's extortions and violent methods had provoked the baronage throughout his reign. In August 1100 he was mysteriously shot through the head by an arrow while hunting in the New Forest, leaving a memory of shameless exactions and infamous morals, but also a submissive realm to his successor. The main progress in his reign was financial; but the new feudal monarchy was also more firmly established, and in territory its sway was wider than at Rufus's accession. The Norman lords whom the Conqueror had settled upon the Welsh Marches had fastened a lasting grip upon Southern Wales. The Northern counties had been finally brought under Norman control, and a military frontier drawn against the Scots. While the rough hands of Rufus chafed and bruised the feudal relationship, they had also enforced the rights of a feudal king.

Prince Henry, the youngest of the royal brothers, had been a member of the fatal hunting party in the New Forest. There is no proof that he was implicated in the death of his brother, but he certainly wasted no time in mourning. He made straight for the royal treasury at Winchester, and gained possession of it after sharp argument with its custodians. Evidently he represented a strong movement of opinion among the leading classes, and he had a policy of his own. For a layman his scholarship deserved the title of Beauclerc which the custom of his day accorded him. He set the precedent, which his successor followed, of proclaiming a charter upon his accession. By this he sought to conciliate those powerful forces in Church and State which had been alienated by the rapacity and tactlessness of his predecessor. He guaranteed that the rights of the baronage and the Church should be respected. At the same time, having seen the value of Saxon loyalty in the reigns of his father and his brother, he promised the conquered race good justice and the laws of Edward the Confessor. He knew that the friction caused by the separation of Normandy from England was by no means soothed. Duke Robert was already on his way back from his Crusade with his mortgage to redeem.

The barons on both sides of the Channel would profit from fraternal strife to drive hard bargains in their own interests. Henry's desire to base himself in part at least upon the Saxon population of England led him, much to the suspicion of the Norman barons, to make a marriage with Matilda, niece of the last surviving Saxon claimant to the English throne and descendant of the old English line of Kings. The barons, mollified by the charter, accepted this decisive step. The ceaseless gigantic process of intermarriage received the highest sanction.

Henry was now ready to face Robert whenever he should return. In September 1100 this event occurred. Immediately the familiar incidents of feudal rebellion were renewed in England, and for the next six years the King had to fight to make good his title under his father's will. The great house of Montgomery formed the head of the opposition in England. By a series of persevering sieges the family's strongholds fell one by one, and Henry at length destroyed their power and annexed their estates to the Crown. But the root evil lay in Normandy, and in 1105, having consolidated his position in England, Henry crossed the Channel. In September 1106 the most important battle since Hastings was fought at Tenchebrai. King Henry's victory was complete. Duke Robert was carried to his perpetual prison in England. Normandy acknowledged Henry's authority, and the control of Anglo-Norman policy passed from Rouen to London. The Saxons, who had fought heartily for Henry, regarded this battle as their military revenge for Hastings. By this new comradeship with the Crown, as well as by the royal marriage with Matilda, they felt themselves relieved from some at least of the pangs of being conquered. The shame was gone; the penalties could be endured. Through these two far-reaching factors a certain broad measure of unity was re-established in the Island.

*   *   *   *   *

There was now no challenged succession. The King of England's authority was established on both sides of the Channel. The Saxon people had proved their loyalty and the more powerful barons had been cowed. Foreign dangers having also been repelled, Henry was free for the time being to devote himself to internal government and to strengthening the power of the Crown throughout the land. He sought to invest the Anglo-Norman kingship with new and powerful attributes. There survived in medieval Europe a tradition of kingship more exalted than that of feudal overlord. The king was not merely the apex of the feudal pyramid, but the anointed Vicegerent of God upon earth. The collapse of the Roman Empire had not entirely destroyed this Roman conception of sovereignty, and Henry now set himself to inject this idea of kingship into the Anglo-Norman State; and in so doing he could not help reviving, whether consciously or not, the English conception of the King as the keeper of the peace and guardian of the people.

The centre of government, the Curia Regis, was an ill-defined body consisting of those tenants-in-chief whose feudal duty it was to attend when summoned, and those personal servants of the monarch who could be used for Government service as well as for their household duties. Henry realised that royal servants who were members of the minor baronage, if formed into a permanent nucleus, would act as a brake upon the turbulence of the greater feudatories. Here were the first beginnings, tentative, modest, but insinuating, of a civil administrative machinery, which within its limits was more efficient and persistent than anything yet known. These officials soon developed a vested interest of their own. Families like the Clintons and the Bassetts, whom the King, as the chronicler put it, had "raised from the dust to do him service," entrenched themselves in the household offices, and created what was in fact an official class.

The power of any Government depends ultimately upon its finances. It was therefore in the business of gathering and administering the revenue that this novel feature first became apparent. There was no distinction in feudal society between the private and public resources of the Crown. The King in feudal theory was only the greatest of the landowners in the State. The sheriffs of counties collected not only the taxes and fines accruing to the Crown, but also the income from the royal estates, and they were responsible, when they appeared yearly at the royal treasury, for the exact payment of what was due from each of their counties. Henry's officials created a special organ to deal with the sheriffs and the business the sheriffs transacted. This was the Exchequer, still regarded simply as the Curia meeting for financial purposes, but gradually acquiring a life of its own. It took its name from the chequered boards used for greater ease of calculation in Roman numerals, and its methods included the keeping of written records, among them the important documents called the Pipe Rolls because they were kept rolled up in the shape of a pipe. Thus the King gained a surer grip over the finances of the realm, and the earliest specialised department of royal administration was born. Its offspring still survives.

Henry took care that the sheriffs of the counties were brought under an increasingly strict control, and several commissions were appointed during the reign to revise their personnel. In troublous times the office of sheriff tended to fall into the hands of powerful barons and to become hereditary. The King saw to it that whenever possible his own men held these key positions. One of the most fertile sources of revenue arose from the fines imposed by the courts upon delinquents. The barons realised this as soon as the King, and their manorial courts provided them with important incomes, which could at once be turned into armed retainers. Within their domains they enjoyed a jurisdiction over nearly all laymen. But in the county courts and in the courts of the hundreds the Crown had at its disposal the old Saxon system of justice. These time-honoured institutions could well be used to rival the feudal courts of the baronage. Henry therefore revised and regularised the holding of the county courts, and made all men see that throughout the land there was a system of royal justice. King's officers—judges, as they became—in their occasional circuits administered this justice, and the very nature of their function brought them often into clash not only with humble suitors and malefactors, but with proud military magnates.

The King entered into a nation-wide competition with the baronage upon who could best deserve the rich spoils of the law. Through his control of the sheriffs he bound together the monarchy and the old Saxon system of local justice. The Conqueror had set the example when in the Domesday survey he combined the Continental system of getting information by means of bodies of men sworn to tell the truth with the English organisation by shire and hundred. His son for other purposes continued and intensified the process, sending officials constantly from his household through the kingdom, and convening the county courts to inquire into the claims of the royal revenue and to hear cases in which the Crown was interested. From these local inquiries by royal officials there were to spring far-reaching consequences in the reign of Henry II. The chroniclers spoke well of Henry I. "Good man he was," they declared, "and there was great awe of him. In his days no man dared to harm another." They bestowed upon him the title "Lion of Justice," and none has sought to rob him of it.

We must regard his reign as a period when the central Government, by adroit and sharp accountancy and clerking, established in a more precise form the structure and resources of the State. In the process the feudatory chiefs upon whom the local government of the land depended were angered. Thus, as the years wore on the stresses grew between the royal authority and the feudal leaders. The King's hand, though it lay heavy upon all, became increasingly a protection of the people against the injustice and caprice of the local rulers. Examples there were of admirable baronial administration, for there was a light in Norman eyes which shone above the squalid pillage and appetites of earlier ages. A country held down and exploited by feudal nobles was none the less the constant victim of local oppression. We see therefore the beginning of an attachment to the King or central Government on the part of the people, which invested the Crown with a new source of strength, sometimes forthcoming and sometimes estranged, but always to be gathered, especially after periods of weakness and disorder, by a strong and righteous ruler.

*　　*　　*　　*　　*

The Anglo-Norman State was now powerful. Henry was lord of England, Normandy, and Maine. In 1109 his only legitimate daughter, Maud, was betrothed to Henry V, Holy Roman Emperor and King of Germany. On the other hand, the reunion of England and Normandy after Tenchebrai had stirred the hostility of France. The early twelfth century saw the revival of a capital authority at Paris. With the accession of Louis VI the real strength of the French monarchy begins. It was essential for the safety of France that the unity of the Anglo-Norman State should be finally ruptured. The Duke of Normandy was technically the feudal subject of the King of France, and the existence of the son of captive Duke Robert provided the French King with innumerable pretexts for interference and offered to discontented Norman barons perennial opportunity. These Norman commitments forced Henry in the later years of his reign to intervene in the politics of Northern France. His position in Normandy was continually threatened by the claims of Robert's son, William Clito, who until his death in 1128 was backed by Louis, and also by the neighbouring state of Anjou, which disputed King Henry's rights in Maine. A wearing warfare darkened the later years of the reign. From the military point of view Henry was easily able to hold his own against any army the French could put into the field.

What may be judged malignant fortune now intervened. The King had a son, his heir apparent, successor indisputable. On this young man of seventeen many hopes and assurances were founded. In the winter of 1120 he was coming back from a visit to France in the royal yacht called the *White Ship*. Off the coast of Normandy the vessel struck a rock and all but one were drowned. The prince had indeed been embarked in a boat. He returned to rescue his sister. In this crisis the principle of equality asserted itself with such violence that at the ships's side so many leaped into the boat that it sank. Two men remained afloat, the ship's butcher and a knight. "Where is the Prince?" asked the knight above the waves. "All are drowned," replied the butcher. "Then," said the knight, "all is lost for England," and threw up his hands. The butcher came safe to shore with the tale. None dared tell it to the King. When at last he heard the tidings "he never smiled again." This was more than the agony of parental grief for an only son. It portended the breakdown of a system and prospect upon the consolidation of which the whole life's work of Henry stood. The spectre of a disputed succession glared again upon England. The forces of anarchy grew, and every noble in his castle balanced his chances upon who would succeed to the Crown.

There were two claimants, each of whom had a fair share of right. The King had a daughter, Matilda, or Maud as the English called her, but although there was no Salic Law in the Norman code this clanking, jangling aristocracy, mailed and

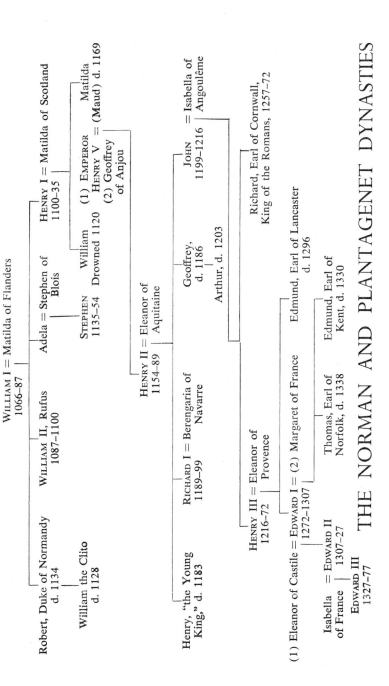

THE NORMAN AND PLANTAGENET DYNASTIES

spurred, did not take kindly to the idea of a woman's rule. Against her stood the claim of Stephen, son of the Conqueror's daughter Adela. Stephen of Blois, no inconsiderable figure on the Continent, with great estates in England added, was, after his elder brother had waived his claim, the rightful male heir. The feudal system lived entirely through the spirit of sworn allegiance. Throughout Christendom the accusation of violating an oath was almost mortal. Only great victories could atone and absolve. But here was a dilemma which every man could settle for himself according to his interests and ambitions. Split—utter, honest, total!

King Henry in the grey close of his life set himself to fill the void with his daughter Maud as female king. He spent his remaining years in trying to establish a kind of "pragmatic sanction" for a family succession which would spare his widespread domains from civil war. At the age of eight Maud had been betrothed to the Holy Roman Emperor. In 1125, five years after the *White Ship* sank, he died, and at twenty-two she was a widow and an Empress. We have many records of this remarkable princess, of whom it was said "she had the nature of a man in the frame of a woman." Fierce, proud, hard, cynical, living for politics above all other passions, however turbulent, she was fitted to bear her part in any war and be the mother of one of the greatest English kings.

Upon this daughter, after mature consideration, Henry founded all his hopes. On two separate occasions he called his murmuring barons together and solemnly swore them to stand by Maud. Subsequently, in order to enhance her unifying authority, and to protect Normandy from the claims of Anjou after his death, he married her to the Count of Anjou, thus linking the interests of the most powerful state in Northern France with the family and natural succession in England. The English mood has never in later ages barred queens, and perhaps queens have served them best. But here at this time was a deep division, and a quarrel in which all parties and all interests could take sides. The gathered political arrays awaited the death of the King. The whole interest of the baronage, supported at this juncture by the balancing weight of the Church, was to limit the power of the Crown and regain their control of their own districts. Now in a division of the royal authority they saw their chance.

After giving the Island thirty years of peace and order and largely reconciling the Saxon population to Norman rule, Henry I expired on December 1, 1135, in the confident hope that his daughter Maud would carry on his work. But she was with her husband in Anjou and Stephen was the first on the spot. Swiftly returning from Blois, he made his way to London and claimed the crown. The secular forces were divided and the decision of the Church would be decisive. Here Stephen had the advantage that his brother Henry was Bishop of Winchester, with a great voice in council. With Henry's help Stephen made terms with the Church, and, thus sustained, was crowned and anointed King. It was however part of the tacit compact that he should relax the severe central control which in the two preceding reigns had so much offended the nobility.

There was an additional complication. Henry I had a bastard son, Robert of Gloucester, a distinguished soldier and a powerful magnate in the West Country, who is usually regarded as one of the rare examples of a disinterested baron. Robert did not rate his chances sufficiently high to compete with either of the legitimate heirs. Almost from the beginning he loyally supported his half-sister Maud, and became one of Stephen's most determined opponents.

A succession established on such disputable grounds could only be maintained unchallenged by skilful sovereignty. The more we reflect upon the shortcomings of modern government the readier we shall be to make allowances for the difficulties of these times. Stephen in the early years of his reign lost the support of the three essential elements of his strength. The baronage, except those favoured by the new monarchy, were sure that this was the long-awaited moment to press their claims. The novel Civil Service, the great officials all linked together by family ties, armed with knowledge, with penmanship, trained to administration, now also began to stand aside from the new King. And many prelates were offended because Stephen violated clerical privilege by imprisoning the great administrative family of Roger, Bishop of Salisbury, whom he suspected of being about to change sides. Thus he had much of the Church against him too. There were grievous discontents among the high, the middle, and the low.

"When the traitors perceived," in the words of the *Anglo-Saxon Chronicle,* that King Stephen was "a mild man and soft and good and *did no justice,* then did they all manner of horrors. They had done homage to him and sworn oaths, but they held no faith." [1]

King David of Scotland, persuaded of the English decay, crossed the Border and laid claim to Northumbria. The Archbishop of York advanced against him, with the support of the mass of the Northern counties. He displayed the standards of St Peter of York, St John of Beverley, and St Wilfred of Ripon, and in a murderous battle at Northallerton, henceforward known as the Battle of the Standard, repulsed and slaughtered the invaders. This reverse, far from discouraging the malcontents, was the prelude to civil war. In 1139 Maud, freed from entanglements that had kept her in France, entered the kingdom to claim her rights. As Stephen had done, she found her chief support in the Church. The men who had governed England under Henry II, antagonised by Stephen's weakness

[1] Douglas, *Age of the Normans,* p. 161.

towards the barons, joined his enemies. In 1141 a more or less general rebellion broke out against his rule, and he himself was taken prisoner at the Battle of Lincoln. The Bishop of Winchester, Stephen's own brother and hitherto his main supporter, now went over to Maud's side. For nearly a year Maud, uncrowned, was in control of England. The Londoners after some trial liked her even less than Stephen. Rising in fury, they drove her out of the capital. She fought on indomitably. But the strain upon the system had been too great. The Island dissolved into confused civil war. During the six years that followed there was neither law nor peace in large parts of the country.

*　　*　　*　　*　　*

The civil war developed into the first successful baronial reaction against the centralising policy of the kings. Stephen, faced with powerful rivals, had failed to preserve the rights of the Crown. The royal revenues decreased, royal control of administration lapsed; much of the machinery itself passed for a time out of use. Baronial jurisdiction reasserted its control; baronial castles overawed the people. It seemed that a divided succession had wrecked the work of the Norman kings.

The sufferings of the Fen Country, where there was a particularly ferocious orgy of destruction during the anarchy, are grimly described in the *Anglo-Saxon Chronicle* by a monk of Peterborough.

"Every powerful man made his castles and held them against the King, . . . and when the castles were made they filled them with devils and evil men. Then they seized those men who they supposed had any possessions, both by night and day, men and women, and put them to prison for their gold and silver, and tortured them with unspeakable tortures. . . . Many thousands they killed with hunger. I neither can nor may tell all the horrors and all the tortures that they did to the wretched men of this land. And it lasted the nineteen winters while Stephen was King; and ever it was worse. They laid gelds [taxes] on the villages from time to time and called it 'Tenserie'; when the wretched men had no more to give they robbed and burnt all the villages, so that you might go a whole day's journey and you would never find a man in a village or land being tilled. Then was corn dear, and meat and cheese and butter, because there was none in the land. Wretched men starved of hunger; some went seeking alms who at one time were rich men; others fled out of the land. . . . Wheresoever men tilled the earth bare no corn, for the land was all ruined by such deeds; and they said that Christ and his saints were asleep."

Another writer, a monk of Winchester, writes in very similar terms of the disasters that came upon his part of England: "With some men the love of country was turned to loathing and bitterness, and they preferred to migrate to distant regions. Others, in the hope of protection, built lowly huts of wattle-work round about the churches, and so passed their lives in fear and anguish. Some for want of food fed upon strange and forbidden meats—the flesh of dogs and horses; others relieved their hunger by devouring unwashed and uncooked herbs and roots. In all the shires a part of the inhabitants wasted away and died in herds from the stress of famine, while others with their wives and children went dismally into a self-inflicted exile. You might behold villages of famous names standing empty, because the country people, male and female, young and old, had left them; fields whitened with the harvest as the year [1143] verged upon autumn, but the cultivators had perished by famine and the ensuing pestilence." [1]

These horrors may not have been typical of the country as a whole. Over large parts of England fighting was sporadic and local in character. It was the central southern counties that bore the brunt of civil war. But these commotions bit deep into

[1] Translated from *Gesta Stephani*, ed. Howlett, p. 99.

the consciousness of the people. It was realised how vital an institution a strong monarchy was for the security of life and property. No better reasons for monarchy could have been found than were forced upon all minds by the events of Stephen's reign. Men looked back with yearning to the efficient government of Henry I. But a greater than he was at hand.

*   *   *   *   *

In 1147 Robert of Gloucester died and the leadership of Maud's party devolved upon her son. Henry Plantagenet was born to empire. His grandfather Fulk had made of the Angevin lands, Anjou, Touraine, and Maine, a principality unsurpassed in France and in resources more than the equal of Normandy. Fulk died in 1143, King of Jerusalem, leaving two sons to succeed him on that precarious throne, and a third, Geoffrey, as heir to his French dominions. Geoffrey's marriage with Maud had united the Norman and Angevin lands, and the child of this marriage was from his birth in 1133 recognised as the "master of many peoples." To contemporaries he was best known as Henry Fitz-Empress; but he carried into English history the emblem of his house, the broom, the *Planta Genesta,* which later generations were to make the name of this great dynasty, the Plantagenets. He embodied all their ability, all their energy, and not a little of that passionate, ruthless ferocity which, it was whispered, came to the house of Anjou from no mortal source, but from a union with Satan himself.

When scarcely fifteen, in 1147, Henry had actively championed his claim to the English throne on English soil. His small band of followers was then defeated by Stephen's forces, and he took refuge in Normandy. The Empress Maud gave up her slender hopes of success in the following year and joined her son in the duchy. Nineteen years of life remained before her, but she never set foot in England again. Works of piety, natural to the times, filled many of her days. But during the years that followed Henry's triumph she played an important political part as regent in Normandy and in his hereditary Angevin dominions. During her interventions in England in quest of the crown the charge of arrogance was often levelled against her; but in her older age she proved a sagacious counsellor to her son.

Henry was involved in a further attempt against England in 1149, but the campaign projected on his behalf by the King of Scots and the Earl of Chester came to nothing. For a few years of comparative peace King Stephen was left in uneasy possession. In the meantime Henry was invested by his parents in 1150 as Duke of Normandy. The next year his father's death made him also Count of Anjou, Touraine, and Maine. In his high feudal capacity Henry repaired to Paris to render homage to his lord the King of France, of which country he already possessed, by the accepted law of the age, a large part.

Louis VII was a French Edward the Confessor; he practised with faithful simplicity the law of Christ. All his days were spent in devotion, and his nights in vigil or penance. When he left his own chapel he would delay the whole Court by waiting till the humblest person present had preceded him. These pious and exemplary habits did not endear him to his queen. Eleanor of Aquitaine was in her own right a reigning princess, with the warmth of the South in her veins. She had already complained that she had "married a monk and not a king" when this square-shouldered, ruddy youth, with his "countenance of fire," sprightly talk, and overflowing energy, suddenly presented himself before her husband as his most splendid vassal. Eleanor did not waste words in coming to a decision. The Papacy bowed to strong will in the high feudal chiefs, and Eleanor obtained a divorce from Louis VII in 1152 on the nominal grounds of consanguinity. But what staggered the French Court and opened the eyes of its prayerful King was the sudden marriage of Eleanor to Henry two months later. Thus half of France passed out of royal control into the hands of Henry. Rarely have passion and policy flowed so buoyantly together. The marriage was one of the most brilliant political strokes of the age. Henry afterwards admitted his designs, and accepted the admiration of Europe for their audacity. He was nineteen and she was probably thirty; and, uniting their immense domains, they made common cause against all comers. To Louis VII were vouchsafed the consolations of the spirit; but even these were jarred upon by the problems of government.

War in all quarters lay before the royal pair. The joining to Normandy and Anjou of Poitou, Saintonge, Périgord, the Limousin, the Angoumois, and Gascony, with claims of suzerainty over Auvergne and Toulouse, fascinated and convulsed the feudal Christian world. Everywhere men shook their heads over this concentration of power, this spectacle of so many races and states, sundered from each other by long feuds or divergent interests, now suddenly flung together by the hot blood of a love intrigue. From all sides the potentates confronted the upstart. The King of France, who certainly had every conceivable cause of complaint; King Stephen of England, who disputed Henry's title to the Norman duchy, though without force to intervene across the Channel; the Count of Champagne; the Count of Perche; and Henry's own brother, Geoffrey—all spontaneously, and with good reason, fell upon him.

A month after the marriage these foes converged upon Normandy. But the youthful Duke Henry beat them back, ruptured and broken. The Norman army proved once again its fighting quality. Before he was twenty Henry had cleared Normandy of rebels and pacified Anjou. He turned forthwith to England.

It was a valiant figure that landed in January 1153, and from all over England, distracted by civil wars, hearts and eyes turned towards him. Merlin had prophesied a deliverer; had he not in his veins blood that ran back to William the Conqueror, and beyond him, through his grandmother Matilda, wife of Henry I, to Cedric and the long-vanished Anglo-Saxon line? A wild surge of hope greeted him from the tormented Islanders, and when he knelt after his landing in the first church he found "to pray for a space, in the manner of soldiers," the priest pronounced the wish of the nation in the words, "Behold there cometh the Lord, the Ruler, and the kingdom is in his hand."

There followed battles: Malmesbury, where the sleet, especially directed by Almighty God, beat upon the faces of his foes; Wallingford, where King Stephen by divine interposition fell three times from his horse before going into action. Glamour, terror, success, attended this youthful, puissant warrior, who had not only his sword, but his title-deeds. The baronage saw their interest favoured by a stalemate; they wanted neither a victorious Stephen nor a triumphant Henry. The weaker the King the stronger the nobles. A treaty was concluded at Winchester in 1153 whereby Stephen made Henry his adopted son and his appointed heir. "In the business of the kingdom," promised Stephen, "I will work by the counsel of the Duke; but in the whole realm of England, as well in the Duke's part as my own, I will exercise royal justice." On this Henry did homage and made all the formal submissions, and when a year later Stephen died he was acclaimed and crowned King of England with more general hope and rejoicing than had ever uplifted any monarch in England since the days of Alfred the Great.

Henry Plantagenet

THE accession of Henry II began one of the most pregnant and decisive reigns in English history. The new sovereign ruled an empire, and, as his subjects boasted, his warrant ran "from the Arctic Ocean to the Pyrenees." England to him was but one—the most solid though perhaps the least attractive—of his provinces. But he gave to England that effectual element of external control which, as in the days of William of Orange, was indispensable to the growth of national unity. He was accepted by English and Norman as the ruler of both races and the whole country. The memories of Hastings were confounded in his person, and after the hideous anarchy of civil war and robber barons all due attention was paid to his commands. Thus, though a Frenchman, with foreign speech and foreign modes, he shaped our country in a fashion of which the outline remains to the present day.

After a hundred years of being the encampment of an invading army and the battleground of its quarrelsome officers and their descendants England became finally and for all time a coherent kingdom, based upon Christianity and upon that Latin civilisation which recalled the message of ancient Rome. Henry Plantagenet first brought England, Scotland, and Ireland into a certain common relationship; he re-established the system of royal government which his grandfather, Henry I, had prematurely erected. He relaid the foundations of a central power, based upon the exchequer and the judiciary, which was ultimately to supersede the feudal system of William the Conqueror. The King gathered up and cherished the Anglo-

Saxon tradition of self-government under royal command in shire and borough; he developed and made permanent "assizes" as they survive to-day. It is to him we owe the enduring fact that the English-speaking race all over the world is governed by the English Common Law rather than by the Roman. By his Constitutions of Clarendon he sought to fix the relationship of Church and State and to force the Church in its temporal character to submit itself to the life and law of the nation. In this endeavour he had, after a deadly struggle, to retreat, and it was left to Henry VIII, though centuries later, to avenge his predecessor by destroying the shrine of St Thomas at Canterbury.

A vivid picture is painted of this gifted and, for a while, enviable man: square, thick-set, bull-necked, with powerful arms and coarse, rough hands; his legs bandy from endless riding; a large, round head and closely cropped red hair; a freckled face; a voice harsh and cracked. Intense love of the chase; other loves, which the Church deplored and Queen Eleanor resented; frugality in food and dress; days entirely concerned with public business; travel unceasing; moods various. It was said that he was always gentle and calm in times of urgent peril, but became bad-tempered and capricious when the pressure relaxed. "He was more tender to dead soldiers than to the living, and found far more sorrow in the loss of those who were slain than comfort in the love of those who remained." He journeyed hotfoot around his many dominions, arriving unexpectedly in England when he was thought to be in the South of France. He carried with him in his tours of each province wains loaded with ponderous rolls which represented the office files of to-day. His Court and train gasped and panted behind him. Sometimes, when he had appointed an early start, he was sleeping till noon, with all the wagons and pack-horses awaiting him fully laden. Sometimes he would be off hours

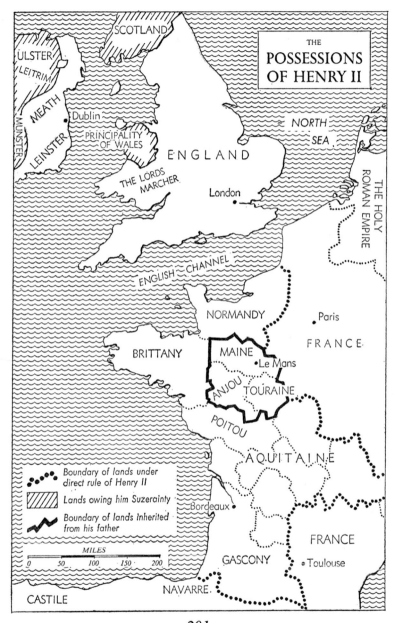

THE

POSSESSIONS
OF HENRY II

SCOTLAND

ULSTER

LEITRIM

MEATH

MUNSTER

LEINSTER

•Dublin

PRINCIPALITY
OF WALES

THE LORDS
MARCHER

E N G L A N D

London

NORTH
SEA

THE HOLY ROMAN EMPIRE

ENGLISH CHANNEL

NORMANDY

•Paris

F R A N C E

BRITTANY

MAINE

•Le Mans

ANJOU

TOURAINE

POITOU

A Q U I T A I N E

Boundary of lands under
direct rule of Henry II

Lands owing him Suzerainty

Boundary of lands Inherited
from his father

•Bordeaux

FRANCE

MILES

0   50   100   150   200

GASCONY

•Toulouse

CASTILE

NAVARRE

before the time he had fixed, leaving everyone to catch up as best they could. Everything was stirred and moulded by him in England, as also in his other much greater estates, which he patrolled with tireless attention.

But this twlefth-century monarch, with his lusts and sports, his hates and his schemes, was no materialist; he was the Lord's Anointed, he commanded, with the Archbishop of Canterbury —"those two strong steers that drew the plough of England" —the whole allegiance of his subjects. The offices of religion, the fear of eternal damnation, the hope of even greater realms beyond the grave, accompanied him from hour to hour. At times he was smitten with remorse and engulfed in repentance. He drew all possible delights and satisfactions from this world and the next. He is portrayed to us in convulsions both of spiritual exaltation and abasement. This was no secluded monarch: the kings of those days were as accessible to all classes as a modern President of the United States. People broke in upon him at all hours with business, with tidings, with gossip, with visions, with complaints. Talk rang high in the King's presence and to His Majesty's face among the nobles and courtiers, and the jester, invaluable monitor, castigated all impartially with unstinted licence.

Few mortals have led so full a life as Henry II or have drunk so deeply of the cups of triumph and sorrow. In later life he fell out with Eleanor. When she was over fifty and he but forty-two he is said to have fallen in love with "Fair Rosamond," a damosel of high degree and transcendent beauty, and generations have enjoyed the romantic tragedy of Queen Eleanor penetrating the protecting maze at Woodstock by the clue of a silken thread and offering her hapless supplanter the hard choice between the dagger and the poisoned cup. Tiresome investigators have undermined this excellent tale, but it certainly should find its place in any history worthy of the name.

Such was the man who succeeded to the troubled and divided inheritance of Stephen. Already before his accession to the English throne Henry had fought the first of his many wars to defend his Continental inheritance. Ever since the emergence of the strong Norman power in North-West France, a hundred years before, the French monarchy had struggled ceaselessly against the encroachments of great dukedoms and countships upon the central Government. The Dukes of Normandy, of Aquitaine, and of Brittany, the Counts of Anjou, Toulouse, Flanders, and Boulogne, although in form and law vassals of the French Crown, together with a host of other feudal tenants-in-chief, aspired to independent sovereignty, and in the eclipse of the monarchy seemed at times near to achieving their ambition. The Battle of Hastings had made the greatest French subject, the Duke of Normandy, also King of England; but Henry II's accession to the Island throne in 1154 threatened France with far graver dangers. Hitherto there had always been political relief in playing off over-mighty subjects one against another. The struggle between Anjou and Normandy in the eleventh century had rejoiced the French king, who saw two of his chief enemies at grips. But when in one hour Henry II was King of England, Duke of Normandy, Lord of Aquitaine, Brittany, Poitou, Anjou, Maine, and Guienne, ruler from the Somme to the Pyrenees of more than half France, all balance of power among the feudal lords was destroyed.

Louis VII found instead of a dozen principalities, divided and jealous, one single imperial Power, whose resources far surpassed his own. He was scarcely the man to face such a combination. He had already suffered the irreparable misfortune of Eleanor's divorce, and of her joining forces and blood with his rival. By him she bore sons; by Louis only daughters. Still, some advantages remained to the French king. He managed to hold out for his lifetime against the Plantagenets; and after nearly four centuries of struggle and devastation the final victory in Europe rested with France. The Angevin Empire was indeed more impressive on the map than in reality. It was a motley, ill-knit collection of states, flung together by the chance of a single marriage, and lacked unity both of purpose and strength. The only tie between England and her Continental empire was the fact that Henry himself and some of his magnates held lands on either side of the Channel. There was no pretence of a single, central Government; no uniformity of administration or custom; no common interests or feelings of loyalty. Weak as Louis VII appeared in his struggle with the enterprising and active Henry, the tide of events flowed with the compact French monarchy, and even Louis left it more firmly established than he found it.

The main method of the French was simple. Henry had inherited vast estates; but with them also all their local and feudal discontents. Louis could no longer set the Count of Anjou against the Duke of Normandy, but he could still encourage both in Anjou and in Normandy those local feuds and petty wars which sapped the strength of the feudal potentates, in principle his vassals. Nor was the exploiting of family quarrels an unfruitful device. In the later years of his reign, the sons of Henry II, eager, turbulent, and proud, allowed themselves to be used by Louis VII and by his successor, the wily and gifted Philip Augustus, against their father.

*   *   *   *   *

How, we may ask, did all this affect the daily life of England and her history? A series of personal feudal struggles fought in distant lands, the quarrels of an alien ruling class, were little understood and less liked by the common folk. Yet these things long burdened their pilgrimage. For many generations their bravest and best were to fight and die by the marshes of the Loire or under the sun-baked hills of Southern France in pursuit of the dream of English dominion over French soil. For this two centuries later Englishmen triumphed at Crécy, Poitiers, and Agincourt, or starved in the terrible Limoges march of the Black Prince. For this they turned fertile France into a desert where even the most needed beasts died of thirst and hunger. Throughout the medieval history of England war with France is the interminable and often the dominant theme. It groped and scraped into every reach of English life, moulding and fretting the shape of English society and institutions.

No episode opens to us a wider window upon the politics of the twelfth century in England than the quarrel of Henry II with his great subject and former friend, Thomas Becket, Archbishop of Canterbury. We have to realise the gravity of this conflict. The military State in feudal Christendom bowed to the Church in things spiritual; it never accepted the idea of the transference of secular power to priestly authority. But the Church, enriched continually by the bequests of hardy barons, anxious in the death agony about their life beyond the grave, became the greatest landlord and capitalist in the community. Rome used its ghostly arts upon the superstitions of almost all the actors in the drama. The power of the State was held in constant challenge by this potent interest. Questions of doctrine might well have been resolved, but how was the government of the country to be carried on under two conflicting powers, each possessed of immense claims upon limited national resources? This conflict was not confined to England. It was the root question of the European world, as it then existed.

Under William the Conqueror schism had been avoided in England by tact and compromise. Under Lanfranc the Church worked with the Crown, and each power reinforced the other against the turbulent barons or the oppressed commonalty.

But now a great personality stood at the summit of the religious hierarchy, Thomas Becket, who had been the King's friend. He had been his Chancellor, or, as Ranke first remarked, "to use a somewhat equivalent expression, his most trusted Cabinet Minister." He had in both home and foreign affairs loyally served his master. He had re-organised the imposition of scutage, a tax that allowed money to commute personal service in arms and thus eventually pierced the feudal system to its core. He had played his part in the acquisition of Brittany. The King felt sure that in Becket he had his own man—no mere servant, but a faithful comrade and colleague in the common endeavour. It was by the King's direct influence and personal effort that Becket was elected Archbishop.

From that moment all his gifts and impulses ran in another channel. Something like the transformation which carried Henry V from a rollicking prince to the august hero-King overnight was now witnessed in Becket. His private life had always been both pious and correct. He had of course been immersed in political affairs; nor was it as a sombre figure behind the throne. But whereas hitherto as a courtier and a prince he had rivalled all in magnificence and pomp, taking his part in the vivid pageant of the times, he now sought by extreme austerities to gather around himself the fame and honour of a saint. Becket pursued the same methods and ambitions in the ecclesiastical as previously he had done in the political sphere; and in both he excelled. He now championed the Church against the Crown in every aspect of their innumerable interleaving functions. He clothed this aggressive process with those universal ideas of the Catholic Church and the Papal authority which far transcended the bounds of our Island, covering Europe and reaching out into the mysterious and the sublime. After a tour upon the Continent and a conclave with the religious dignitaries of France and Italy he returned to England imbued with the resolve to establish the independence of the Church hierarchy on the State as represented by the King. Thus he opened the conflict which the wise Lanfranc had throughout his life striven to avoid. At this time the mood in England was ripe for strife upon this issue.

In a loose and undefined way Saxon England had foreshadowed the theory to which the Elizabethan reformers long afterwards returned. Both thought of the monarch as appointed by God, not only to rule the State, but to protect and guide the Church. In the eleventh century however the Papacy had been reinvigorated under Hildebrand, who became Pope Gregory VII in 1073, and his successors. Rome now began to make claims which were hardly compatible with the traditional notions of the mixed sovereignty of the King in all matters temporal and spiritual. The Gregorian movement held that the government of the Church ought to be in the hands of the clergy, under the supervision of the Pope. According to this view, the King was a mere layman whose one religious function was obedience to the hierarchy. The Church was a body apart, with its own allegiance and its own laws. By the reign of Henry II the bishop was not only a spiritual officer; he was a great landowner, the secular equal of earls; he could put forces in the field; he could excommunicate his enemies, who might be the King's friends. Who, then, was to appoint the bishop? And, when once appointed, to whom, if the Pope commanded one thing and the King another, did he owe his duty? If the King and his counsellors agreed upon a law contrary to the law of the Church, to which authority was obedience due? Thus there came about the great conflict between Empire and Papacy symbolised in the question of Investiture, of which the dispute between Henry II and Becket is the insular counterpart.

The struggle between Henry II and Becket is confused by

the technical details over which it was fought. There was however good reason why the quarrel should have been engaged upon incidents of administration rather than upon the main principles which were at stake. The Crown resented the claim of the Church to interfere in the State; but in the Middle Ages no king dared to challenge the Church outright, or, much as he might hope to limit its influence, thought of a decisive breach. It was not till the sixteenth century that an English king in conflict with the Papacy dared to repudiate the authority of Rome and nakedly declare the State supreme, even in spiritual matters. In the twelfth century the only practicable course was compromise. But the Church at this time was in no mood for a bargain. In every country the secular power took up the challenge; but it was hard to meet, and in Central Europe at least the struggle ended only in the exhaustion of both Empire and Papacy.

The Church in England, like the baronage, had gained greatly in power since the days of William the Conqueror and his faithful Archbishop Lanfranc. Stephen in his straits had made sweeping concessions to the Church, whose political influence then reached its zenith. These concessions, Henry felt, compromised his royal rights. He schemed to regain what had been lost, and as the first step in 1162 appointed his trusted servant Becket to be Archbishop of Canterbury, believing he would thus secure the acquiescence of the Episcopacy. In fact he provided the Church with a leader of unequalled vigour and obstinacy. He ignored or missed the ominous signs of the change in Becket's attitude, and proceeded to his second step, the publication in 1164 of the Constitutions of Clarendon. In these Henry claimed, not without considerable truth, to be re-stating the customs of the kingdom as they had been before the anarchy of Stephen's reign. He sought to retrace thirty years and to annul the effects of

Stephen's surrender. But Becket resisted. He regarded Stephen's yieldings as irrevocable gains by the Church. He refused to let them lapse. He declared that the Constitutions of Clarendon did not represent the relations between Church and Crown. When, in October 1164, he was summoned to appear before the Great Council and explain his conduct he haughtily denied the King's authority and placed himself under the protection of the Pope and God.

Thus he ruptured that unity which had hitherto been deemed vital in the English realm, and in fact declared war with ghostly weapons upon the King. Stiff in defiance, Becket took refuge on the Continent, where the same conflict was already distracting both Germany and Italy. The whole thought of the ruling classes in England was shaken by this grievous dispute. It endured for six years, during which the Archbishop of Canterbury remained in his French exile. Only in 1170 was an apparent reconciliation brought about between him and the King at Fréteval, in Touraine. Each side appeared to waive its claims in principle. The King did not mention his rights and customs. The Archbishop was not called upon to give an oath. He was promised a safe return and full possession of his see. King and Primate met for the last time in the summer of 1170 at Chaumont. "My lord," said Thomas at the end, "my heart tells me that I part from you as one whom you shall see no more in this life." "Do you hold me as a traitor?" asked the King. "That be far from thee, my lord," replied the Archbishop; but he returned to Canterbury resolved to seek from the Pope unlimited powers of excommunication wherewith to discipline his ecclesiastical forces. "The more potent and fierce the prince is," he wrote, "the stronger stick and harder chain is needed to bind him and keep him in order." "I go to England," he said, "whether to peace or to destruction I know not; but God has decreed what fate awaits me."

Meanwhile, in Becket's absence, Henry had resolved to secure the peaceful accession of his son, the young Henry, by having him crowned in his own lifetime. The ceremony had been performed by the Archbishop of York, assisted by a number of other clerics. This action was bitterly resented by Becket as an infringement of a cherished right of his see. After the Fréteval agreement Henry supposed that bygones were to be bygones. But Becket had other views.

His welcome home after the years of exile was astonishing. At Canterbury the monks received him as an angel of God. "I am come to die among you," he said in his sermon, and again, "In this church there are martyrs, and God will soon increase their number." He made a triumphal progress through London, scattering alms to the beseeching and exalted people. Then hotfoot he proceeded to renew his excommunication of the clergy who had taken part in the crowning of young Henry. These unfortunate priests and prelates traveled in a bunch to the King, who was in Normandy. They told a tale not only of an ecclesiastical challenge, but of actual revolt and usurpation. They said that the Archbishop was ready "to tear the crown from the young King's head."

Henry Plantagenet, first of all his line, with all the fire of his nature, received these tidings when surrounded by his knights and nobles. He was transported with passion. "What a pack of fools and cowards," he cried, "I have nourished in my house, that not one of them will avenge me of this turbulent priest!" Another version says "of this upstart clerk." A council was immediately summoned to devise measures for reasserting the royal authority. In the main they shared the King's anger. Second thoughts prevailed. With all the stresses that existed in that fierce and ardent society, it was not possible that the realm could support a fearful conflict between the two sides of life represented by Church and State.

But meanwhile another train of action was in process. Four knight had heard the King's bitter words spoken in the full circle. They travelled fast to the coast. They crossed the Channel. They called for horses and rode to Canterbury. There on December 29, 1170, they found the Archbishop in the cathedral. The scene and the tragedy are famous. He confronted them with Cross and mitre, fearless and resolute in warlike action, a master of the histrionic arts. After haggard parleys they fell upon him, cut him down with their swords, and left him bleeding like Julius Cæsar, with a score of wounds to cry for vengeance.

This tragedy was fatal to the King. The murder of one of the foremost of God's servants, like the breaking of a feudal oath, struck at the heart of the age. All England was filled with terror. They acclaimed the dead Archbishop as a martyr; and immediately it appeared that his relics healed incurable diseases, and robes that he had worn by their mere touch relieved minor ailments. Here indeed was a crime, vast and inexpiable. When Henry heard the appalling news he was prostrated with grief and fear. All the elaborate process of law which he had sought to set on foot against this rival power was brushed aside by a brutal, bloody act; and though he had never dreamed that such a deed would be done there were his own hot words, spoken before so many witnesses, to fasten on him, for that age at least, the guilt of murder, and, still worse, sacrilege.

The immediately following years were spent in trying to recover what he had lost by a great parade of atonement for his guilt. He made pilgrimages to the shrine of the murdered Archbishop. He subjected himself to public penances. On several anniversaries, stripped to the waist and kneeling humbly, he submitted to be scourged by the triumphant monks. We may however suppose that the corporal chastisement, which apparently from the contemporary pictures was administered with birch rods, was mainly symbolic. Under this display of contrition and submission the King laboured perseveringly to regain the rights of State. By the Compromise of Avranches in 1172 he made his peace with the Papacy on comparatively easy terms. To many deep-delving historians it seems that in fact, though not in form, he had by the end of his life re-established the main principles of the Constitutions of Clarendon, which are after all in harmony with what the English nation or any virile and rational race would mean to have as their law. Certainly the Papacy supported him in his troubles with his sons. The knights, it is affirmed, regained their salvation in the holy wars. But Becket's sombre sacrifice had not been in vain. Until the Reformation the Church retained the system of ecclesiastical courts independent of the royal authority, and the right of appeal to Rome, two of the major points upon which Becket had defied the King.

It is a proof of the quality of the age that these fierce contentions, shaking the souls of men, should have been so rigorously and yet so evenly fought out. In modern conflicts and revolutions in some great states bishops and archbishops have been sent by droves to concentration camps, or pistolled in the nape of the neck in the well-warmed, brilliantly lighted corridor of a prison. What claim have we to vaunt a superior civilisation to Henry II's times? We are sunk in a barbarism all the deeper because it is tolerated by moral lethargy and covered with a veneer of scientific conveniences.[1]

*   *   *   *   *

Eighteen years of life lay before the King after Becket's death. In a sense, they were years of glory. All Europe marvelled at the extent of Henry's domains, to which in 1171 he had added the Lordship of Ireland. Through the marriages of his daughters he was linked with the Norman King of Sicily,

[1] Written in 1938.

the King of Castile, and Henry the Lion of Saxony, who was a most powerful prince in Germany. Diplomatic agents spread his influence in the Lombard cities of northern Italy. Both Emperor and Pope invited him in the name of Christ and all Europe to lead a new Crusade and to be King of Jerusalem. Indeed, after the Holy Roman Emperor, Frederick Barbarossa, Henry stood next in Christendom. It was suspected by his contemporaries that his aim was to win for himself a kingdom in Italy and even to wear the imperial crown.

Yet Henry knew well that his splendour was personal in origin, tenuous and transient in quality; and he had also deep clouding family sorrows. During these years he was confronted with no less than four rebellions by his sons. For the three eldest he had provided glittering titles; Henry held Normandy, Maine and Anjou; Richard was given Aquitaine, and to Geoffrey went Brittany. These boys were typical sprigs of the Angevin stock. They wanted power as well as titles, and they bore their father no respect. Urged on by their mother, Queen Eleanor, who now lived in Poitiers apart from her husband, between 1173 and 1186 they rose in revolt in various combinations. On each occasion they could count on the active support of the watchful King of France. Henry treated his ungrateful children with generosity, but he had no illusions. The royal chamber at Westminster at this time was adorned with paintings done at the King's command. One represented four eaglets preying upon the parent bird, the fourth one poised at the parent's neck, ready to pick out the eyes. "The four eaglets," the King is reported to have said, "are my four sons who cease not to persecute me even unto death. The youngest of them, whom I now embrace with so much affection will sometime in the end insult me more grievously and more dangerously than any of the others."

So it was to be. John, whom he had striven to provide with

an inheritance equal to that of his brothers, joined the final plot against him. In 1188 Richard, his eldest surviving son, after the death of young Henry, was making war upon him in conjunction with King Philip of France. Already desperately ill, Henry was defeated at Le Mans and recoiled to Normandy. When he saw in the list of conspirators against him the name of his son John, upon whom his affection had strangely rested, he abandoned the struggle with life. "Let things go as they will," he gasped. "Shame, shame on a conquered King." So saying, this hard, violent, brilliant and lonely man expired at Chinon on July 6, 1189. The pious were taught to regard this melancholy end as the further chastisement of God upon the murderer of Thomas Becket. Such is the bitter taste of worldly power. Such are the correctives of glory.

The English Common Law

THE Plantagenets were rough masters, and the temper of the age was violent. It was the violence however of vigour, not of decadence. England has had greater soldier-kings and subtler diplomatists than Henry II, but no man has left a deeper mark upon our laws and institutions. His strange outbursts of frenzied energy did not exhaust themselves in politics, war, and the chase. Like his Norman predecessors and his sons, Henry II possessed an instinct for the problems of government and law, and it is here that his achievement lies. The names of his battles have vanished with their dust, but his fame will live with the English Constitution and the English Common Law.

This great King was fortunate in his moment. William I and Henry I had brought to England or preserved there all those instruments through which their successor was to work. They themselves could move but slowly and with caution. The land must settle itself to its new rules and rulers. In 1154 however Henry of Anjou had come to a country which nearly twenty years of anarchy had prepared for the acceptance of a strong hand at the centre. Himself a Frenchman, the ruler of more than half France, he brought to his task the qualities of vision, wide experience, and a strength that did not scruple to stoop to cunning. The disasters of Stephen's reign determined Henry not only to curb baronial independence and regain the ground lost by his predecessor, but to go much further. In place of a multitude of manorial courts where local magnates dispensed justice whose quality and character varied with the customs and temper of the neighbourhood, he planned a system of royal courts which would administer a law common to all England and all men.

The policy was not without peril. The King was wise enough to avoid a direct assault, for he knew, as the Conqueror had known, that to lay a finger upon the sanctity of customary rights would provoke disaster. Faced with this barrier, Henry shrewdly opposed custom to custom and cloaked innovation in the respected garb of conservatism. He was careful to respect existing forms. His plan was to stretch old principles to take on new meanings. In an unwritten Constitution the limits of the King's traditional rights were vaguely defined. This opened a shrewd line of advance. For centuries before the Conquest, Church and King had been the enemies of seigneurial anarchy, but there had been no question of swiftly extending the Crown's jurisdiction. Fastening upon the elastic Saxon concept of the King's Peace, Henry used it to draw all criminal cases into his courts. Every man had his own Peace, which it was a crime to break, and the more important the man the graver the breach. The King's Peace was the most important of all, and those who broke it could be tried in the King's court. But the King's Peace was limited, and often embraced only offences committed in the King's presence or on the King's highway or land. When the King died his Peace died with him and men might do as they willed. Cautiously and quietly Henry began to claim that the King's Peace extended over all England, and that no matter where it was broken offenders should be tried in the King's courts. Civil cases he attracted by straining a different principle, the old right of the King's court to hear appeals in cases where justice had been refused and to protect men in possession of their lands. He did not brandish what he was about; the changes that he made were introduced gradually and without legislation, so that at first they were hardly perceived. Rarely is it possible to state the date at which any innovation was made; yet at the King's death a clever man might have looked back and seen how much had been altered in the thirty-five years that Henry II had sat on the English throne.

But if Henry was to pose as a conservative in the legal sphere he must be consistent. Compulsion could play little part in his programme; it had to be the first principle of his policy to attract cases to his courts rather than to compel them. A bait was needed with which to draw litigants to the royal courts; the King must offer them better justice than they could have at the hands of their lords. Henry accordingly threw open to litigants in the royal courts a startling new procedure —trial by jury. *Regale quoddam beneficium,* a contemporary called it—a royal boon; and the description illuminates both the origin of the jury and the part it played in the triumph of the Common Law. Henry did not invent the jury; he put it to a new purpose. The idea of the jury is the one great contribution of the Franks to the English legal system, for, unknown in this country before the Conquest, the germ of it lies far back in the practice of the Carolingian kings. In origin the jury was a royal instrument of administrative convenience: the King had the right to summon a body of men to bear witness under oath about the truth of any question concerning the royal interest. It was through this early form of jury that William the Conqueror had determined the Crown rights in the great Domesday survey. The genius of Henry II, perceiving new possibilities in such a procedure, turned to regular use in the courts an instrument which so far had only been used for administrative purposes.

Only the King had the right to summon a jury. Henry accordingly did not grant it to private courts, but restricted it to those who sought justice before the royal judges. It was an astute move. Until this time both civil and criminal cases had been decided through the oath, the ordeal, or the duel. The court would order one of the litigants to muster a body of men who would swear to the justice of his cause and whom it was hoped God would punish if they swore falsely; or condemn him, under the supervision of a priest, to carry a red-hot iron, or eat a morsel of bread, or be plunged in a pool of water. If the iron did not burn or the bread choke or the water reject him so that he could not sink, then Divine Providence was adjudged to have granted a visible sign that the victim was innocent. The duel, or trial by battle, was a Norman innovation based on the modern theory that the God of Battles will strengthen the arm of the righteous, and was at one time much favoured for deciding disputes about land. Monasteries and other substantial landowners took the precaution however of assisting the Almighty by retaining professional champions to protect their property and their rights. All this left small room for debate on points of law. In a more rational age men were beginning to distrust such antics, and indeed the Church refused to sanction the ordeal during the same year that Magna Carta was sealed. Thus trial by jury quickly gained favour. But the old processes were long in dying. If a defendant preferred to take his case before God man could not forbid him, and the ordeal therefore was not abolished outright. Hence a later age was to know the horrors of the *peine forte et dure*—the compulsion of the accused by slow pressure to death to agree to put himself before a jury. Time swept this away; yet so late as 1818 a litigant nonplussed the judges by an appeal to trial by battle and compelled Parliament to abolish this ancient procedure.

The jury of Henry II was not the jury that we know. There

were various forms of it; but in all there was this essential difference: the jurymen were witnesses as well as judges of the facts. Good men and true were picked, not yet for their impartiality, but because they were the men most likely to know the truth. The modern jury which knows nothing about the case till it is proved in court was slow in coming. The process is obscure. A jury summoned to Westminster from distant parts might be reluctant to come. The way was long, the roads unsafe, and perhaps only three or four would arrive. The court could not wait. An adjournment would be costly. To avoid delay and expense the parties might agree to rely on a jury *de circumstantibus,* a jury of bystanders. The few jurors who knew the truth of the matter would tell their tale to the bystanders, and then the whole body would deliver their verdict. In time the jurors with local knowledge would cease to be jurors at all and become witnesses, giving their evidence in open court to a jury entirely composed of bystanders. Such, we may guess, or something like it, was what happened. Very gradually, as the laws of evidence developed, the change came. By the fifteenth century it was under way; yet the old idea lingered, and even under the Tudor kings jurymen might be tried for perjury if they gave a wrongful verdict.

The jury system has come to stand for all we mean by English justice, because so long as a case has to be scrutinised by twelve honest men, defendant and plaintiff alike have a safeguard from arbitrary perversion of the law. It is this which distinguishes the law administered in English courts from Continental legal systems based on Roman law. Thus amidst the great process of centralisation the old principle was preserved, and endures to this day, that law flows from the people. Land is not given by the King.

These methods gave good justice. Trial by jury became popular. Professional judges removed from local prejudice, whose outlook ranged above the interested or ignorant lord or his steward, armed with the King's power to summon juries, secured swifter decisions, and a strong authority to enforce them. Henry accordingly had to build up almost from nothing a complete system of royal courts, capable of absorbing a great rush of new work. The instrument to which he turned was the royal Council, the organ through which all manner of governmental business was already regularly carried out. It was to be the common parent of Chancery and Exchequer, of Parliament, of the Common Law courts and those Courts of Prerogative on which the Tudors and Stuarts relied. At the outset of Henry II's reign, it dealt almost indiscriminately with every kind of administrative business. On the judicial side the Court of the Exchequer, which tried cases affecting the royal revenue, was beginning to take shape; but in the main the Council in this aspect was scarcely more than the King's feudal court, where he did justice, like any other lord, among his vassals. Under Henry II all this was changed. The functions of the King's justices became more and more specialised. During the reigns of his sons the Council began to divide into two great courts, the King's Bench and the Common Pleas. They did not become fully separate till a century later. Thereafter, with the Court of the Exchequer, they formed the backbone of the Common Law system down to the nineteenth century. In addition, travelling justices— justices "in eyre"—were from time to time appointed to hear all manner of business in the shires, whose courts were thus drawn into the orbit of royal justice.

But all this was only a first step. Henry also had to provide means whereby the litigant, eager for royal justice, could remove his case out of the court of his lord into the King's court. The device which Henry used was the royal writ. At all costs baronial rights must be formally respected; but by straining the traditional rights of the Crown it was possible to claim that particular types of case fell within the King's province. Upon this principle Henry evolved a number of set formulæ, or writs, each fitted to a certain type of case; and any man who could by some fiction fit his own case to the wording of one of the royal writs might claim the King's justice. The wording of writs was rigid, but at this date new forms of writ might still be given. For about eighty years they increased in number, and with each new form a fresh blow was struck at the feudal courts. It was not until de Montfort's revolt against the third Henry in the thirteenth century that the multiplication of writs was checked and the number fixed at something under two hundred. This system then endured for six hundred years. However the times might change, society had to adapt itself to that unbending framework. Inevitably English law became weighted with archaisms and legal fictions. The whole course of a case might depend on the writ with which it was begun, for every writ had its special procedure, mode of trial, and eventual remedy. Thus the Saxon spirit of formalism survived. Henry II had only been able to break down the primitive methods of the early courts by fastening upon the law a procedure which became no less rigid. Yet, cumbersome though it was, the writ system gave to English law a conservative spirit which guarded and preserved its continuity from that time on in an unbroken line.

* * * * *

It is a maxim of English law that legal memory begins with the accession of Richard I in 1189. The date was set for a technical reason by a statute of Edward I. It could scarcely have been more appropriately chosen however, for with the close of the reign of Henry II we are on the threshold of a new epoch in the history of English law. With the establishment of a system of royal courts, giving the same justice all over the country, the old diversity of local law was rapidly broken down, and a law common to the whole land and to all men soon took its place. A modern lawyer, transported to the England of Henry's predecessor, would find himself in strange surroundings; with the system that Henry bequeathed to his son he would feel almost at home. That is the measure of the great King's achievement. He had laid the foundations of the English Common Law, upon which succeeding generations would build. Changes in the design would arise, but its main outlines were not to be altered.

It was in these fateful and formative years that the English-speaking peoples began to devise methods of determining legal disputes which survive in substance to this day. A man can only be accused of a civil or criminal offence which is clearly defined and known to the law. The judge is an umpire. He adjudicates on such evidence as the parties choose to produce. Witnesses must testify in public and on oath. They are examined and cross-examined, not by the judge, but by the litigants themselves or their legally qualified and privately hired representatives. The truth of their testimony is weighed not by the judge by by twelve good men and true, and it is only when this jury has determined the facts that the judge is empowered to impose sentence, punishment, or penalty according to law. All might seem very obvious, even a platitude, until one contemplates the alternative system which still dominates a large portion of the world. Under Roman law, and systems derived from it, a trial in those turbulent centuries, and in some countries even to-day, is often an inquisition. The judge makes his own investigation into the civil wrong or the public crime, and such investigation is largely uncontrolled. The suspect can be interrogated in private. He must answer all questions put to him. His right to be represented by a legal adviser is restricted. The witnesses against him can testify in secret and in his absence. And only when these processes have been accomplished is the accusation or charge against him formulated and published. Thus often arises secret intimidation, enforced confessions, torture, and blackmailed pleas of guilty. These sinister dangers were extinguished from the Common Law of England more than six centuries ago. By the time Henry II's great-grandson, Edward I had died English criminal and civil procedure had settled into a mould and tradition which in the mass govern the English-speaking peoples to-day. In all claims and disputes, whether they concerned the grazing lands of the Middle West, the oilfields of California, the sheep-runs and gold-mines of Australia, or the territorial rights of the Maoris, these rules have obtained, at any rate in theory, according to the procedure and mode of trial evolved by the English Common Law.

Nor was this confined to how trials were conducted. The law that was applied to such multitudinous problems, some familiar, others novel, was in substance the Common Law of England. The law concerning murder, theft, the ownership of land, and the liberty of the individual was all transported, together with much else, to the New World, and, though often modified to suit the conditions and temper of the times, descends in unbroken line from that which governed the lives and fortunes of twelfth-century Englishmen.

Most of it was then unwritten, and in England much still remains so. The English statutes, for example, still contain no definition of the crime of murder, for this, like much other law, rested on the unwritten custom of the land as declared by the inhabitants and interpreted, developed, and applied by the judges. Lawyers could only ascertain it by studying reports and records of ancient decisions. For this they had already in this early age made their own arrangements. A century after Henry's death they began to group themselves into professional communities in London, the Inns of Court, half colleges, half law-schools, but predominantly secular, for the presence of clerics learned in the laws of Rome and the Canon Law of the Roman Church was not encouraged, and here they produced annual laws reports, or "Year Books," as they were then called, whose authority was recognised by the judges, and which continued in almost unbroken succession for nearly three centuries. In all this time however only one man attempted a general and comprehensive statement of the English Common Law. About the year 1250 a Judge of Assize named Henry of Bracton produced a book of nearly nine hundred pages entitled *A Tract on the Laws and Customs of England*. Nothing like it was achieved for several hundred years, but Bracton's method set an example, since followed throughout the English-speaking world, not so much of stating the Common Law as of explaining and commenting on it, and thus encouraging and helping later lawyers and judges to develop and expand it. Digests and codes imposed in the Roman manner by an omnipotent state on a subject people were alien to the spirit and tradition of England. The law was already there, in the customs of the land, and it was only a matter of discovering it by diligent study and comparison of recorded decisions in earlier cases, and applying it to the particular dispute before the court. In the course of time the Common Law changed. Lawyers of the reign of Henry II read into the statements of their predecessors of the tenth century meanings and principles which their authors never intended, and applied them to the novel conditions and problems of their own day. No matter. Here was a precedent. If a judge could be shown that a custom or something like it had been recognised and acted upon in an earlier and similar case he would be more ready, if it accorded with his sense of what was just and with the current feelings of the community, to follow it in the dispute before him. This slow but continuous growth of what is popularly known as "case law" ultimately achieved much the same freedoms and rights for the individual as are enshrined in other countries by written instruments such as the Declarations of the Rights of Man and the spacious and splendid provisions of the American Declaration of Independence and constitutional guarantees of civil rights. But English justice advanced very cautiously. Even the framers of Magna Carta did not attempt to lay down new law or proclaim any broad general principles. This was because both sovereign and subject were in practice bound by the Common Law, and the liberties of Englishmen rested not on any enactment of the State, but on immemorial slow-growing custom declared by juries of free men who gave their verdicts case by case in open court.

Cœur de Lion

THE Christian kingdom founded at Jerusalem after the First Crusade had stood precariously for a century, guarded by the military orders of the Knights Templars and Hospitallers. Its continued existence was largely due to the disunity that prevailed among the Moslem lands surrounding it. At length the rise of a great national leader of the Turks, or Saracens, united the Moslem power. In 1169 Saladin became Vizier of Egypt. Shortly afterwards he proclaimed himself Sultan. By origin he was a Kurd, and by culture a Damascene. Soon his power was stretching out into Syria, encircling the Crusaders' principalities on the Levantine coast. He took Damascus in 1174 and Aleppo in 1183. In their anxieties at these gathering dangers the Christian community in Jerusalem, and Guy of Lusignan, the King, offered the threatened crown first to Philip of France and then to Henry II, and made the West ring with cries for help. But the quarrels of the Western princes prevented effective measures being taken in time. In 1186 Saladin in his turn proclaimed a Holy War. He promised his warlike hordes booty and adventure in this world and bliss eternal in the next, and advanced upon Jerusalem. The Christian army of occupation which took the field against him, perhaps ten thousand strong, was caught at a disadvantage in the thirsty desert and cut to pieces by greatly superior numbers at Hattin. The King, the Grand Master of the Templars, and many of the greatest nobles were taken prisoners. In October 1187 Jerusalem surrendered, and thereafter all Palestine and Syria, except Tyre, Antioch, and Tripoli, fell again into Moslem hands.

The shock of these events resounded throughout Europe. The Pope shared the general horror of the Christian West. His legates traversed the Courts enjoining peace among Christians and war against the infidel. The sovereigns of the three greatest nations of the West responded to the call, and an intense movement stirred the chivalry of England, France, and Germany. Pictures were shown of the Holy Sepulchre defiled by the horses of the Saracen cavalry. Not only the gentle folk but to some extent all classes were swept by deep emotion. Not without sorrow, as the literature of those times shows, did many of the young Crusaders leave home and loved ones for a journey into the dangers of the distant and the unknown. The magnetism of war and adventure mingled with a deep counterpart of sacrifice and mysticism which lights the age and its efforts with the charm of true romance. In Germany the solemn Diet of Mainz "swore the expedition" to the Holy Land. The Kings of France and England agreed upon a joint Crusade, without however ceasing their immediate strife. To the religious appeal was added the spur of the tax-gatherer. The "Saladin tithe" was levied upon all who did not take the Cross. On the other hand, forgiveness of taxes and a stay in the payment of debts were granted to all Crusaders. The strongest armies every yet sent to the East were raised. Germany marshalled a large array round the standard of Frederick Barbarossa. A Scandinavian fleet bore twelve thousand Norsemen through the Straits of Gibraltar. Thus did armoured Europe precipitate itself upon Asia. Meanwhile the first of the rescuers, Conrad of Montferrat, who, hastening from Constantinople, had saved Tyre, was already besieging Acre.

In the midst of these surgings Henry II died in sorrow and

disaster. He made no attempt to prescribe the succession, and it passed naturally to Richard. The new King affected little grief at the death of a father against whom he was in arms. He knelt beside his bier no longer than would have been necessary to recite the Lord's Prayer, and turned at once to the duties of his realm. In spite of many harsh qualities, men saw in him a magnanimity which has added lustre to his military renown. At the outset of his reign he gave an outstanding example. During his rebellion against his father he had pressed hard upon Henry II's rout at Le Mans in the very forefront of the cavalry without even wearing his mail. In the rearguard of the beaten army stood Henry's faithful warrior, William the Marshal. He confronted Richard and had him at his mercy. "Spare me!" cried Richard in his disadvantage; so the Marshal turned his lance against the prince's horse and killed it, saying with scorn, "I will not slay you. The Devil may slay you." This was humiliation and insult worse than death. It was not therefore without anxiety that the Marshal and his friends awaited their treatment at the hands of the sovereign to whom their loyalties must now be transferred. But King Richard rose at once above the past. He spoke with dignity and detachment of the grim incident so fresh and smarting in his mind. He confirmed his father's true servant in all his offices and honours, and sent him to England to act in his name. He gave him in marriage the rich Crown heiress of Pembroke, and at a stroke the Marshal became one of the most powerful of English barons. Indeed it was noted that the King's favour lighted upon those who had stood loyally by his father against him, even to the detriment of those who had been his own fellow-rebels.

*   *   *   *   *

Richard, with all his characteristic virtues and faults cast in a heroic mould, is one of the most fascinating medieval figures. He has been described as the creature and embodiment of the age of chivalry. In those days the lion was much admired in heraldry, and more than one king sought to link himself with its repute. When Richard's contemporaries called him "Cœur de Lion" they paid a lasting compliment to the king of beasts. Little did the English people owe him for his services, and heavily did they pay for his adventures. He was in England only twice for a few short months in his ten years' reign; yet his memory has always stirred English hearts, and seems to present throughout the centuries the pattern of the fighting man. In all deeds of prowess as well as in large schemes of war Richard shone. He was tall and delicately shaped; strong in nerve and sinew, and most dexterous in arms. He rejoiced in personal combat, and regarded his opponents without malice as necessary agents in his fame. He loved war, not so much for the sake of glory or political ends, but as other men love science or poetry, for the excitement of the struggle and the glow of victory. By this his whole temperament was toned; and, united with the highest qualities of the military commander, love of war called forth all the powers of his mind and body.

Although a man of blood and violence, Richard was too impetuous to be either treacherous or habitually cruel. He was as ready to forgive as he was hasty to offend; he was openhanded and munificent to profusion; in war circumspect in design and skilful in execution; in politics a child, lacking in subtlety and experience. His political alliances were formed upon his likes and dislikes; his political schemes had neither unity nor clearness of purpose. The advantages gained for him by military genius were flung away through diplomatic ineptitude. When on the journey to the East Messina in Sicily was won by his arms he was easily persuaded to share with his polished, faithless ally, Philip Augustus, fruits of a victory which more wisely used might have foiled the French king's artful schemes. The rich and tenable acquisition of Cyprus was cast away even more easily than it was won. His life was one magnificent parade, which, when ended, left only an empty plain.

The King's heart was set upon the new Crusade. This task seemed made for him. It appealed to every need of his nature. To rescue the Holy Land from the pollution of the infidel, to charge as a king at the head of knightly squadrons in a cause at once glorious to man and especially acceptable to God, was a completely satisfying inspiration. The English would greatly have liked their King to look after their affairs, to give them peace and order, to nourish their growing prosperity, and to do justice throughout the land. But they understood that the Crusade was a high and sacred enterprise, and the Church taught them that in unseen ways it would bring a blessing upon them. Richard was crowned with peculiar state, by a ceremonial which, elaborating the most ancient forms and traditions of the Island monarchy, is still in all essentials observed to-day. Thereafter the King, for the sake of Christ's sepulchre, virtually put the realm up for sale. Money he must have at all costs for his campaign in far-off Palestine. He sold and re-sold every office in the State. He made new and revolutionarily heavy demands for taxation. He called for "scutage," or the commutation of military service for a money payment, and later re-introduced "carucage," a levy on every hundred acres of land. Thus he filled his chests for the Holy War.

Confiding the government to two Justiciars, William Longchamp, Bishop of Ely, and Hugh Puiset, Bishop of Durham, under the supervision of the one trustworthy member of his family, his mother, the old Queen, Eleanor of Aquitaine, he started for the wars in the summer of 1190. He had promised

Philip of France to marry his sister Alice, about whom, except for her looks, the tales were none too good. Philip claimed that Richard had tried to seduce her, and there was bad feeling between the monarchs. However that may be, after Richard had marched across France and sailed to Sicily, where he rested for the winter, his mother brought out to him Berengaria, daughter of the King of Navarre, whom he had known and admired, and now resolved to marry. It was fitting that the "Lion-heart" should marry for love and not for policy, but the rejection of Alice prevented a tie between the Kings of France and England which had been deemed essential to their comradeship in the Crusade. Philip was little soothed for the affront by a compensation of ten thousand marks. The quarrels of England and France were not so lightly set aside, and jealousies and bickerings distressed the winter sojourn of the two allies in Sicily.

Meanwhile Frederick Barbarossa had led his German host from Regensburg in May 1189 through Hungary to Constantinople. As soon as the frontiers of the Byzantine Empire were reached difficulties arose. The successors of Constantine still ruled over an extensive realm in Balkan Europe and in Asia Minor. The Emperor Isaac II at this time had allied himself with Saladin, and it was only under the threat of a Crusade against these Greek schismatics that by the end of March 1190 the Germans were allowed a free passage across the Bosphorus to the Asiatic shore. Barbarossa marched through Asia Minor and reached Cilicia. Here this veteran of the Second Crusade, of forty years before, was drowned in the river Calycadnus, either through his horse slipping at the ford or through the imprudence of bathing after dining. Some of his troops turned back, many died of plague at Antioch, and of his great army, the flower of Germany, barely a thousand, under his son, reached the Crusaders' camp before Acre in October 1190. But these kept tryst. The Anglo-French armies did not quit Sicily till the spring of 1191. Philip sailed direct to Acre. Richard paused in Cyprus. He quarrelled with the local Greek ruler, declared that an insult had been offered to his betrothed, conquered the island, and there wedded Berengaria. It was not until June 8, 1191, that he arrived with powerful forces before Acre.

The glamours of chivalry illumine the tale of the Third Crusade. All the chief princes of Europe were now in line around the doomed stronghold of Saladin, rivalling each other in prowess and jealousy. The sanctity of their cause was no bar to their quarrels and intrigues. King Richard dominated the scene. Fighting always in the most dangerous places, striking down the strongest foes, he negotiated all the time with Saladin. An agreement was in fact almost reached. To save his garrison Saladin offered to surrender his Christian captives, to pay a large indemnity, and to give up the cross, captured by him in Jerusalem, on which Christ—though this after twelve hundred years was not certain—had suffered. But the negotiations failed, and Richard in his fury massacred in cold blood the two thousand Turkish hostages who had been delivered as guarantees. Within five weeks of his arrival he brought the two years' siege to a successful conclusion.

By the time Acre fell King Richard's glory as a warrior and also his skill as a general were the talk of all nations. But the quarrels of the allies paralysed the campaign. Guy of Lusignan, the exiled King of Jerusalem, was disputing with Conrad of Montferrat for the crown. Richard took the one side and Philip the other. A compromise was arranged, but immediately the French king returned home to prosecute his designs in Flanders and to intrigue with Prince John against his absent brother. Duke Leopold of Austria, whom Richard had personally insulted, also took his departure. In these circum-

stances the Crusading army, ably led by Richard, in spite of
the victory at Arsuf, where many thousand infidels were slain,
could do no more than reach an eminence which commanded
a distant view of the Holy City. The King veiled his eyes, not
bearing to look upon the city he could not enter. He resolved
to retreat to the coast. In the next year, 1192, he captured
Jaffa. Once again the distant prospect of Jerusalem alone rewarded the achievements of the Crusaders, and once again
they fell back frustrated.

By now the news from England was so alarming that the
King felt it imperative to return home. He renewed his negotiations with Saladin, even offering his sister Joanna in marriage to Saladin's brother as the cement of a lasting peace. In
the hard fighting the Saracens had won the respect of their
martial foes. A peace or truce for three years was at length
effected, by which the coastal towns were divided and the
Holy Sepulchre opened as a place of pilgrimage to small
parties of Crusaders. It was as tourists only that they reached
their goal. The hard struggle between Guy and Conrad for
the Kingdom of Jerusalem settled itself, for Conrad, at the
moment when his claims had at length been recognised by
Richard, was murdered by the assassins belonging to a Moslem
sect ruled by "the Old Man of the Mountain." Guy, despairing
of regaining his inheritance, purchased Cyprus from the English king. He settled there, and founded a dynasty which, aided
by the military orders of knighthood, was to maintain itself
against the Turks for nearly four hundred years.

Early in 1193 the King set out for home. Wrecked in the
Adriatic, he sought to make his way through Germany in
disguise, but his enemy the Duke of Austria was soon upon
his track. He was arrested, and held prisoner in a castle. So
valuable a prize was not suffered to remain in the Duke's
hands. The Emperor himself demanded the famous captive.

For many months his prison was a secret of the Imperial Court, but, as a pretty legend tells us, Blondel, Richard's faithful minstrel, went from castle to castle striking the chords which the King loved best, and at last was rewarded by an answer from Richard's own harp.

*   *   *   *   *

William Longchamp, Bishop of Ely, and, with magnificent pluralism, Papal Legate, Chancellor, and Justiciar, had addressed himself with fidelity and zeal to the task of governing England, entrusted to him by Richard in 1189. Emulating the splendour of a monarch, he moved about the country with a pompous retinue, and very soon drew upon himself the envy and then the active hatred of the whole nobility. As the King's faithful servant he saw that the chief danger lay in the over-mighty position of Prince John. The indulgence of Richard had allowed his brother to form a state within a state. John held the shires of Derby, Nottingham, Somerset, Dorset, Devon, and Cornwall; the Earldom of Gloucester, with wide lands in South Wales; the honours of Lancaster, Wallingford, Eye, and Peverel. For the revenues which John drew from these lands he rendered no account to the Exchequer. Their sheriffs were responsible to him alone; their judicial business was transacted by his servants, their writs issued by his chancery and in his name. The royal officers and judges dared not enter John's shires. Bishop Longchamp determined to resist this dual system of government. His personal ostentation and arrogant airs had already multiplied his difficulties. Socially of humble origin, and by race a foreigner, he antagonised the other members of the Council, and provoked them to side with John, who knew well how to turn all this to his profit.

In the summer of 1191 there was open conflict between the two parties, and Longchamp marched against a revolt of

John's adherents in the North Midlands. This was a serious crisis. Fortunately however the King, far off in the Levant, had sent home Walter de Coutances, the Archbishop of Rouen, to watch the royal interests. The Archbishop formed a third party, loyal to the King, offended by Longchamp, but unwilling to support John; and presently he succeeded to Longchamp's position when the latter fled from England in October. The return of Philip Augustus from the Crusade in this same autumn brought new opportunities to John's ambition. The French king saw in Richard's absence the chance of breaking up the Angevin power and driving the English out of France. In John he found a willing partner. It was agreed between them that Philip Augustus should attack Normandy, while John raised a revolt in England.

Early in 1193, at a moment already full of peril, the grave news reached England that the King was prisoner "somewhere in Germany." There was general and well-founded consternation among the loyal bulk of his subjects. John declared that Richard was dead, appeared in arms, and claimed the crown. That England was held for Richard in his long absence against all these powerful and subtle forces is a proof of the loyalties of the feudal age. A deep sense of his heroic character and sacred mission commanded the allegiance of a large number of resolute, independent people whose names are unknown to history. The Church never flinched; Walter de Coutances of Rouen stood firm; the Queen-Mother with septuagenarian vigour stood by her eldest son; these dominated the Council, and the Council held the country. The coasts were guarded against an impending French invasion. John's forces melted. In April the strain was relieved by the arrival of authoritative news that Richard was alive. Prince John put the best face he could upon it and stole away to France.

* * * * *

The Holy Roman Emperor demanded the prodigious ransom of 150,000 marks, twice the annual revenue of the English Crown. One hundred thousand was to be ready in London before the King was liberated. Richard approved and the English Council agreed. Meanwhile Philip and John were active on the other side. They offered the Emperor 80,000 marks to keep the English king under lock and key till Michaelmas 1194, or 1500 marks a month for each month he was kept, or 150,000 marks to deliver him into their hands. But the Emperor felt that his blackmailing honour was engaged to Richard, with whom he had, perhaps precipitately, settled the figure. Once Philip knew that the Emperor would not go back upon his bargain he sent John his notorious message: "Have a care—the Devil is unloosed."

It remained to collect the ransom. The charge staggered the kingdom. Yet nothing was more sacred than the feudal obligation to ransom the liege lord, above all when he enjoyed the sanctity of a Crusader. The Justiciar, the Archbishops, and Queen Eleanor addressed themselves to their grievous task. The Church faced its duty. It was lawful to sacrifice even the most holy ornaments of the cathedrals for the ransom of a Christian lost in the Holy War. From all the lands a new "scutage" was taken. All laymen had to give a quarter of their movables. The Church lands bore an equal burden; they gave their plate and treasure, and three of the monastic orders yielded unresistingly a year's wool crop. Prince John of course set an example in collecting these taxes throughout his shires. His agents dwelt upon the sacred duty of all to pay, and he kept the proceeds of their faith and loyalty for himself. Three separate attempts were made to gather the money, and although England and Normandy, taxed to the limit, could not scrape together the whole of the 150,000 marks required, the

Emperor, satisfied that he could get no more, resolved to set his captive at liberty.

At the end of 1193 the stipulated first instalment was paid, and at the beginning of February 1194 Richard Cœur de Lion was released from bondage. He picked his way, we may be assured, with care across Europe, avoiding his French domains, and on March 16 arrived again in London among citizens impoverished but still rejoiced to see him and proud of his fame. He found John again in open rebellion, having seized castles and raised forces with French aid. The new Justiciar and the Council were already acting against the traitor prince, and Richard lent the weight of his strong right arm as well as the majesty of his name to the repression of the revolt. John fled once more to France. The King was recrowned in London with even more elaborate ceremony than before. As he was now plainly at war with Philip Augustus, his first, last, and only measures of government were to raise money and gather knights. These processes well started, he crossed the Channel to defend his French possessions. He never set foot in England again. But the Islanders owed him no grudge. All had been done as was right and due.

The mere arrival of the mighty warrior in France was enough to restore the frontiers and to throw King Philip and his forces upon an almost abject defensive. John sought pardon from the brother and liege lord he had so foully wronged. He did not sue in vain. With the full knowledge that if John had had his way he would still be a captive in a German castle, dethroned, or best of all dead—with all the long story of perfidy and unnatural malice in his mind, Cœur de Lion pardoned John, embraced him in fraternal love, and restored him to some of his estates, except certain fortresses which the barest prudence obliged him to reserve. This gesture was admired for its grandeur, though not perhaps for its wisdom, by the whole society, lay and spiritual, of Christendom.

* * * * *

The five remaining years of Richard's reign were spent in defending his French domains and raising money for that purpose from England. Once again the country was ruled by a deputy, this time Hubert Walter, a man bred in the traditions of Henry II's official household as the right-hand man of Ranulf of Glanville; no feudal amateur, but a professional administrator by training and experience. Hubert Walter was now Archbishop of Canterbury, and Richard's Justiciar. He was to become King John's Chancellor. Thus for ten years he was the kingdom's chief Minister. He had been extremely useful to Richard on the Crusade, on which he had accompanied him, and had been prominent in the organisation of the ransom. With determination, knowledge, and deft touch he developed the system of strong centralised government devised by Henry II. Hubert Walter stands out as one of the great medieval administrators. The royal authority was reasserted in the North; commissions of inquiry dealt with unfinished judicial and financial business; other commissions, with the help of local juries, carried out exhaustive inquiries into royal rights and the administration of justice. A new machinery for keeping the peace was devised, to which the origin of the Justices of the Peace can be traced, and the office of Coroner now emerged clearly for the first time. As head of the Exchequer, Walter of Coutances, Archbishop of Rouen, attempted the revision of taxation and of the existing military system. New assessments of land were begun, weights and measures standardised, and the frauds of cloth-workers and dealers purged or curbed. New concessions, involving the precious privilege of local self-government, were granted to London and the principal towns. Throughout the length and breadth of the land the machinery of government was made to work easily and quietly. If there was discontent at the taxes few dared to voice it. One man, a demagogue, "William of the Beard," uttered sentiments which would in similar circumstances readily occur to modern politicians. He was hanged.

Although Richard was an absentee King whose causes and virtues had proved a drain and disappointment to his subjects, his realm had not suffered so much as it would have seemed. The intrigues of the nobles and the treacheries of Prince John had been restrained by an impersonal Government ruling with the force and in the name of high and also well-grounded principles. The system of administration devised by Henry II—the Civil Service as we may call it—had stood the test, and, undisturbed by royal interventions, consolidated itself, to the general convenience and advantage. It was proved that the King, to whom all allegiance had been rendered, was no longer the sole guarantee for law and order. There were other sureties upon which in addition the English nation could rely.

In France the war with Philip proceeded in a curious fashion. The negotiations were unceasing. Every year there was a truce, which every year was broken as the weather and general convenience permitted. Richard, studying the strategic defence of Normandy, saw in a high crag which rises at the bend of the Seine by Andelys the key to Rouen. Although inhibited by the truce from fortifying it, and regardless of an interdict launched against him by the bishop of the diocese, the King set himself during 1196 to build the most perfect fortress which his experience could devise. He called it Château Gaillard, or "Saucy Castle," and "my fair child"; and as it rose with all its outworks, bridges, and water-defences into the immense triple-walled stone structure which still scowls upon the roofs of Andelys he rejoiced that it was beyond question the strongest fortress in the world. "If its walls were iron," said Philip in his wrath, "I would take it." "If they were of butter," retorted Richard, "I would hold it." But fate was to give Philip the last word.

In 1197 the skirmishing and parleying, truce-making and truce-breaking, which had become habitual were slashed by a fierce event. Something like a battle was fought, and Richard drove the King of France and his army in headlong rout through the streets of Gisors, where the solemn oaths of the Third Crusade had been sworn barely ten years before by the Kings of France and England.

In 1199, when the difficulties of raising revenue for the endless war were at their height, good news was brought to King Richard. It was said there had been dug up near the castle of Chaluz, on the lands of one of his vassals, a treasure of wonderful quality; a group of golden images of an emperor, his wife, sons, and daughters, seated round a table, also of gold, had been unearthed. The King claimed this treasure as lord paramount. The lord of Chaluz resisted the demand, and the King laid siege to his small, weak castle. On the third day, as he rode daringly near the wall, confident in his hard-tried luck, a bolt from a crossbow struck him in the left shoulder by the neck. The wound, already deep, was aggravated by the necessary cutting out of the arrow-head. Gangrene set in, and Cœur de Lion knew that he must pay a soldier's debt. He prepared for death with fortitude and calm, and in accordance with the principles he had followed. He arranged his affairs; he divided his personal belongings among his friends or bequeathed them to charity. He sent for his mother, the redoubtable Eleanor, who was at hand. He declared John to be his heir, and made all present swear fealty to him. He ordered the archer who had shot the fatal bolt, and who was now a prisoner, to be brought before him. He pardoned him, and made him a gift of money. For seven years he had not confessed for fear of being compelled to be reconciled to Philip, but now he received the offices of the Church with sincere and exemplary piety, and died in the forty-second year of his age on April 6, 1199, worthy, by the consent of all men, to sit with King Arthur and Roland and other heroes of martial romance at some Eternal Round Table, which we trust the Creator of the Universe in His comprehension will not have forgotten to provide.

The archer was flayed alive.

Magna Carta

T HE character of the prince who now ascended the throne
of England and became lord of Normandy, Anjou, Touraine, and Maine, claimant to Brittany and heir to Queen
Eleanor's Aquitaine, was already well known. Richard had
embodied the virtues which men admire in the lion, but there
is no animal in nature that combines the contradictory qualities
of John. He united the ruthlessness of a hardened warrior with
the craft and sublety of a Machiavellian. Although from time
to time he gave way to furious rages, in which "his eyes darted
fire and his countenance became livid," his cruelties were conceived and executed with a cold, inhuman intelligence. Monkish chroniclers have emphasised his violence, greed, malice,
treachery, and lust. But other records show that he was often
judicious, always extremely capable, and on occasions even
generous. He possessed an original and inquiring mind, and
to the end of his life treasured his library of books. In him the
restless energy of the Plantagenet race was raised to a furious
pitch of instability. A French writer,[1] it is true, has tried to
throw the sombre cloak of madness over his moral deformities,
but a study of his actions shows John gifted with a deep and
persistent sagacity, of patience and artifice, and with an un-
shakable resolve, which he fulfilled, to maintain himself upon
the throne while the breath was in his body. The difficulties
with which he contended, on the whole with remarkable success, deserve cool and attentive study. Moreover, when the
long tally is added it will be seen that the British nation and

[1] *Taine.*

the English-speaking world owe far more to the vices of John than to the labours of virtuous sovereigns; for it was through the union of many forces against him that the most famous milestone of our rights and freedom was in fact set up.

Although Richard had declared John to be King there were two views upon the succession. Geoffrey, his elder brother, had left behind him a son, Arthur, Prince of Brittany. It was already possible to hold that this grandson of Henry II of an elder branch had a prior right against John, and that is now the law of primogeniture. William the Marshal put the point before the Archbishop of Canterbury, but they both decided that John had the right. Queen Eleanor stood by her son against the grandson, whose mother she had never liked. John was accepted without demur in England. In the French provinces however the opposite view prevailed. Brittany in particular adopted Arthur. The King of France and all French interests thought themselves well served by a disputed succession and the espousal of a minor's cause. Those who had supported Richard against his father, and John against Richard, found it logical to support Arthur against John. Moreover, John's irreverence on high State occasions gave offence to the Church. An evil omen sprang at the outset from his levity. When in Rouen he was handed the symbolic lance of the Dukes of Normandy he turned to make some jocular remark to his attendant courtiers and let the weapon fall to the ground.

With the accession of John there emerges plainly in the northern French provinces a sense of unity with one another and with the kingdom of France; at the same time on this side of the Channel the English baronage became ever more inclined to insular and even nationalistic ideas. Ties with the Continent were weakening through the gradual division of honours and appanages in England and Normandy between different branches of Anglo-Norman families. Moreover, the growing brilliance of the French Court and royal power in the late twelfth century was a powerful magnet which drew Continental loyalties to Paris. King John found himself compelled to fight at even greater odds than his predecessors for his possessions on the Continent. He was also opposed by an increasing resistance to taxation for that purpose in England. In his coronation sermon the Archbishop is said to have mentioned that the English monarchy was in essence elective rather than hereditary. If, as was generally held, continuity with Edward the Confessor and the Anglo-Saxon kings was to be respected, many good precedents, Alfred the Great among them, could be cited for the doctrine. If the Archbishop preached in this sense there is no doubt he did so with John's full consent. But the principle of picking and choosing among the royal personages by no means weakened the claims of Arthur in regions where his sovereignty was desired.

From the first John feared Arthur. He had been in Brittany and at Arthur's Court when the news of Richard's death reached him. He had made good haste out of so dangerous an area. Arthur was received at Le Mans with enthusiasm. He did homage to Philip for Anjou, Maine, and Touraine. John's strength lay only in Aquitaine and in Normandy. The war and negotiations continued in the fitful style of the preceding reign, but without the prestige of Cœur de Lion on the side of the English Crown. In 1202 Philip, as John's overlord in respect of certain territories, issued a summons in due form citing John before his Court to answer charges made against him by the barons of Poitou. John replied that he was not amenable to such a process. Philip answered that he was summoned as Count of Poitou. John declared that the King of England could not submit himself to such a trial. Philip rejoined that the King of France could not lose his rights over a vassal because that vassal happened to acquire another dignity. All legal expedients being exhausted, John, who was not even promised safe-conduct for his return, refused to attend the Court, and was accordingly sentenced to be deprived of all the lands which he held in France because of his failure of service to his overlord. Thus armed with a legal right recognised by the jurists of the period, Philip invaded Normandy in the summer of 1202, capturing many towns with practically no resistance. The French king knighted Arthur, invested him with all the fiefs of which John had been deprived, except Normandy and Guienne, and betrothed him to his daughter Mary. Arthur was now sixteen.

When we reflect that the French provinces counted just as much with the Plantagenet kings as the whole realm of England it is obvious that a more virtuous man than John would be incensed at such treatment, and its consequences. His pent-up feelings roused in him an energy unexpected by his foes.

Arthur, hearing that his grandmother Eleanor was at the castle of Mirebeau in Poitou with a scanty escort, surrounded the castle, stormed the outworks, and was about to gain custody of this important and hostile old Queen. Eleanor contrived in the nick of time to send word to John, who was at Le Mans. Her son with ample forces covered the eighty miles between them in forty-eight hours, surprised Arthur and the besiegers at daybreak, and, as he declared, "by the favour of God" got the lot. Arthur and all who stood with him, Hugh Lusignan and a cluster of barons who had revolted, two hundred knights or more, fell at a stroke into John's power, and his mother was delivered from her dangerous plight.

Arthur was imprisoned at Falaise and then at Rouen. No one doubted that he lay in mortal peril. All those barons of Brittany who were still loyal to John asked that the Prince should be released, and on John's refusal went into immediate rebellion. John felt that he would never be safe so long as Arthur lived. This was certainly true. The havoc of disunity that was being wrought throughout the French provinces by the French king using Arthur as a pawn might well have weighed with a better man than John. Arthur, caught in open fight besieging his own grandmother, was a prisoner of war. The horrid crime of murder has often been committed for reasons of state upon lesser temptations than now assailed this exceptionally violent king. No one knows what happened to Arthur. An impenetrable veil descends upon the tragedy of Rouen. The officer commanding the fortress, one Hubert de Burgh, of whom more and better hereafter, gave out that upon the King's order he had delivered his prisoner at Easter 1203 to the hands of agents sent by John to castrate him, and that Arthur had died of the shock, This explanation by no means allayed the ill-feeling aroused in Brittany and elsewhere. Hubert then declared that Arthur was still alive, and John stated that he was glad his orders had been disobeyed. However, it may be, Arthur was never seen again. That he was murdered by John's orders was not disputed at the time nor afterwards, though the question whether or not he was mutilated or blinded beforehand remains unanswered.

Although high nobles and common people in large numbers were in those times frequently put to death without trial and for reasons of hate or policy, the murder by a king of an equal confirmed the bad impression which all the world had formed of John. Moreover, the odious crime did not prevent but rather hastened the loss of Normandy.

Arthur had been removed, but John failed to profit by his crime. For Arthur was no more than Philip Augustus's tool, and his disappearance left unchanged the iron purpose of the French king. Against this persistency Richard had roused men's devotion, but John's nature inspired none. Brittany and the central provinces of the Angevin Empire revolted. Philip had come to terms with each province, and at Easter 1203 he made a voyage down the Loire to Saumur. A deep wedge had already been driven between the northern and the southern halves of John's Continental possessions. Having encircled Normandy, Philip prepared to strike at the stronghold of the Angevin power. John, awake to his danger, poured in treasure and supplies to strengthen his defences. The military position was not yet desperate, and if John had not at the end of 1203 after a series of savage but ineffectual raids precipitately quitted Normandy he might, drawing supplies from England, have held the duchy indefinitely. But, as Philip took fortress after fortress in Central Normandy, John's nerve failed, and the Normans, not unwilling to find an excuse for surrender, made English indifference their justification. In March 1204 Richard's "fair child," the frowning Château Gaillard, fell, and the road to Rouen lay open. Three months later the capital itself was taken, and Normandy finally became French.

No English tears need have been shed over this loss. The Angevin Empire at its peak had no real unity. Time and geography lay on the side of the French. The separation proved as much in the interest of England as of France. It rid the Island of a dangerous, costly distraction and entanglement, turned its thought and energies to its own affairs, and above all left a ruling class of alien origin with no interest henceforth that was not English or at least insular. These consolations did not however dawn on John's contemporaries, who saw only disastrous and humiliating defeat, and blamed a King already distrusted by the people and at variance with the nobility.

*   *   *   *   *

The very success of Henry II in re-establishing order and creating an efficient central administration had left new difficulties for those who came after him. Henry II had created an instrument so powerful that it needed careful handling. He had restored order only at the cost of offending privilege. His fiscal arrangements were original, and drastic in their thoroughness. His work had infringed feudal custom at many points. All this had been accepted because of the King's tactful management and in the reaction from anarchy. Richard I, again, had left England in the hands of able administrators, and the odium of their strict government and financial ingenuity fell on them directly, and stopped short of the King, radiant in the halo of a Crusader and fortunate in his absence. John was at hand to bear the brunt in person.

John, like William Rufus, pressed to logical limits the tendencies of his father's system. There were arrears in the payment of scutage from Richard's reign, and more money was needed to fight the French King, Philip Augustus. But a division had opened in the baronage. The English barons of John's reign had become distinct from his Norman feudatories and not many families now held lands on both sides of the Channel. Even King Richard had met with refusals from his English nobles to fight abroad. Disputes about foreign service and payment of scutage lay at the root of the baronial agitation. By systematic abuse of his feudal prerogatives John drove the baronage to violent resistance. English society was steadily developing. Class interests had assumed sharper definition. Many barons regarded attendance or suit at Court as an opportunity for exerting influence rather than for rendering dutiful service. The sense of Church unity grew among the clergy, and corporate feeling in the municipalities. All these classes were needed by the new centralised Government; but John preferred to emphasise the more ruthless aspects of the royal power.

The year 1205 brought a crisis. The loss of Normandy was followed by the death of John's mother, Eleanor, to whose influence he had owed much of his position on the mainland.

The death of Hubert Walter, who for the last ten years had controlled the whole machinery of administration, deprived him of the only statesman whose advice he respected and whose authority stood between the Crown and the nation. It also reopened the thorny question of who should elect the Archbishop of Canterbury.

The Papal throne at this time was occupied by Innocent III, one of the greatest of the medieval Popes, renowned for his statecraft and diplomacy, and intent on raising to its height the temporal power of the Church. The dispute between John and the monastery of Canterbury over the election to the Archbishopric offered Innocent the very chance he sought for asserting Papal authority in England. Setting aside the candidates both of the Crown and of the Canterbury clergy, he caused Stephen Langton to be selected with great pomp and solemnity at Rome in December 1206. King John, confident of sufficient influence in the Papal Court to secure the election of his own candidate, had imprudently acknowledged the validity of the Papal decision beforehand. It was with pardonable anger that he learned how neatly Innocent had introduced a third and successful candidate, whose qualifications were unimpeachable. Stephen Langton was an English cardinal of the highest character, and one of the most famous doctors of the Paris schools. In his wrath, and without measuring the strength of his opponents, the King proceeded to levy a bloodless war upon the Church. Innocent III and Stephen Langton were not men to be browbeaten into surrender, and they possessed in an age of faith more powerful weapons than any secular monarch. When John began to persecute the clergy and seize Church lands the Pope retaliated by laying all England under an interdict. For more than six years the bells were silent, the doors of the churches were closed against the devout; the dead must be buried in unconsecrated ground and

without the last communion. Many of John's subjects were assured of damnation for themselves or their loved ones on this
account alone.

When John hardened his heart to the interdict and re-
doubled the attacks upon Church property, the Pope, in 1209,
took the supreme step of excommunication. The King's subjects were thereby absolved from their allegiance; his enemies
received the blessing of the Church and were sanctified as
Crusaders. But John was stubborn and unabashed. Interdict
and excommunication brought no ghostly terrors to his soul.
Indeed they aggravated the violence of his measures to a point
which his contemporaries could only attribute to insanity.
The royal administration, never more efficient, found little
difficulty in coping with the fiscal and legal problems presented to it or in maintaining order. The interdict, if a menace,
was also an opportunity for which John's plans were well
matured. The ecclesiastical property of clerics who fled abroad
was seized as forfeit by the Crown; and as more and more
bishoprics and abbeys fell vacant their revenues were exploited by royal custodians. Thus the Exchequer overflowed
with the spoils. But for the combination of the Church quarrel
with stresses of mundane politics, the Crown might have established a position not reached till the days of Henry VIII.

After the loss of Normandy John had embarked upon a
series of grandiose schemes for a Continental alliance against
Philip Augustus. He found allies in the Emperor Otto IV and
the Counts of Toulouse and Flanders; but his breach with the
Church hastened a far more formidable league between the
King of France and the Papacy, and in 1213 he had to choose
between submission and a French invasion, backed by all the
military and spiritual resources which Innocent III could set
in motion. The King's insecurity at home forced him to bow

to the threat, and Innocent rejoiced in victory upon his own terms.

John however was not at the end of his devices, and by a stroke of cunning choice enough to be called political genius he turned defeat into something very like triumph. If he could not prevail he would submit; if he submitted he would repent; if he repented there must be no limits to his contrition. At all costs he must break the closing circle of his foes. He spread before Innocent III the lure of temporal sovereignty which he knew that the Pontiff could never resist. He offered to make England a fief of the Papacy, and to do homage to the Pope as his feudal lord. Innocent leapt at this addition to his worldly dignities. He forgave the penitent King; he took him and the realm of England under his especial protection. He accepted the sovereignty of England from the hands of John, and returned it to him as his vassal with his blessing.

This turned the tables upon John's secular enemies. He was now the darling of the Church. Philip Augustus, who at heavy expense had gathered his armies to invade England as a Crusader for his own purposes, thought himself ill-used by the sudden tergiversation of his spiritual ally. He was indignant, and not at all inclined to relinquish the prey he had so long held in view. The barons also found meagre comfort in this transformation. Their grievances remained unredressed, their anger unappeased. Even in the English Church there was a keen division. The English Episcopacy saw themselves now carried into a subjection to Rome far beyond what their piety or interests required, and utterly at variance with the tradition in which they had been reared. Obedience to the Supreme Pontiff was a sacred duty, but it could be carried into excessive interpretations. Stephen Langton himself, the Pope's elect, was as good an Englishman as he was a Churchman. He foresaw the unbridled exploitation by Rome of the patronage of the English Church and the wholesale engrossment of its benefices by Italian nominees. He became almost immediately an opposing force to the Pope. King John, who had lain at Dover, quaking but calculating, may have laughed while he pulled all these strings and threw his enemies into confusion.

Both John and Innocent persevered in their new partnership, and the disaffected barons drew together under the leadership of Stephen Langton. The war with the French king was continued, and John's demands in money and service kept the barons' anger hot. In 1214 an English expedition which John had led to Poitou failed. In Northern France the army led by his nephew, Otto of Saxony, and by the Earl of Salisbury, was defeated by King Philip at Bouvines. This battle destroyed in a day the whole Continental combination on which John's hopes had been based. Here again was the opportunity of the King's domestic enemies. They formed plans to restrain the rule of a despotic and defeated King, and openly threatened revolt unless their terms were accepted. Left to themselves, they might have ruined their cause by rancorous opposition and selfish demands, but Archbishop Langton, anxious for a just peace, exercised a moderating influence upon them. Nor could John, as a Papal vassal, openly disregard Langton's advice.

But John had still one final resource. Encouraged by the Pope, he took the vows of a Crusader and invoked sentence of excommunication upon his opponents. This was not denied him. The conditions of 1213 were now entirely reversed. The barons, who had thought to be Crusaders against an excommunicated King, were now under the ban themselves. But this agile use of the Papal thunders had robbed them of some of their virtues as a deterrent. The barons, encouraged by the King's defeat abroad, persisted in their demands in spite of the

Papal Bull. A great party in the Church stood with them. In vain did John manœuvre, by the offer to grant freedom of election to the Church, to separate the clergy from the barons. Armed revolt seemed the only solution. Although in the final scene of the struggle the Archbishop showed himself unwilling to go to the extreme of civil war, it was he who persuaded the barons to base their demands upon respect for ancient custom and law, and who gave them some principle to fight for besides their own class interests. After forty years' experience of the administrative system established by Henry II the men who now confronted John had advanced beyond the magnates of King Stephen's time. They had learned to think intelligently and constructively. In place of the King's arbitrary despotism they proposed, not the withering anarchy of feudal separatism, but a system of checks and balances which would accord the monarchy its necessary strength, but would prevent its perversion by a tyrant or a fool. The leaders of the barons in 1215 groped in the dim light towards a fundamental principle. Government must henceforward mean something more than the arbitrary rule of any man, and custom and the law must stand even above the King. It was this idea, perhaps only half understood, that gave unity and force to the barons' opposition and made the Charter which they now demanded imperishable.

On a Monday morning in June, between Staines and Windsor, the barons and Churchmen began to collect on the great meadow at Runnymede. An uneasy hush fell on them from time to time. Many had failed to keep their tryst; and the bold few who had come knew that the King would never forgive this humiliation. He would hunt them down when he could, and the laymen at least were staking their lives in the cause they served. They had arranged a little throne for the King and a tent. The handful of resolute men had drawn up, it seems, a short document on parchment. Their retainers and the groups and squadrons of horsemen in sullen steel kept at some distance and well in the background. For was not armed rebellion against the Crown the supreme feudal crime? Then events followed rapidly. A small cavalcade appeared from the direction of Windsor. Gradually men made out the faces of the King, the Papal Legate, the Archbishop of Canterbury, and several bishops. They dismounted without ceremony. Someone, probably the Archbishop, stated briefly the terms that were suggested. The King declared at once that he agreed. He said the details should be arranged immediately in his chancery. The original "Articles of the Barons" on which Magna Carta is based exist to-day in the British Museum. They were sealed in a quiet, short scene, which has become one of the most famous in our history, on June 15, 1215. Afterwards the King returned to Windsor. Four days later, probably, the Charter itself was probably engrossed. In future ages it was to be used as the foundation of principles and systems of government of which neither King John nor his nobles dreamed.

*   *   *   *   *

At the beginning of the year 1216 there had seemed to be every chance that John would still defeat the baronial opposition and wipe out the humiliation of Runnymede. Yet before the summer was out the King was dead, and the Charter survived the denunciation of the Pope and the arbitrament of war. In the next hundred years it was reissued thirty-eight times, at first with a few substantial alterations, but retaining its original characteristics. Little more was heard of the Charter until the seventeenth century. After more than two hundred years a Parliamentary Opposition struggling to check the encroachments of the Stuarts upon the liberty of the subject rediscovered it and made of it a rallying cry against oppression.

Thus was created the glorious legend of the "Charter of an Englishman's liberties."

If we set aside the rhetorical praise which has been so freely lavished upon the Charter, and study the document itself, we may find it rather surprising reading. It is in a form resembling a legal contract, and consists of sixty-one clauses, each dealing either with the details of feudal administration and custom or with elaborate provisions for securing the enforcement of the promises which it embodies. It is entirely lacking in any spacious statement of the principles of democratic government or the rights of man. It is not a declaration of constitutional doctrine, but a practical document to remedy current abuses in the feudal system. In the forefront stand the questions of scutage, of feudal reliefs and of wardship. The word "freeman" was a technical feudal term, and it is doubtful whether it included even the richer merchants, far less the bondmen or humbler classes who make up the bulk of a nation. It implies on the King's part a promise of good government for the future, but the terms of the promise are restricted to the observance of the customary privileges and interests of the baronial class. The barons on their part were compelled to make some provision for their tenants, the limits forced on John being vaguely applied to the tenants-in-chief as well; but they did as little as they safely and decently could. The villeins, in so far as they were protected, received such solicitous attention as befitted valuable chattels attached to the manor and not as free citizens of the realm.

The thirteenth century was to be a great age of Parliamentary development and experiment, yet there is no mention in Magna Carta of Parliament or representation of any but the baronial class. The great watchwords of the future here find no place. The actual Charter is a redress of feudal grievances extorted from an unwilling king by a discontented ruling class insisting on its privileges, and it ignored some of the most important matters which the King and baronage had to settle, such as the terms of military service.

Magna Carta must not however be dismissed lightly, in the words of a modern writer, as "a monument of class selfishness." Even in its own day men of all ranks above the status of villeins had an interest in securing that the tenure of land should be secure from arbitrary encroachment. Moreover, the greatest magnate might hold, and often did hold, besides his estate in chief, parcels of land under the most diverse tenures, by knight service, by the privileges of "socage," or as a tenant at will. Therefore in securing themselves the barons of Runnymede were in fact establishing the rights of the whole landed class, great and small—the simple knight with two hundred acres, the farmer or small yeoman with sixty. And there is evidence that their action was so understood throughout the country. In 1218 an official endeavoured to upset by writ a judgment given in the county court of Lincolnshire. The victim was a great landowner, but the whole county rallied to his cause and to the "liberty sworn and granted," stating in their protest that they acted "with him, and for him, and for ourselves, and the community of the whole realm."

If the thirteenth-century magnates understood little and cared less for popular liberties or Parliamentary democracy, they had all the same laid hold of a principle which was to be of prime importance for the future development of English society and English institutions. Throughout the document it is implied that here is a law which is above the King and which even he must not break. This reaffirmation of a supreme law and its expression in a general charter is the great work of Magna Carta; and this alone justifies the respect in which men have held it. The reign of Henry II, according to the most respected authorities, initiates the rule of law. But the work as yet was incomplete: the Crown was still above the law; the legal system which Henry had created could become, as John showed, an instrument of oppression.

Now for the first time the King himself is bound by the law. The root principle was destined to survive across the generations and rise paramount long after the feudal background of 1215 had faded in the past. The Charter became in the process of time an enduring witness that the power of the Crown was not absolute.

The facts embodied in it and the circumstances giving rise to them were buried or misunderstood. The underlying idea of the sovereignty of law, long existent in feudal custom, was raised by it into a doctrine for the national State. And when in subsequent ages the State, swollen with its own authority, has attempted to ride roughshod over the rights or liberties of the subject it is to this doctrine that appeal has again and again been made, and never, as yet, without success.

On the Anvil

KING JOHN died in the toils; but he died at bay. The misgovernment of his reign had brought against him what seemed to be an overwhelming combination. He was at war with the English barons who had forced him to grant the Charter. They had invited Louis, son of the implacable Philip, King of France, into the country to be their liege lord, and with him came foreign troops and hardy adventurers. The insurgent barons north of the Humber had the support of Alexander, King of Scots; in the West the rebellion was sustained by Llewellyn, the powerful Prince of North Wales. The towns were mainly against the King; London was vehemently hostile. The Cinque Ports were in enemy hands. Winchester, Worcester, and Carlisle, separated by the great distances of those times, were united in opposition to the Crown.

On the other hand, the recreant King had sacrificed the status of the realm to purchase the unswerving aid of the Papacy. A strong body of mercenaries, the only regular troops in the kingdom, were in John's pay. Some of the greatest warrior-nobles, the venerable William the Marshal, and the famous, romantic Ranulf, Earl of Chester, with a strong following of the aristocracy, adhered to his cause. The mass of the people, bewildered by this new quarrel of their masters, on the whole inclined to the King against the barons, and certainly against the invading foreigners. Their part was only to suffer at the hands of both sides. Thus the forces were evenly balanced; everything threatened a long, stubborn civil war and a return to the anarchy of Stephen and Maud. John himself, after a lifetime of subtleties and double-dealing, of illegal devices and sharp, unexpected twists of religious policy, showed himself possessed, in the last months of his life, of a warlike energy and resource which astonished friend and foe. It was at this moment that he died of dysentery, aggravated by fatigue and too much food and drink. Shakespeare has limned his final agony:

> And none of you will bid the winter come
> To thrust his icy fingers in my maw. . . .
> I beg cold comfort, and you are so strait
> And so ungrateful, you deny me that.

The death of the King in this convulsion of strife changed the conditions of the conflict without ending it. The rival interests and factions that were afoot had many purposes beyond the better government of England. Louis was in the Island, and fighting. Many had plighted him their faith, already once forsworn. The rebel lords were deeply involved with their Scottish and Welsh allies; none was in the humour for peace. Yet the sole reason and justification for revolt died with John. Henry, a child of nine, was the undoubted heir to all the rights and loyalties of his grandfather's wide empire. He was the rightful King of England. Upon what grounds could the oppressions of the father be visited upon his innocent son? A page of history had been violently turned; the new parchment was blank and clear. All parties were profoundly sensible of these considerations. Nevertheless John for the moment was missed by those whose lives and fortunes were devoted to the national cause. William the Marshal acted with honesty and decision. Had he failed in his duty to the Crown the strong centralised monarchy which Henry II had created, and upon which the growing civilisation of the realm depended, might have degenerated into a heptarchy of feudal princes, or even worse. The Papal Legate, sure of the unchanging policy of Rome, aided William the Marshal. The boy King was crowned at Gloucester and began his reign of fifty-six years on October 28, 1216. He was anointed by the Legate, and in default of the diadem which John had lost in crossing the Wash a plain gold circlet was placed upon his brow. This was to prove no inadequate symbol of his rule.

William the Marshal, aged seventy, reluctantly undertook what we should now call the Regency. He joined to himself the Earl of Chester, who might well have been his rival but did not press his claims, and Hubert de Burgh, John's faithful servant. The wisdom and the weakness of the new Government were alike revealed in the reissue of the Charter, which had been too rashly quashed by the Pope in 1215. The religious character of the King's party had become predominant. The Royalists wore white crosses, the Church preached a virtual Crusade, and the chiefs of the opposing faction were excommunicated. "At a time," said Henry in after-years to Bishop Grosseteste, "when we were orphan and minor, when our subjects were not only alienated from us, but were organised against us, it was our mother, the Roman Church, which brought this realm once more under our authority, which consecrated us King, crowned us and placed us on the throne."

It was a reign of turmoil and distress and yet the forces of progress moved doggedly forward. Redhot iron was smitten on the anvil, and the hammer-blows forged a metal more tense than had yet been seen. In this period the common people, with their Anglo-Saxon tradition of ancient rights and law running back to remote antiquity, lay suffering under the armoured feet of the nobility and of the royal mercenaries, reinforced in the main by the power of the Church. But the people's masters were disunited; not only did their jealousies and ambitions and their taste for war keep them at variance, but several rending fissures were opening among them. They were divided into parties; they were cross-cut obliquely by a strong nationalism. It is an age of impulse and experiment, not controlled by any general political theory.

* * * * *

The confusion and monotony of the barons' warfare, against each other, or against the King, sometimes with the Church, more often against the Church, have repelled many readers of history. But the fact is that King Henry III survived all his troubles and left England enjoying a prosperity and peace unknown when he was a child. The cruel war and anarchy lay only upon the surface; underneath, unformulated and largely unrealised by the hard-pressed actors, coursed all the tides which were to flow in Europe five hundred years later; and almost all the capital decisions which are demanded of the modern world were rife in this medieval society. From out of the conflict there rise the figures of heroes, both warriors and statesmen, from whose tribulations we are separated by long ages, but whose work and outlook unite them to us, as if we read their acts and words in the morning newspaper.

We must examine some of these figures at close quarters. Stephen Langton, the great Archbishop, was the indomitable, unwearying, builder of the rights of Englishmen against royal, baronial, and even ecclesiastical pretensions. He stood against King John; he stood against the Pope. Both cast upon him at times their utmost displeasure, short of taking his life. Here is a man who worked for the unity of Christendom through the Catholic Church; but also for the interests of England against the Papacy. Here is a faithful servant of the Crown, but at the same time a champion of the Charter, and all it meant, and still means. A commanding central figure, practical, resourceful, shifting from side to side as evils forced him, but quite unchanging and unchangeable in his broad, wise, brave, workaday, liberal purpose. Here was, if not an architect of our Constitution, at least a punctual and unfailing Clerk of the Works.

The second personality which emerges from the restless scene is Hubert de Burgh. Shakespeare, whose magic finger touches in succession most of the peaks of English history and lights them with the sunrise so that all can see them standing out above the mountainous disorder, has brought Hubert to our ken. Here is a soldier and a politician, armed with the practical wisdom which familiarity with courts and camps, with high authorities, ecclesiastical and armoured, may infuse into a man's conduct, and even nature. John's Justiciar, identified with the crimes and the follies of the reign, was yet known to all men as their constant resolute opponent. Under the Marshal, who was himself a star of European chivalry, Hubert was an outstanding leader of resistance to the rebellion against the monarchy. At the same time, above the warring factions, he was a solid champion of the rights of England. The Island should not be ravaged by greedy nobles, nor pillaged by foreign adventurers, nor mutilated unduly even for the high interests of the Papacy, which so often were the interests of Christendom itself.

The rebellion of the barons was quelled by fights on land and sea. At Lincoln the King's party had gained a fantastic but none the less decisive victory. In the streets of Lincoln, during a whole day, we are told that four hundred royal knights jostled and belaboured six hundred of the baronial party. Only three were killed in the combat. Contemporary opinion declined to accord the name of battle to this brawl. It was called "the Fair of Lincoln." It is difficult to form a picture of what happened. One must suppose that the knights had upon the average at least eight or ten stalwart retainers each, and that the almost invulnerable, chain-mailed monsters waddled about in the throng, chasing away or cutting down the unarmoured folk, and welting each other when they met, hard, but perhaps not too hard. On this basis there were intricate manœuvres and stratagems, turnings of flanks, takings in rear, entry through privy ports by local treachery, odd confrontations; all kinds of devices. But in the upshot the Royalists outwitted and out-walloped the insurgents. Accidents will happen in the best regulated faction fights, and one of the leading rebel barons, Thomas, Count of Perche, had the misfortune to be killed by a sword-thrust which penetrated his visor and sank deep into his brain. But for almost all the rest of the armoured crew it was a joyous adventure. The vengeance of the victors was wreaked mainly upon their rivals' retainers and upon the civil population, who were plundered and slaughtered on a considerable scale.

"The Fair of Lincoln" gave the infant Henry III a victory on land, and de Burgh's sea-victory off Dover against French reinforcements for Louis cut the revolt from its Continental root. Negotiations proceeded continually amid the broils. They were strenuously disputed, and meanwhile each side devastated the estates of the opposing party, to the intense misery of their inhabitants. Hubert, supported by Archbishop Langton and the Papal Legate, never lost his hold upon the Charter, although this was the nominal bond of union of their opponents. There were unavoidable stresses between the devout English Royalists and the interests of the universal Church, as interpreted by the Pope. These stresses did not however take a physical form. Compromises were reached, not only between Crown and barons, but in the ecclesiastical sphere, between England and Rome.

After a year of fighting, Louis of France was compelled to leave the country in 1217, his hopes utterly dashed. The Great Charter was now re-issued for the second time in order to show that the Government meant its word. In 1219 the old victorious Marshal died, and Hubert ruled the land for twelve years. He was a stern ruler. When Fawkes de Breauté, who had been the chief mercenary of John and William the Marshal during all these recent tumults, grew overmighty and attempted to disturb the new-found peace of the land, Hubert determined to expel him. On taking Fawkes's stronghold of Bedford Castle in 1224, after two months' siege, Hubert hanged in front of its walls the twenty-four surviving knights who had commanded the garrison. In the following year, as a sign of pacification, the Great Charter was again re-issued in what was substantially its final form. Thus it became an unchallenged part of English law and tradition. But for the turbulent years of Henry III's minority, it might have mouldered in the archives of history as a merely partisan document.

No long administration is immune from mistakes and every statesman must from time to time make concessions to wrongheaded superior powers. But Hubert throughout his tenure stood for the policy of doing the least possible to recover the King's French domains. This he carried out not only by counsel, but by paralysing action, and by organising ignominious flight before the enemy when battle seemed otherwise unavoidable. He hampered the preparation for fresh war; he stood firm against the incursions of foreign favourites and adventurers. He resisted the Papacy in its efforts to draw money at all costs out of England for its large European schemes. He maintained order, and as the King grew up he restrained the Court party which was forming about him from making inroads upon the Charter. His was entirely the English point of view.

At last in 1229 he had exhausted his goodwill and fortune and fate was upon him. The King, now twenty-two years of age, crowned and acting, arrived at Portsmouth with a large